THE FOLLIES OF RICHARD WADSWORTH

NICK MAANDAG

DRAWN & QUARTERLY

drawnandquarterly.com

978-1-77046-361-5 | First edition: June 2019 | Printed in Canada | 10 9 8 7 6 5 4 3 2 1

Cataloguing data available from Library and Archives Canada.

Published in the USA by Drawn & Quarterly, a client publisher of Farrar, Straus and Giroux.
Published in Canada by Drawn & Quarterly, a client publisher of Raincoast Books.
Published in the United Kingdom by Drawn & Quarterly, a client publisher of Publishers Group UK.

Canadä Drawn & Quarterly acknowledges the support of the Government of Canada and the Canada Council for the Arts for our publishing program.

CONTENTS

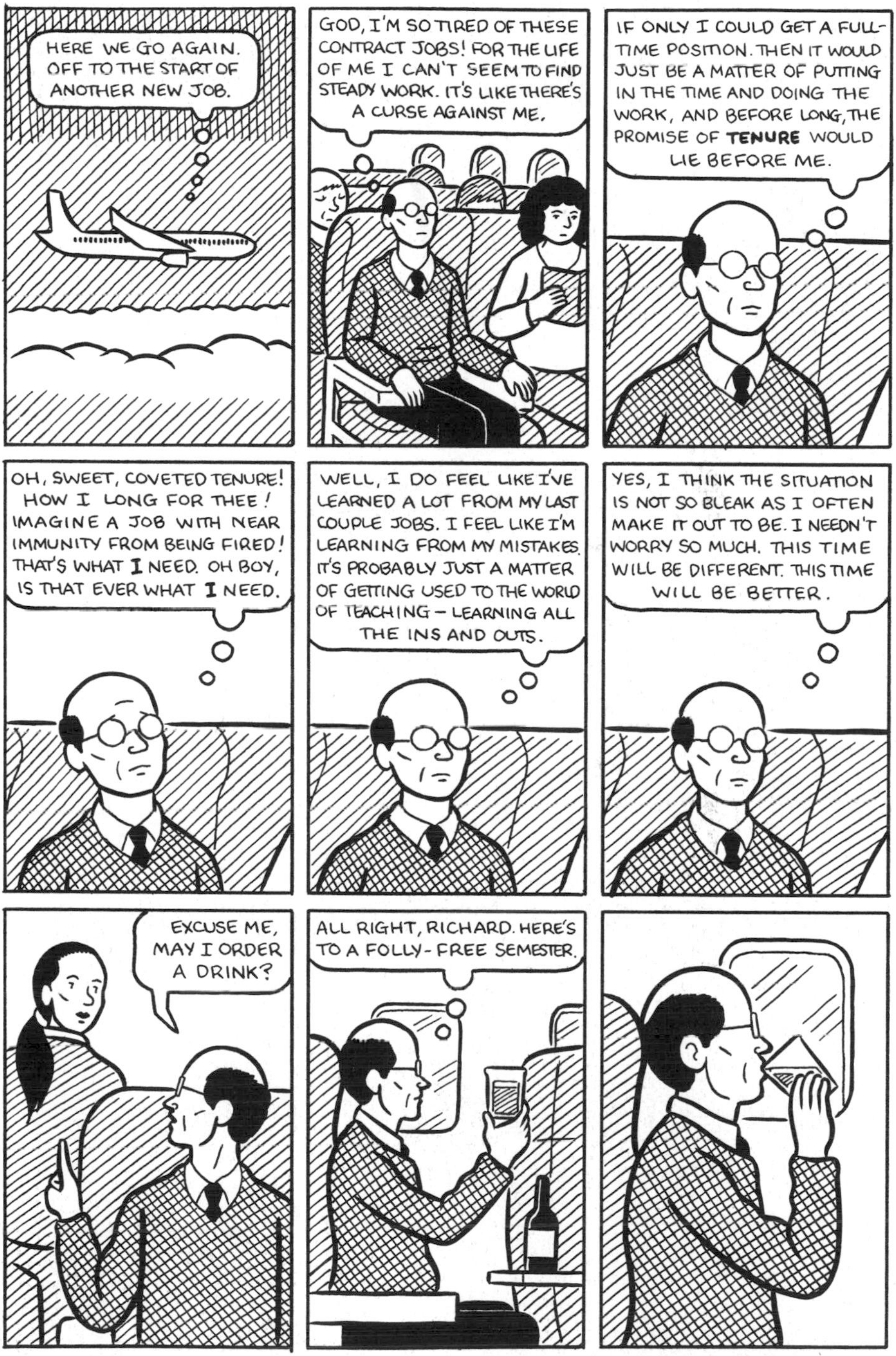
HERE WE GO AGAIN. OFF TO THE START OF ANOTHER NEW JOB.
GOD, I'M SO TIRED OF THESE CONTRACT JOBS! FOR THE LIFE OF ME I CAN'T SEEM TO FIND STEADY WORK. IT'S LIKE THERE'S A CURSE AGAINST ME.
IF ONLY I COULD GET A FULL-TIME POSITION. THEN IT WOULD JUST BE A MATTER OF PUTTING IN THE TIME AND DOING THE WORK, AND BEFORE LONG, THE PROMISE OF **TENURE** WOULD LIE BEFORE ME.
OH, SWEET, COVETED TENURE! HOW I LONG FOR THEE! IMAGINE A JOB WITH NEAR IMMUNITY FROM BEING FIRED! THAT'S WHAT **I** NEED. OH BOY, IS THAT EVER WHAT **I** NEED.
WELL, I DO FEEL LIKE I'VE LEARNED A LOT FROM MY LAST COUPLE JOBS. I FEEL LIKE I'M LEARNING FROM MY MISTAKES. IT'S PROBABLY JUST A MATTER OF GETTING USED TO THE WORLD OF TEACHING – LEARNING ALL THE INS AND OUTS.
YES, I THINK THE SITUATION IS NOT SO BLEAK AS I OFTEN MAKE IT OUT TO BE. I NEEDN'T WORRY SO MUCH. THIS TIME WILL BE DIFFERENT. THIS TIME WILL BE BETTER.
EXCUSE ME, MAY I ORDER A DRINK?
ALL RIGHT, RICHARD. HERE'S TO A FOLLY-FREE SEMESTER.

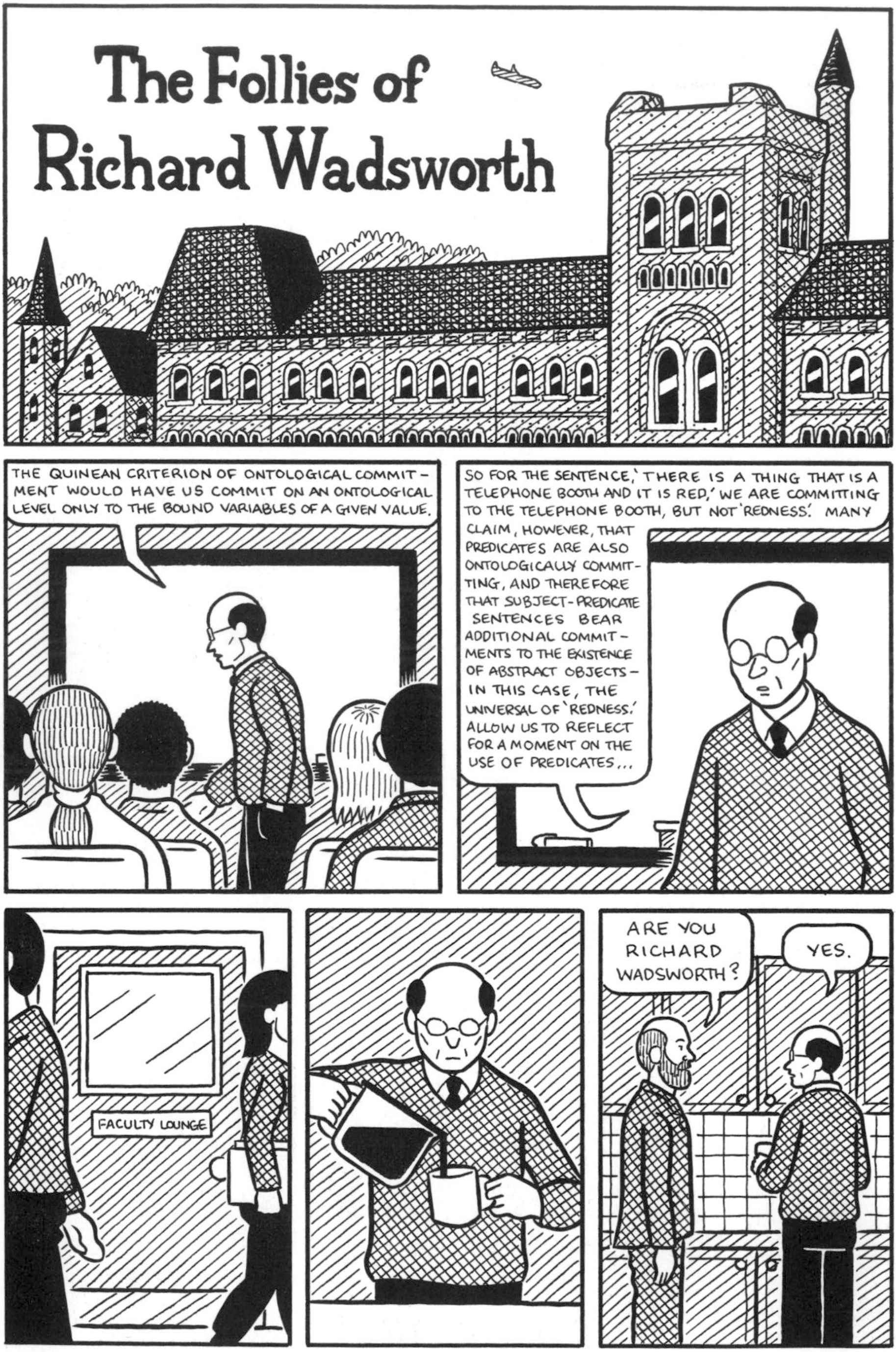
The Follies of Richard Wadsworth
THE QUINEAN CRITERION OF ONTOLOGICAL COMMIT-MENT WOULD HAVE US COMMIT ON AN ONTOLOGICAL LEVEL ONLY TO THE BOUND VARIABLES OF A GIVEN VALUE.
SO FOR THE SENTENCE, 'THERE IS A THING THAT IS A TELEPHONE BOOTH AND IT IS RED,' WE ARE COMMITTING TO THE TELEPHONE BOOTH, BUT NOT 'REDNESS.' MANY CLAIM, HOWEVER, THAT PREDICATES ARE ALSO ONTOLOGICALLY COMMIT-TING, AND THEREFORE THAT SUBJECT-PREDICATE SENTENCES BEAR ADDITIONAL COMMIT-MENTS TO THE EXISTENCE OF ABSTRACT OBJECTS - IN THIS CASE, THE UNIVERSAL OF 'REDNESS.' ALLOW US TO REFLECT FOR A MOMENT ON THE USE OF PREDICATES...
FACULTY LOUNGE
ARE YOU RICHARD WADSWORTH?
YES.

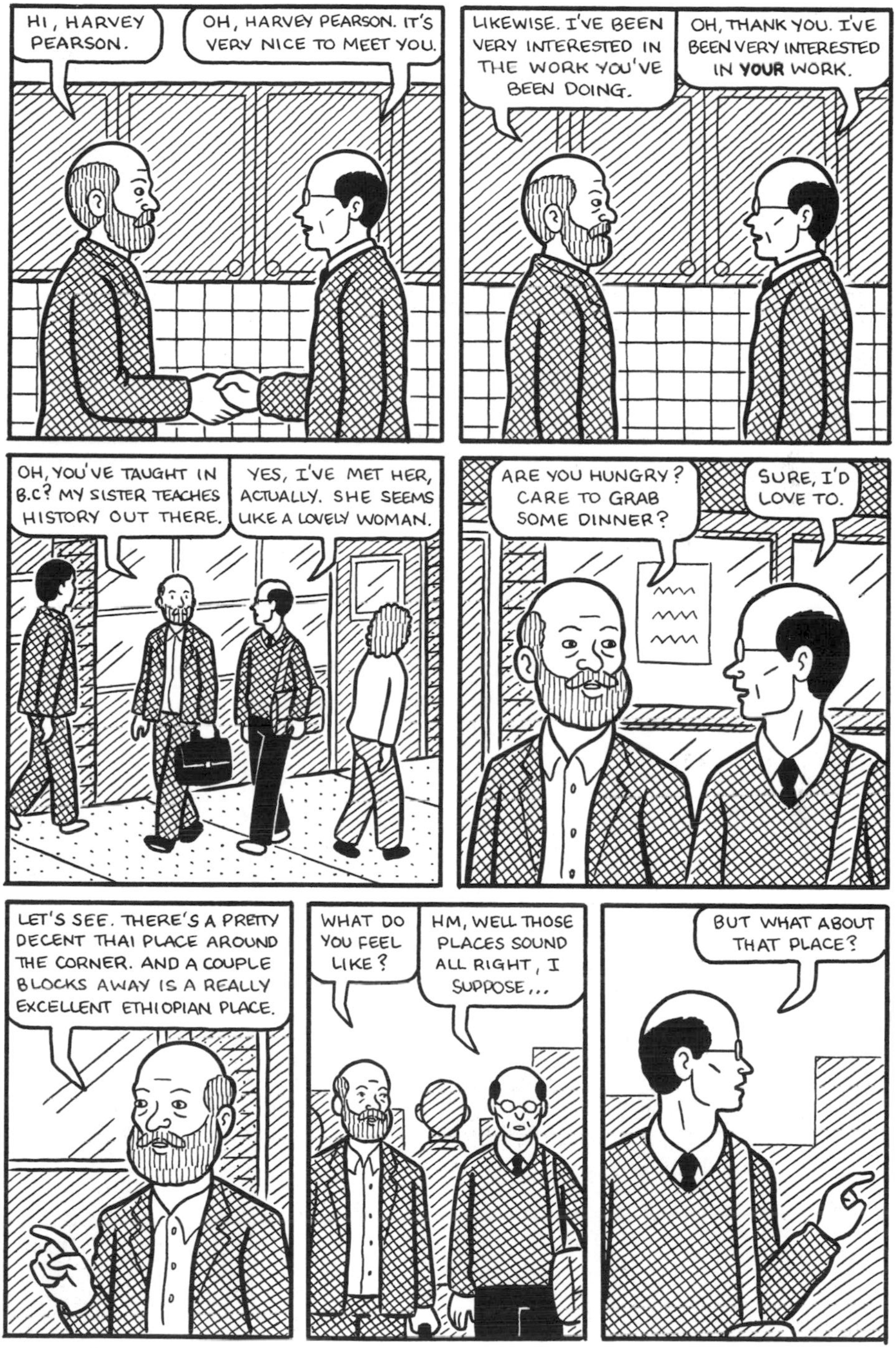
HI, HARVEY PEARSON.
OH, HARVEY PEARSON. IT'S VERY NICE TO MEET YOU.
LIKEWISE. I'VE BEEN VERY INTERESTED IN THE WORK YOU'VE BEEN DOING.
OH, THANK YOU. I'VE BEEN VERY INTERESTED IN **YOUR** WORK.
OH, YOU'VE TAUGHT IN B.C? MY SISTER TEACHES HISTORY OUT THERE.
YES, I'VE MET HER, ACTUALLY. SHE SEEMS LIKE A LOVELY WOMAN.
ARE YOU HUNGRY? CARE TO GRAB SOME DINNER?
SURE, I'D LOVE TO.
LET'S SEE. THERE'S A PRETTY DECENT THAI PLACE AROUND THE CORNER. AND A COUPLE BLOCKS AWAY IS A REALLY EXCELLENT ETHIOPIAN PLACE.
WHAT DO YOU FEEL LIKE?
HM, WELL THOSE PLACES SOUND ALL RIGHT, I SUPPOSE...
BUT WHAT ABOUT THAT PLACE?

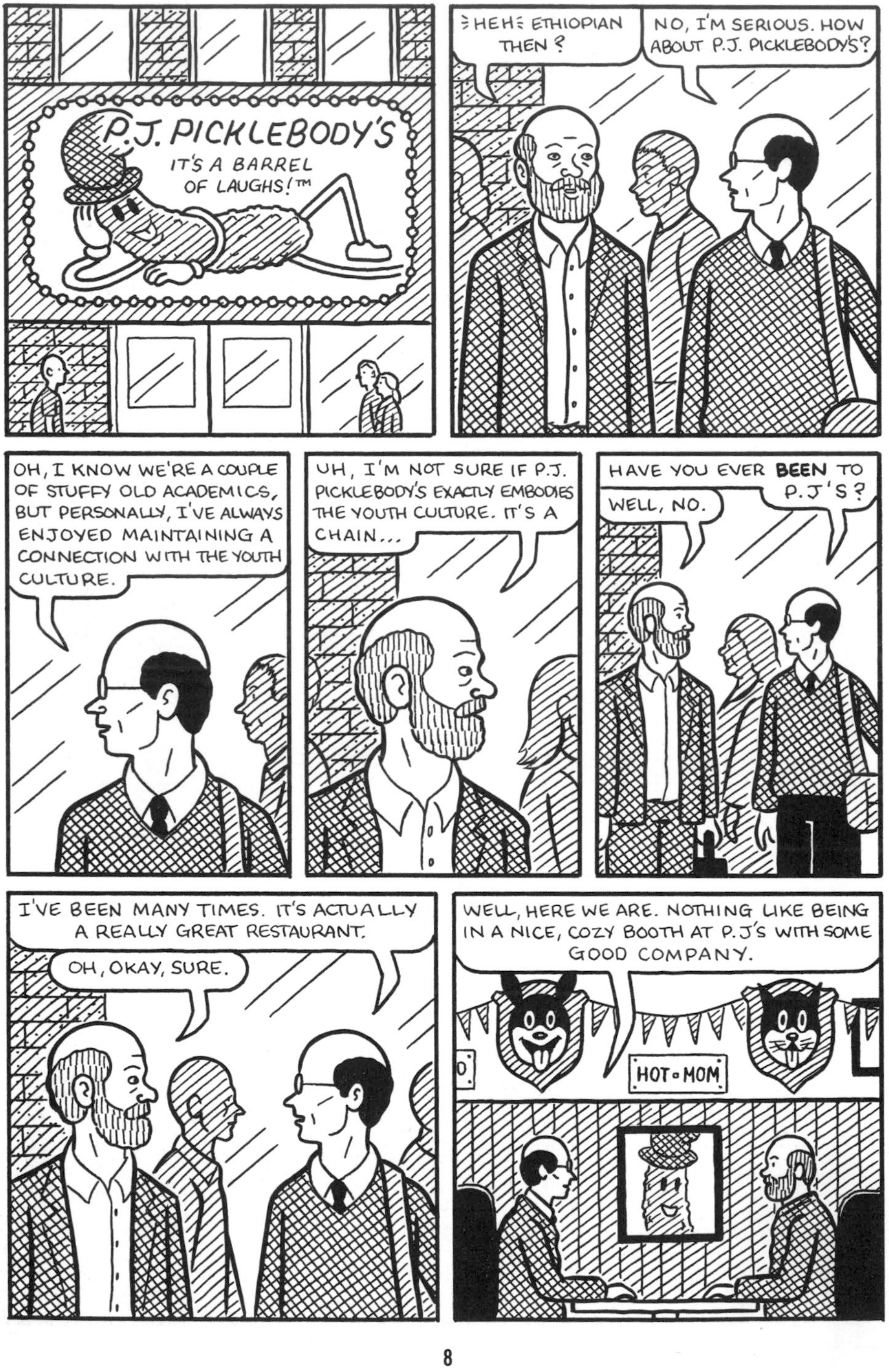
P.J. PICKLEBODY'S
IT'S A BARREL OF LAUGHS!™
HEH ETHIOPIAN THEN?
NO, I'M SERIOUS. HOW ABOUT P.J. PICKLEBODY'S?
OH, I KNOW WE'RE A COUPLE OF STUFFY OLD ACADEMICS, BUT PERSONALLY, I'VE ALWAYS ENJOYED MAINTAINING A CONNECTION WITH THE YOUTH CULTURE.
UH, I'M NOT SURE IF P.J. PICKLEBODY'S EXACTLY EMBODIES THE YOUTH CULTURE. IT'S A CHAIN...
HAVE YOU EVER BEEN TO P.J'S?
WELL, NO.
I'VE BEEN MANY TIMES. IT'S ACTUALLY A REALLY GREAT RESTAURANT.
OH, OKAY, SURE.
WELL, HERE WE ARE. NOTHING LIKE BEING IN A NICE, COZY BOOTH AT P.J'S WITH SOME GOOD COMPANY.
HOT MOM

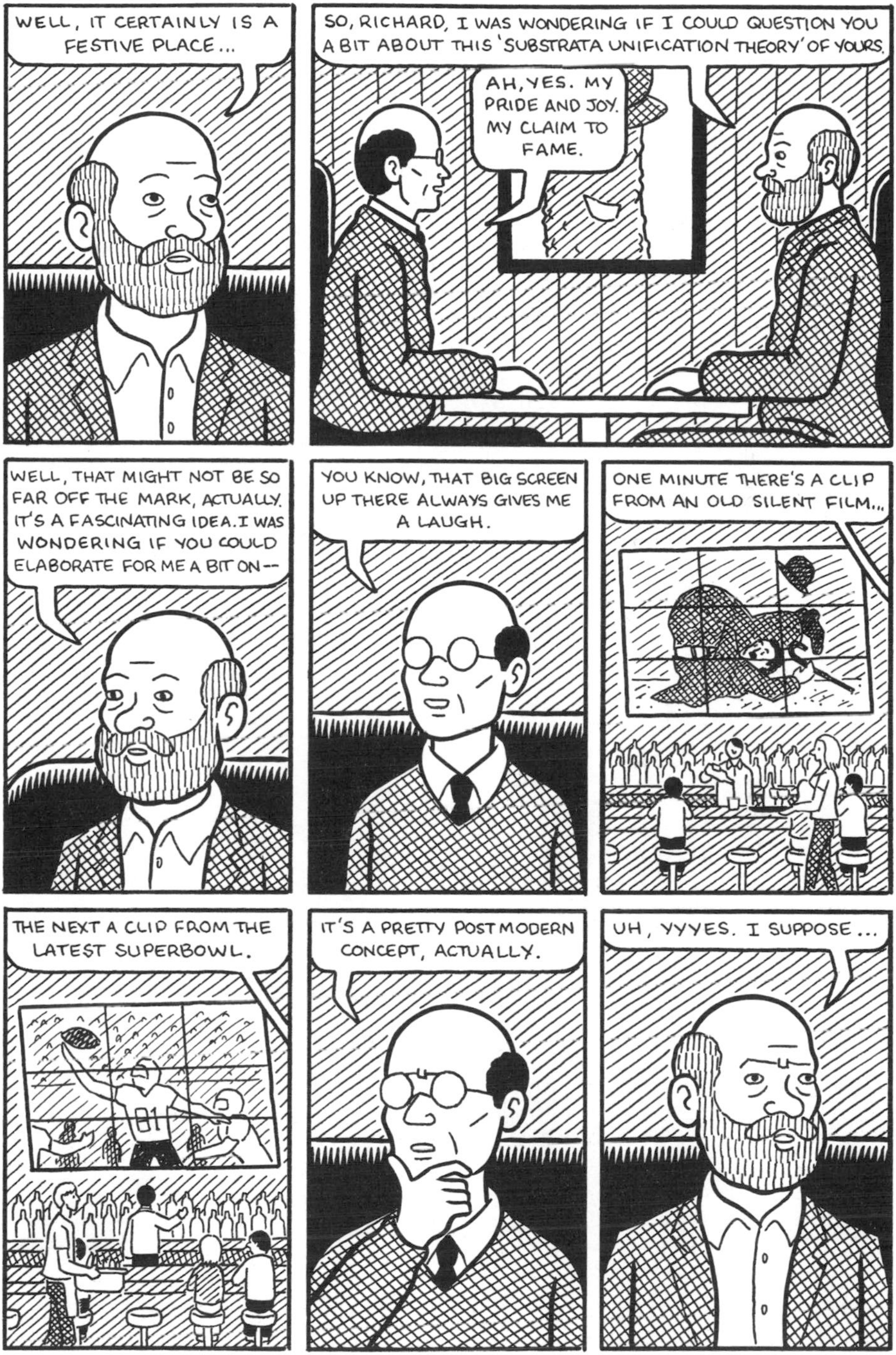
WELL, IT CERTAINLY IS A FESTIVE PLACE...
SO, RICHARD, I WAS WONDERING IF I COULD QUESTION YOU A BIT ABOUT THIS 'SUBSTRATA UNIFICATION THEORY' OF YOURS.
AH, YES. MY PRIDE AND JOY. MY CLAIM TO FAME.
WELL, THAT MIGHT NOT BE SO FAR OFF THE MARK, ACTUALLY. IT'S A FASCINATING IDEA. I WAS WONDERING IF YOU COULD ELABORATE FOR ME A BIT ON--
YOU KNOW, THAT BIG SCREEN UP THERE ALWAYS GIVES ME A LAUGH.
ONE MINUTE THERE'S A CLIP FROM AN OLD SILENT FILM...
THE NEXT A CLIP FROM THE LATEST SUPERBOWL.
81
IT'S A PRETTY POSTMODERN CONCEPT, ACTUALLY.
UH, YYYES. I SUPPOSE...

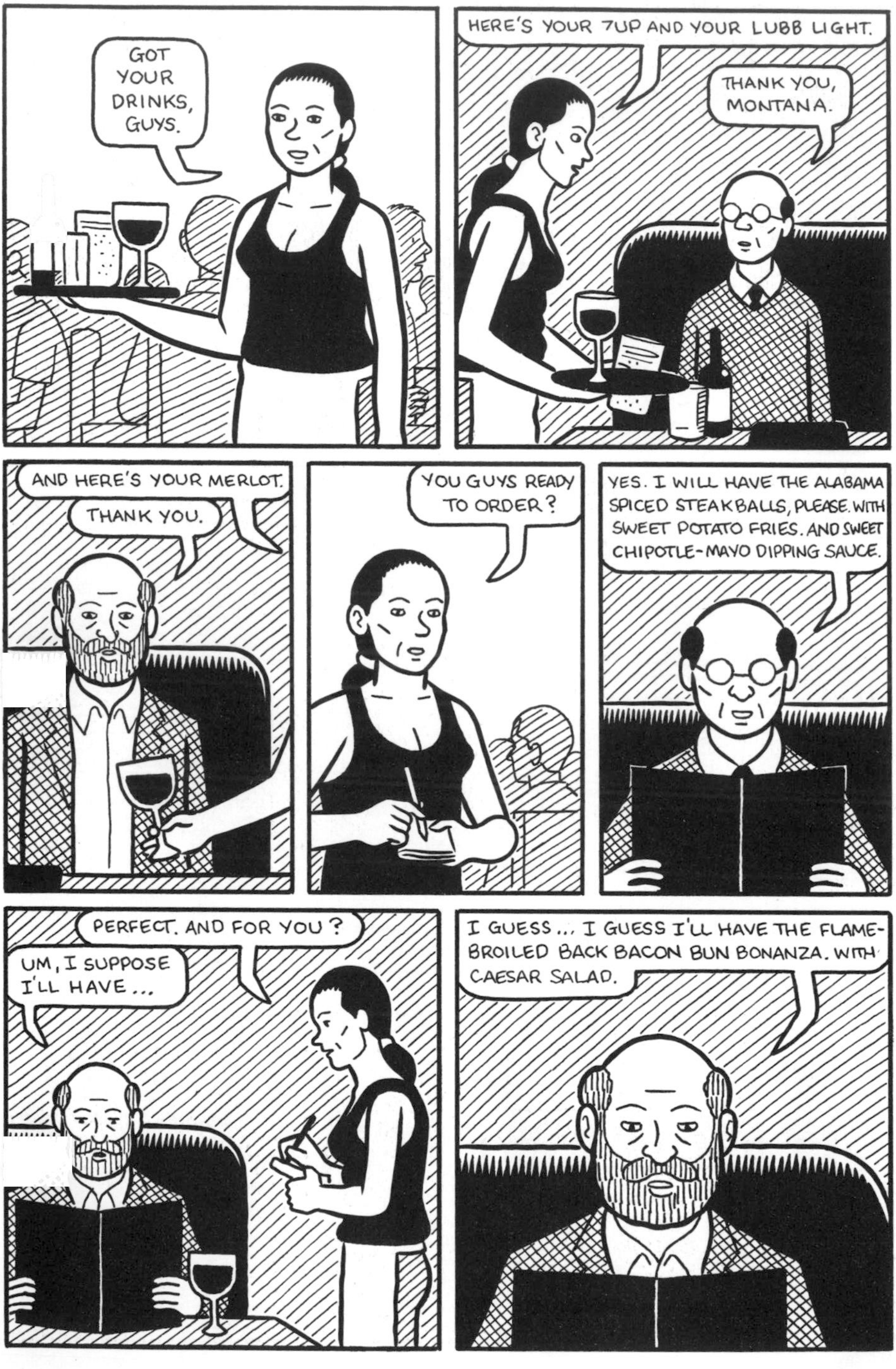
GOT YOUR DRINKS, GUYS.
HERE'S YOUR 7UP AND YOUR LUBB LIGHT.
THANK YOU, MONTANA.
AND HERE'S YOUR MERLOT.
THANK YOU.
YOU GUYS READY TO ORDER?
YES. I WILL HAVE THE ALABAMA SPICED STEAKBALLS, PLEASE. WITH SWEET POTATO FRIES. AND SWEET CHIPOTLE-MAYO DIPPING SAUCE.
PERFECT. AND FOR YOU?
UM, I SUPPOSE I'LL HAVE ...
I GUESS ... I GUESS I'LL HAVE THE FLAME-BROILED BACK BACON BUN BONANZA. WITH CAESAR SALAD.

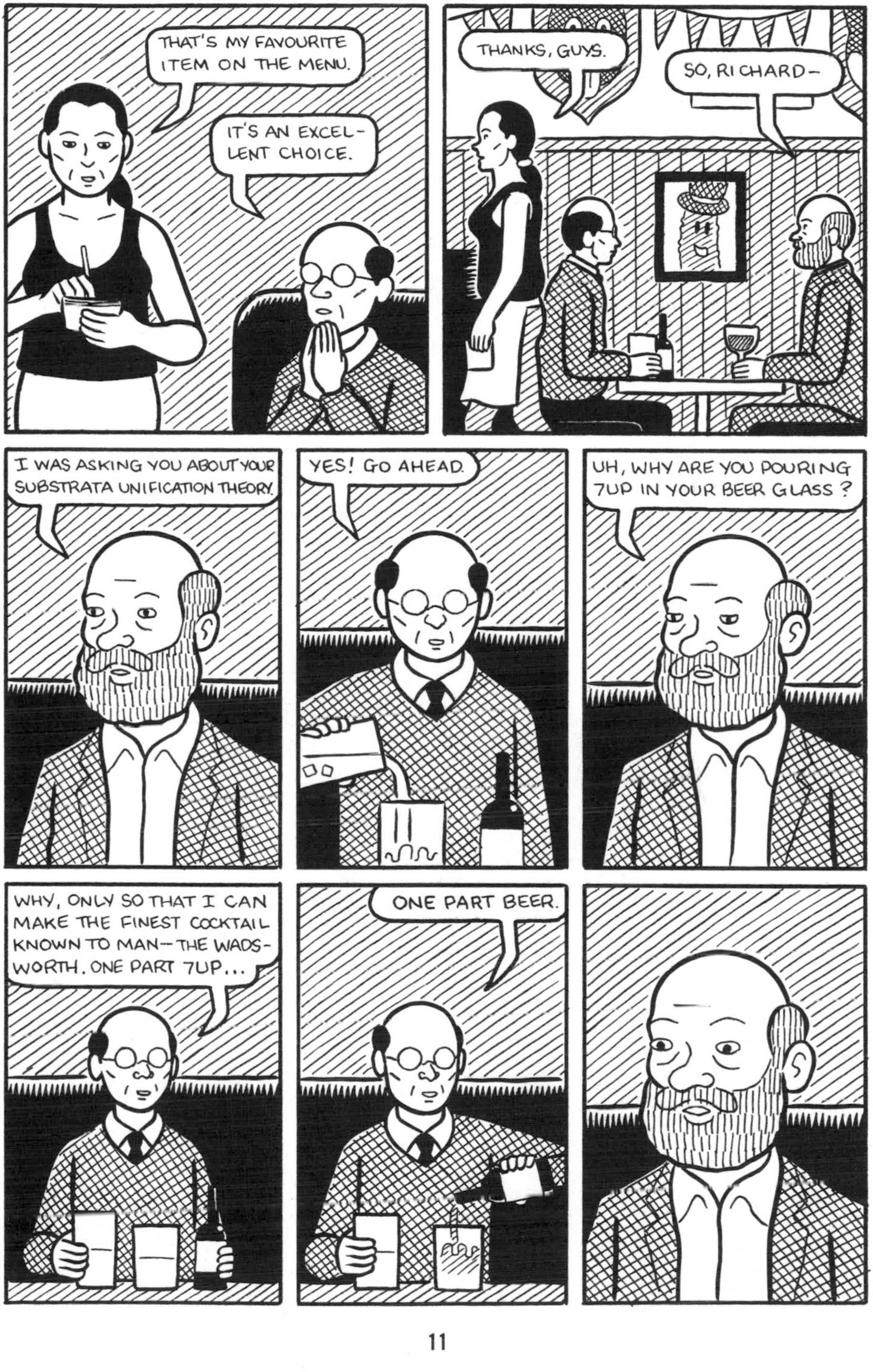
THAT'S MY FAVOURITE ITEM ON THE MENU.
IT'S AN EXCEL-LENT CHOICE.
THANKS, GUYS.
SO, RICHARD—
I WAS ASKING YOU ABOUT YOUR SUBSTRATA UNIFICATION THEORY.
YES! GO AHEAD.
UH, WHY ARE YOU POURING 7UP IN YOUR BEER GLASS?
WHY, ONLY SO THAT I CAN MAKE THE FINEST COCKTAIL KNOWN TO MAN—THE WADS-WORTH. ONE PART 7UP...
ONE PART BEER.

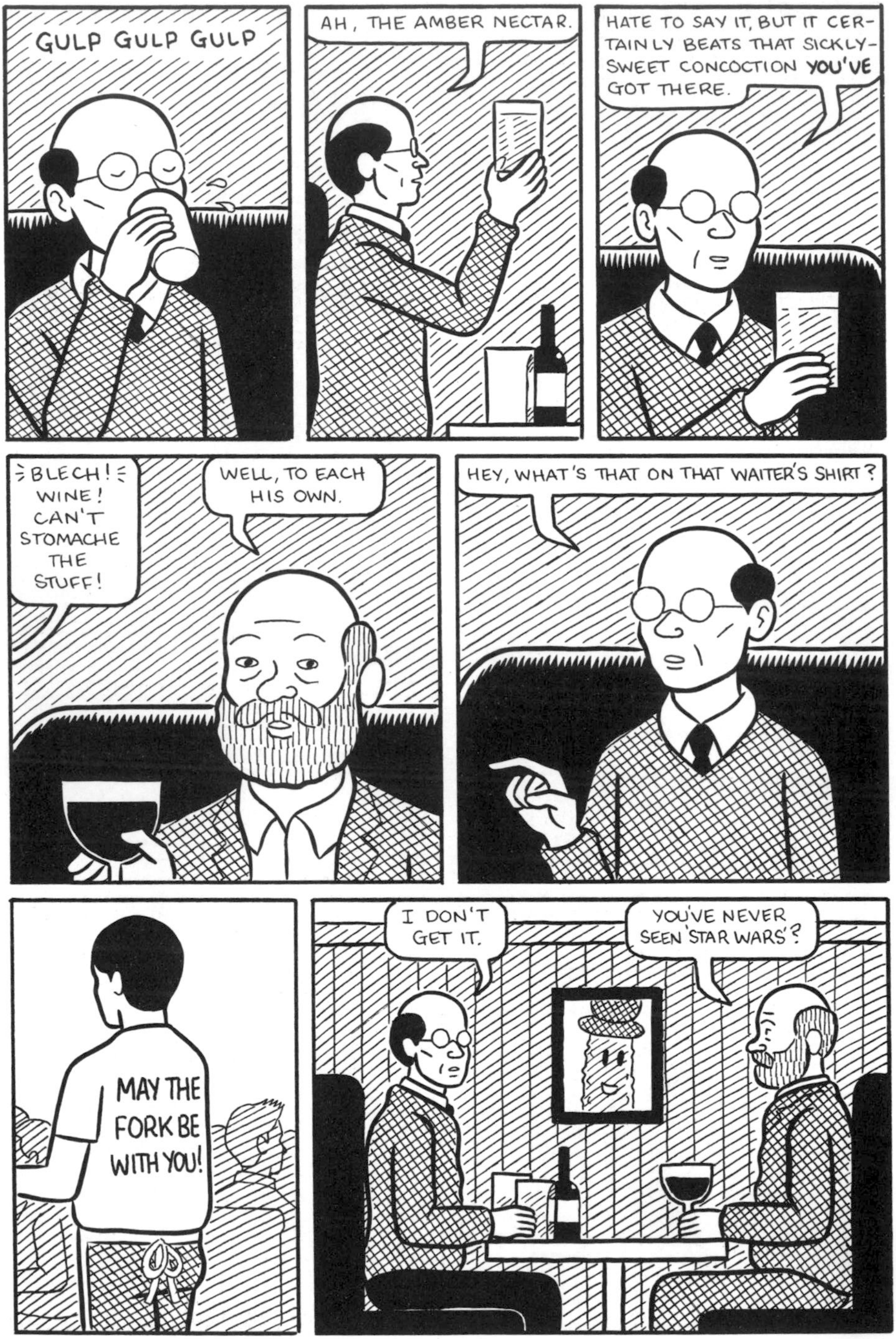
GULP GULP GULP
AH, THE AMBER NECTAR.
HATE TO SAY IT, BUT IT CERTAINLY BEATS THAT SICKLY-SWEET CONCOCTION **YOU'VE** GOT THERE.
BLECH! WINE! CAN'T STOMACHE THE STUFF!
WELL, TO EACH HIS OWN.
HEY, WHAT'S THAT ON THAT WAITER'S SHIRT?
MAY THE FORK BE WITH YOU!
I DON'T GET IT.
YOU'VE NEVER SEEN 'STAR WARS'?

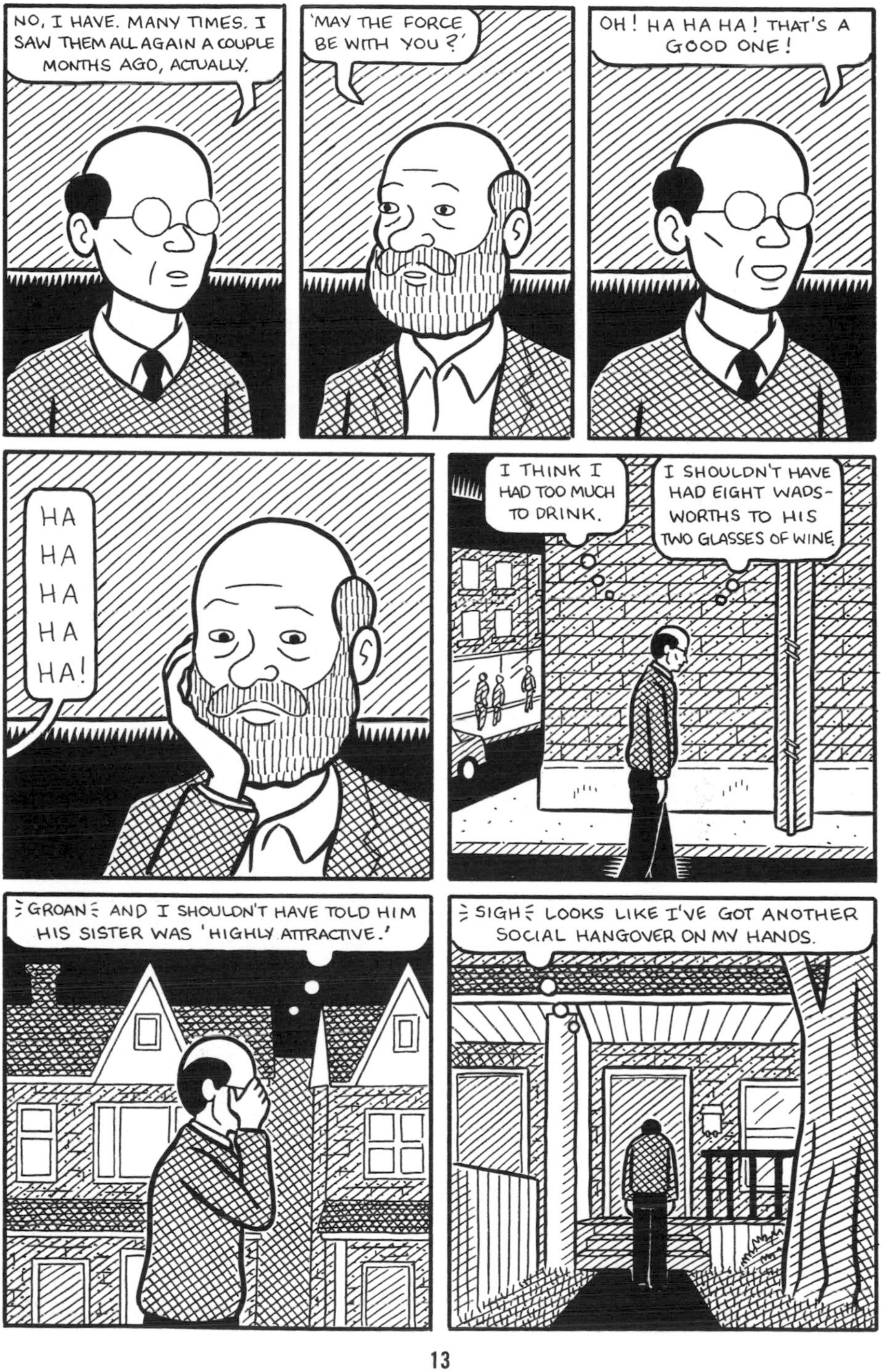
NO, I HAVE. MANY TIMES. I SAW THEM ALL AGAIN A COUPLE MONTHS AGO, ACTUALLY.
'MAY THE FORCE BE WITH YOU?'
OH! HA HA HA! THAT'S A GOOD ONE!
HA HA HA HA HA!
I THINK I HAD TOO MUCH TO DRINK.
I SHOULDN'T HAVE HAD EIGHT WADSWORTHS TO HIS TWO GLASSES OF WINE.
GROAN AND I SHOULDN'T HAVE TOLD HIM HIS SISTER WAS 'HIGHLY ATTRACTIVE.'
SIGH LOOKS LIKE I'VE GOT ANOTHER SOCIAL HANGOVER ON MY HANDS.

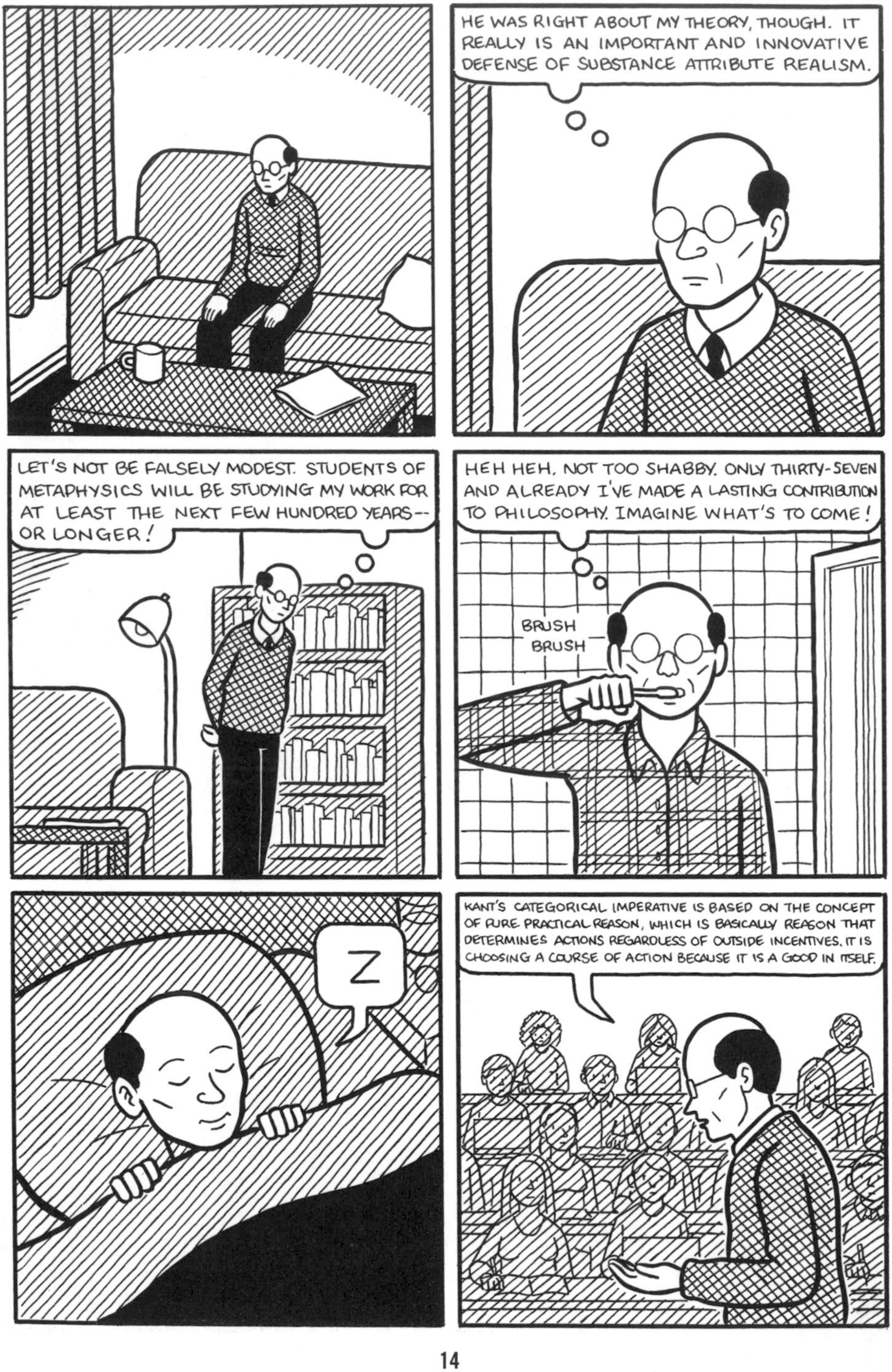
HE WAS RIGHT ABOUT MY THEORY, THOUGH. IT REALLY IS AN IMPORTANT AND INNOVATIVE DEFENSE OF SUBSTANCE ATTRIBUTE REALISM.
LET'S NOT BE FALSELY MODEST. STUDENTS OF METAPHYSICS WILL BE STUDYING MY WORK FOR AT LEAST THE NEXT FEW HUNDRED YEARS-- OR LONGER!
HEH HEH, NOT TOO SHABBY. ONLY THIRTY-SEVEN AND ALREADY I'VE MADE A LASTING CONTRIBUTION TO PHILOSOPHY. IMAGINE WHAT'S TO COME!
BRUSH
BRUSH
Z
KANT'S CATEGORICAL IMPERATIVE IS BASED ON THE CONCEPT OF PURE PRACTICAL REASON, WHICH IS BASICALLY REASON THAT DETERMINES ACTIONS REGARDLESS OF OUTSIDE INCENTIVES. IT IS CHOOSING A COURSE OF ACTION BECAUSE IT IS A GOOD IN ITSELF.

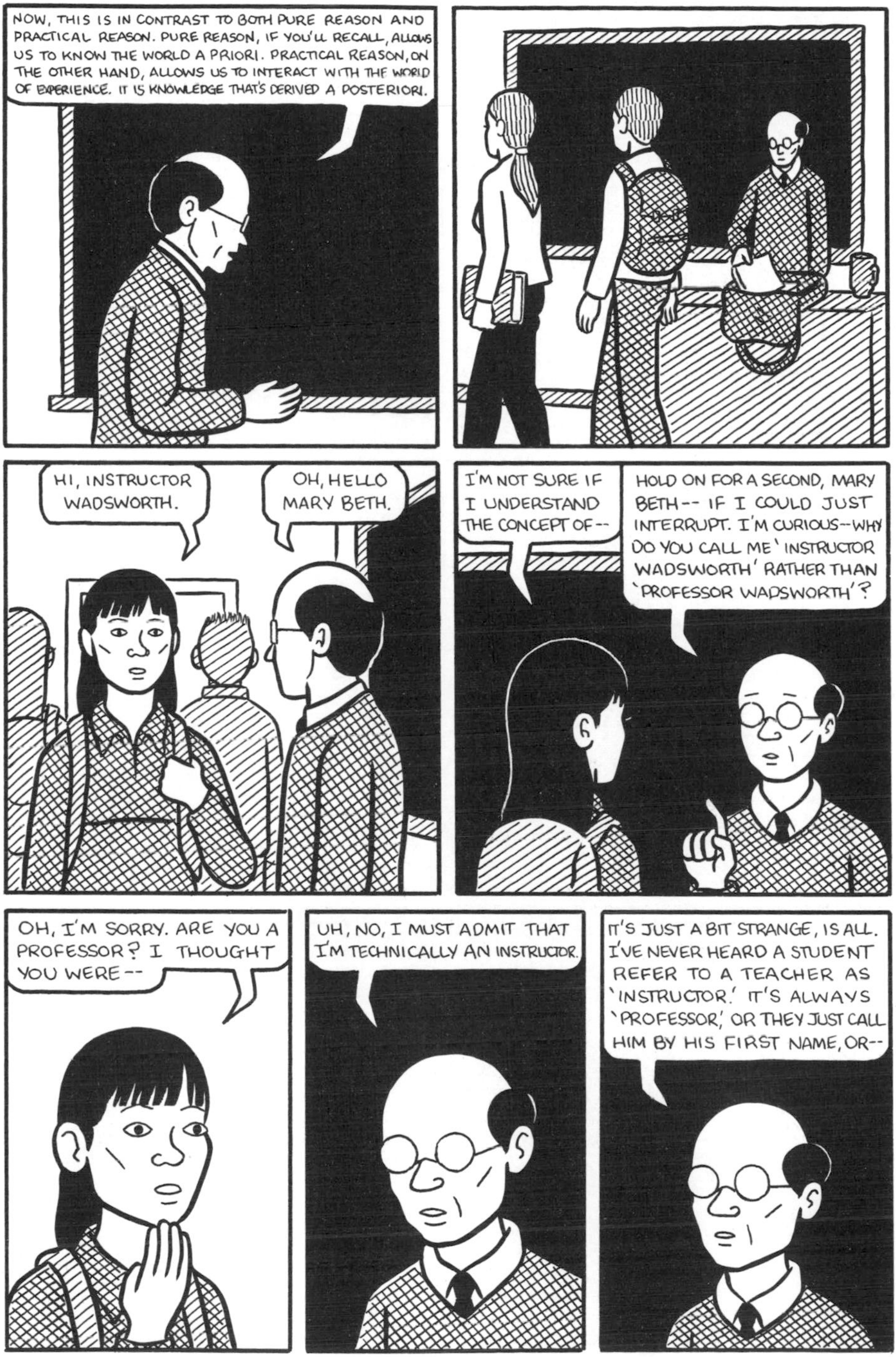
NOW, THIS IS IN CONTRAST TO BOTH PURE REASON AND PRACTICAL REASON. PURE REASON, IF YOU'LL RECALL, ALLOWS US TO KNOW THE WORLD A PRIORI. PRACTICAL REASON, ON THE OTHER HAND, ALLOWS US TO INTERACT WITH THE WORLD OF EXPERIENCE. IT IS KNOWLEDGE THAT'S DERIVED A POSTERIORI.
HI, INSTRUCTOR WADSWORTH.
OH, HELLO MARY BETH.
I'M NOT SURE IF I UNDERSTAND THE CONCEPT OF--
HOLD ON FOR A SECOND, MARY BETH-- IF I COULD JUST INTERRUPT. I'M CURIOUS--WHY DO YOU CALL ME 'INSTRUCTOR WADSWORTH' RATHER THAN 'PROFESSOR WADSWORTH'?
OH, I'M SORRY. ARE YOU A PROFESSOR? I THOUGHT YOU WERE--
UH, NO, I MUST ADMIT THAT I'M TECHNICALLY AN INSTRUCTOR.
IT'S JUST A BIT STRANGE, IS ALL. I'VE NEVER HEARD A STUDENT REFER TO A TEACHER AS 'INSTRUCTOR.' IT'S ALWAYS 'PROFESSOR,' OR THEY JUST CALL HIM BY HIS FIRST NAME, OR--

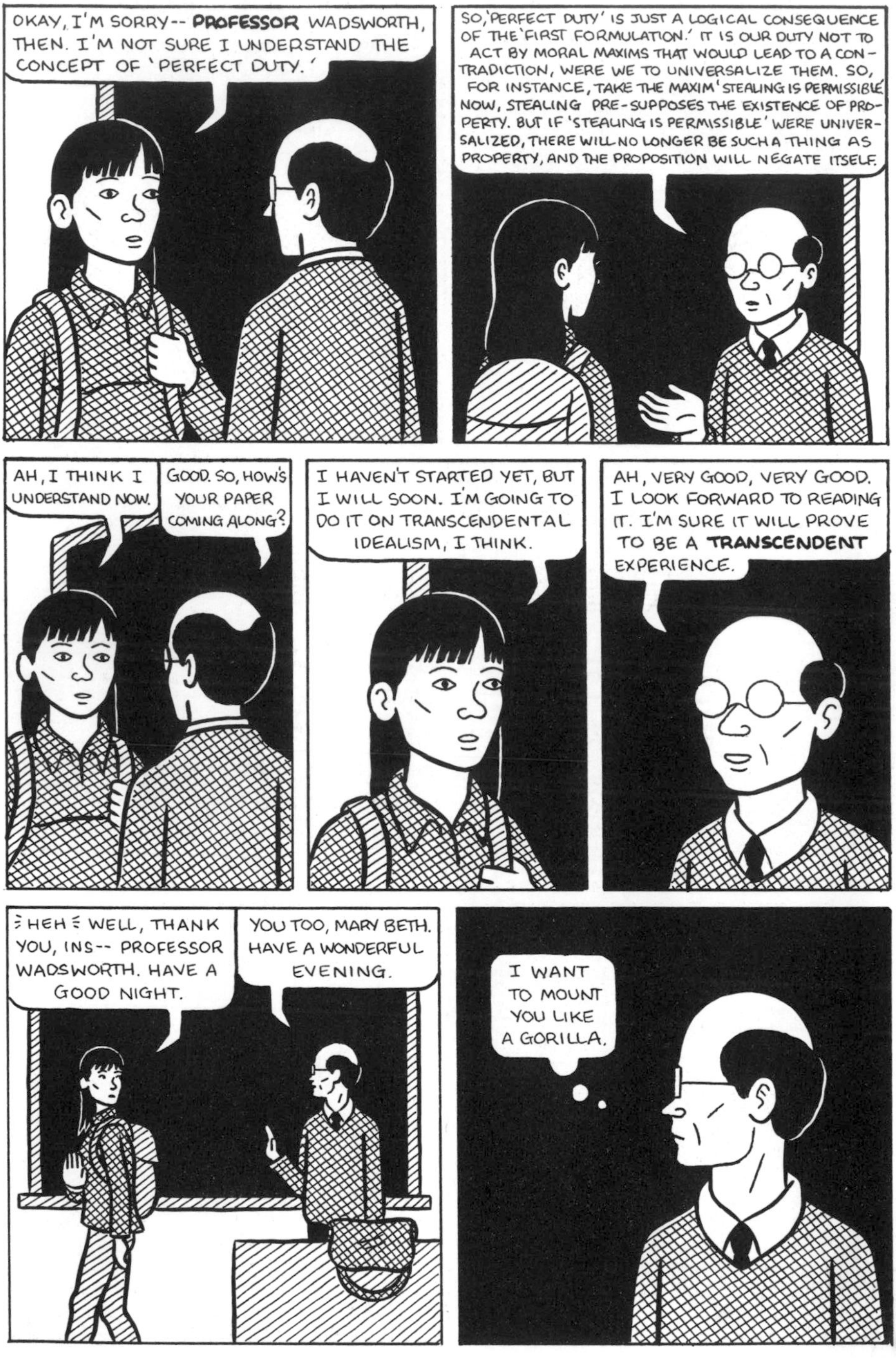
OKAY, I'M SORRY-- **PROFESSOR** WADSWORTH, THEN. I'M NOT SURE I UNDERSTAND THE CONCEPT OF 'PERFECT DUTY.'
SO, 'PERFECT DUTY' IS JUST A LOGICAL CONSEQUENCE OF THE 'FIRST FORMULATION.' IT IS OUR DUTY NOT TO ACT BY MORAL MAXIMS THAT WOULD LEAD TO A CONTRADICTION, WERE WE TO UNIVERSALIZE THEM. SO, FOR INSTANCE, TAKE THE MAXIM 'STEALING IS PERMISSIBLE.' NOW, STEALING PRE-SUPPOSES THE EXISTENCE OF PROPERTY. BUT IF 'STEALING IS PERMISSIBLE' WERE UNIVERSALIZED, THERE WILL NO LONGER BE SUCH A THING AS PROPERTY, AND THE PROPOSITION WILL NEGATE ITSELF.
AH, I THINK I UNDERSTAND NOW.
GOOD. SO, HOW'S YOUR PAPER COMING ALONG?
I HAVEN'T STARTED YET, BUT I WILL SOON. I'M GOING TO DO IT ON TRANSCENDENTAL IDEALISM, I THINK.
AH, VERY GOOD, VERY GOOD. I LOOK FORWARD TO READING IT. I'M SURE IT WILL PROVE TO BE A **TRANSCENDENT** EXPERIENCE.
HEH WELL, THANK YOU, INS-- PROFESSOR WADSWORTH. HAVE A GOOD NIGHT.
YOU TOO, MARY BETH. HAVE A WONDERFUL EVENING.
I WANT TO MOUNT YOU LIKE A GORILLA.

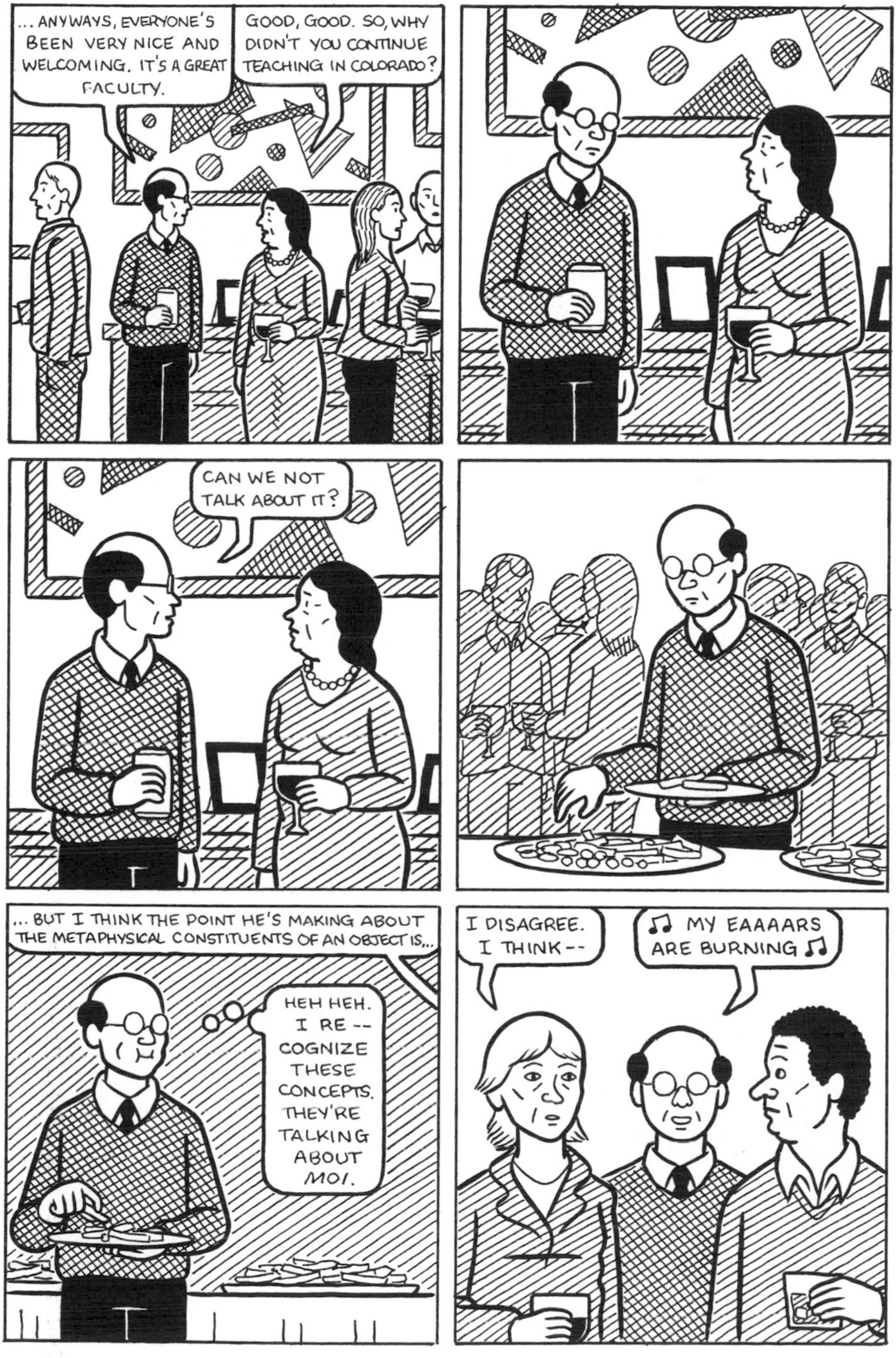
... ANYWAYS, EVERYONE'S BEEN VERY NICE AND WELCOMING. IT'S A GREAT FACULTY.
GOOD, GOOD. SO, WHY DIDN'T YOU CONTINUE TEACHING IN COLORADO?
CAN WE NOT TALK ABOUT IT?
... BUT I THINK THE POINT HE'S MAKING ABOUT THE METAPHYSICAL CONSTITUENTS OF AN OBJECT IS,...
HEH HEH. I RE -- COGNIZE THESE CONCEPTS. THEY'RE TALKING ABOUT MOI.
I DISAGREE. I THINK --
♫ MY EAAAARS ARE BURNING ♫

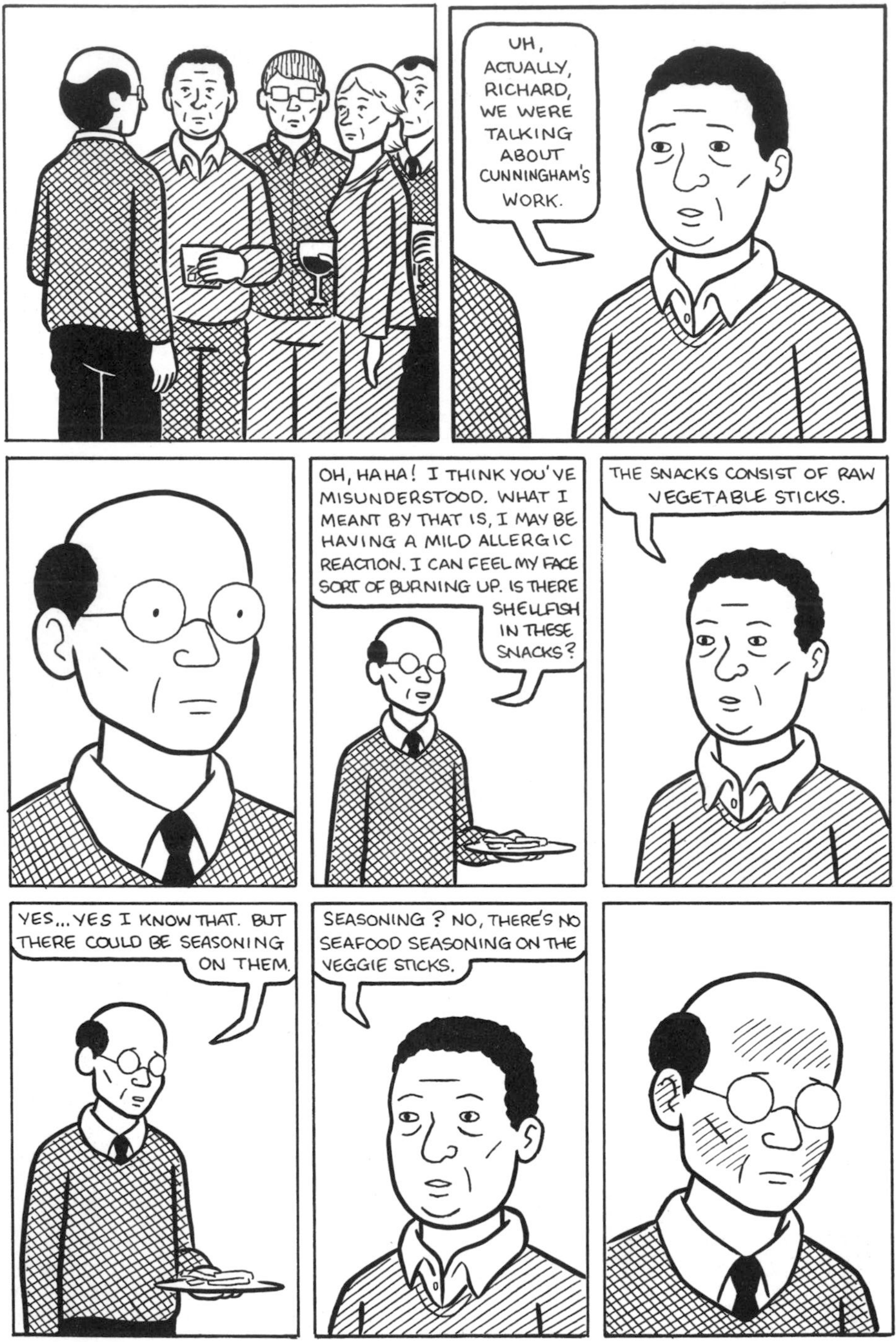
UH, ACTUALLY, RICHARD, WE WERE TALKING ABOUT CUNNINGHAM'S WORK.
OH, HAHA! I THINK YOU'VE MISUNDERSTOOD. WHAT I MEANT BY THAT IS, I MAY BE HAVING A MILD ALLERGIC REACTION. I CAN FEEL MY FACE SORT OF BURNING UP. IS THERE SHELLFISH IN THESE SNACKS?
THE SNACKS CONSIST OF RAW VEGETABLE STICKS.
YES... YES I KNOW THAT. BUT THERE COULD BE SEASONING ON THEM.
SEASONING? NO, THERE'S NO SEAFOOD SEASONING ON THE VEGGIE STICKS.

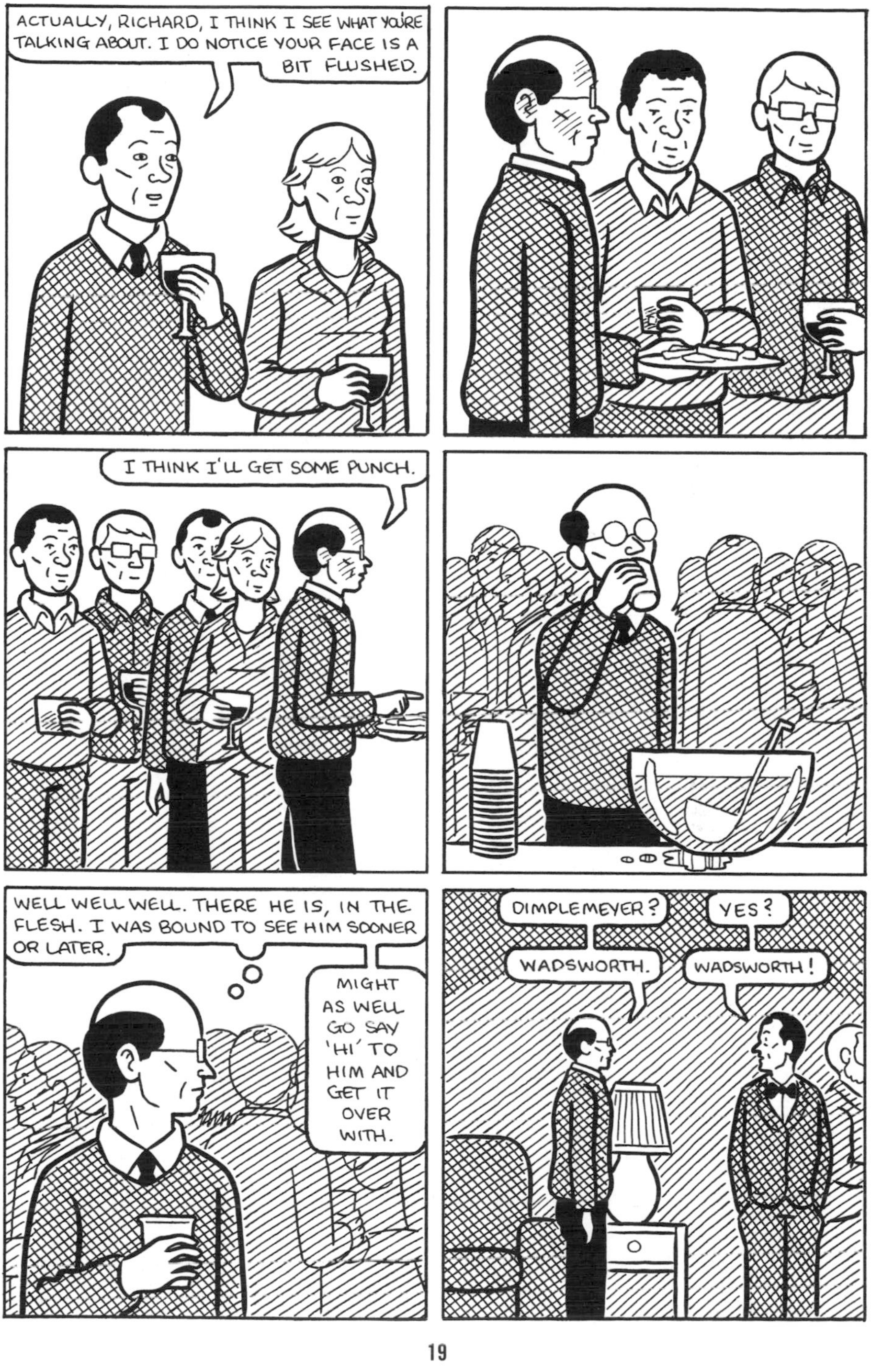
ACTUALLY, RICHARD, I THINK I SEE WHAT YOU'RE TALKING ABOUT. I DO NOTICE YOUR FACE IS A BIT FLUSHED.
I THINK I'LL GET SOME PUNCH.
WELL WELL WELL. THERE HE IS, IN THE FLESH. I WAS BOUND TO SEE HIM SOONER OR LATER.
MIGHT AS WELL GO SAY 'HI' TO HIM AND GET IT OVER WITH.
DIMPLEMEYER?
YES?
WADSWORTH.
WADSWORTH!

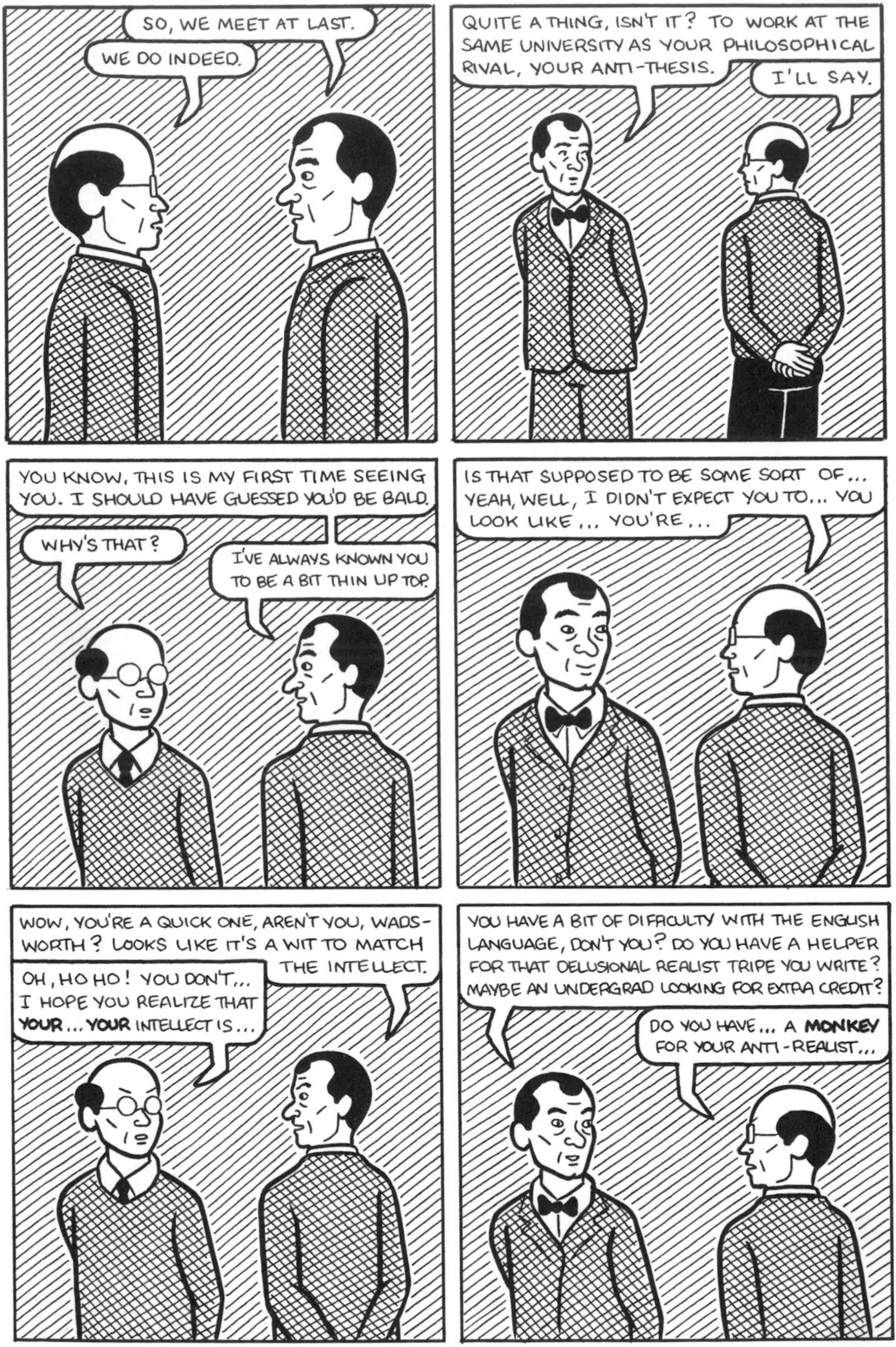
SO, WE MEET AT LAST.
WE DO INDEED.
QUITE A THING, ISN'T IT? TO WORK AT THE SAME UNIVERSITY AS YOUR PHILOSOPHICAL RIVAL, YOUR ANTI-THESIS.
I'LL SAY.
YOU KNOW, THIS IS MY FIRST TIME SEEING YOU. I SHOULD HAVE GUESSED YOU'D BE BALD.
WHY'S THAT?
I'VE ALWAYS KNOWN YOU TO BE A BIT THIN UP TOP.
IS THAT SUPPOSED TO BE SOME SORT OF... YEAH, WELL, I DIDN'T EXPECT YOU TO... YOU LOOK LIKE... YOU'RE...
WOW, YOU'RE A QUICK ONE, AREN'T YOU, WADSWORTH? LOOKS LIKE IT'S A WIT TO MATCH THE INTELLECT.
OH, HO HO! YOU DON'T... I HOPE YOU REALIZE THAT **YOUR**... **YOUR** INTELLECT IS...
YOU HAVE A BIT OF DIFFICULTY WITH THE ENGLISH LANGUAGE, DON'T YOU? DO YOU HAVE A HELPER FOR THAT DELUSIONAL REALIST TRIPE YOU WRITE? MAYBE AN UNDERGRAD LOOKING FOR EXTRA CREDIT?
DO YOU HAVE... A **MONKEY** FOR YOUR ANTI-REALIST...

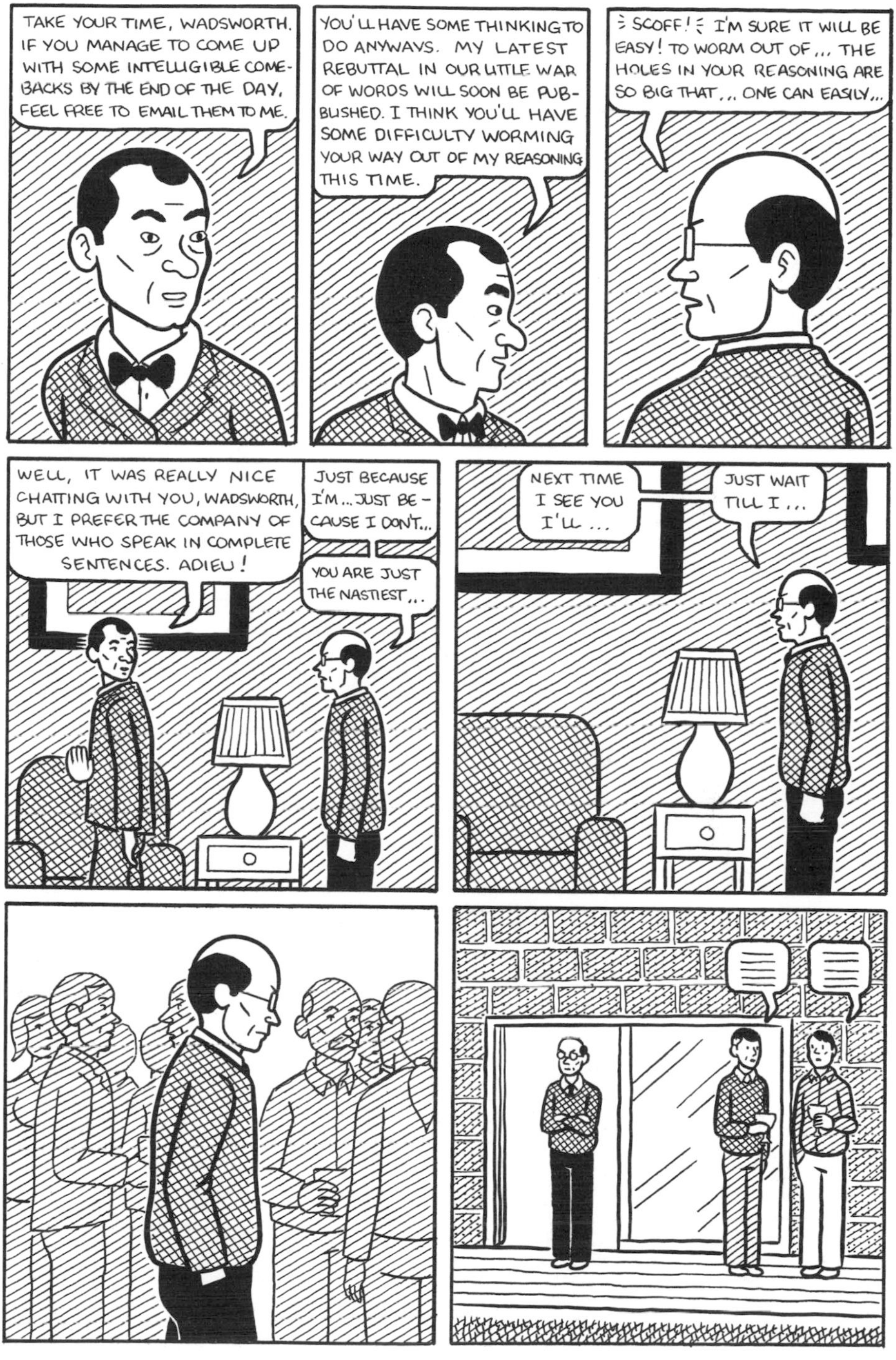
TAKE YOUR TIME, WADSWORTH. IF YOU MANAGE TO COME UP WITH SOME INTELLIGIBLE COME-BACKS BY THE END OF THE DAY, FEEL FREE TO EMAIL THEM TO ME.
YOU'LL HAVE SOME THINKING TO DO ANYWAYS. MY LATEST REBUTTAL IN OUR LITTLE WAR OF WORDS WILL SOON BE PUB-BLISHED. I THINK YOU'LL HAVE SOME DIFFICULTY WORMING YOUR WAY OUT OF MY REASONING THIS TIME.
SCOFF! I'M SURE IT WILL BE EASY! TO WORM OUT OF... THE HOLES IN YOUR REASONING ARE SO BIG THAT... ONE CAN EASILY...
WELL, IT WAS REALLY NICE CHATTING WITH YOU, WADSWORTH, BUT I PREFER THE COMPANY OF THOSE WHO SPEAK IN COMPLETE SENTENCES. ADIEU!
JUST BECAUSE I'M... JUST BE-CAUSE I DON'T...
YOU ARE JUST THE NASTIEST...
NEXT TIME I SEE YOU I'LL ...
JUST WAIT TILL I...

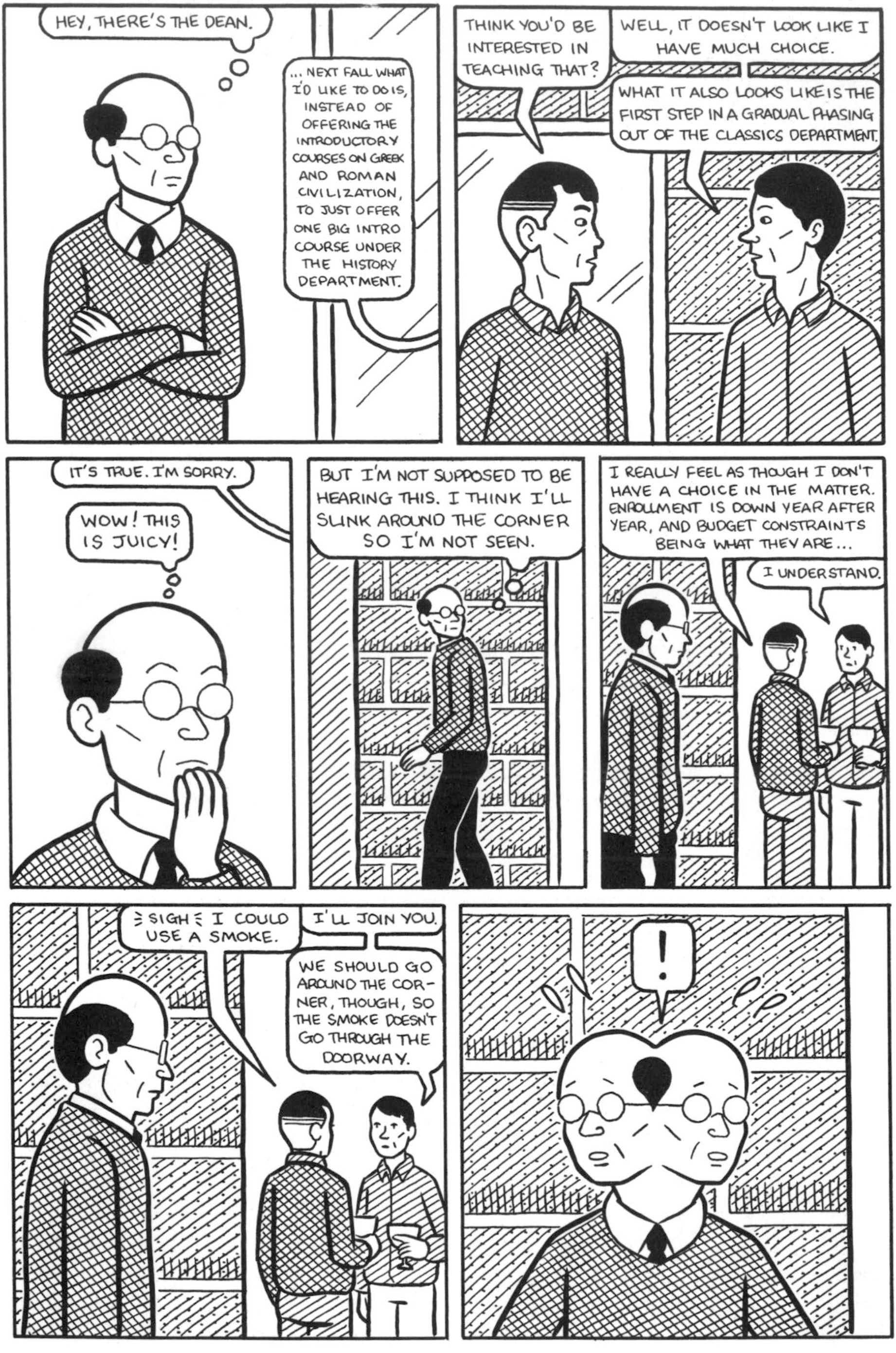
HEY, THERE'S THE DEAN.
... NEXT FALL WHAT I'D LIKE TO DO IS, INSTEAD OF OFFERING THE INTRODUCTORY COURSES ON GREEK AND ROMAN CIVILIZATION, TO JUST OFFER ONE BIG INTRO COURSE UNDER THE HISTORY DEPARTMENT.
THINK YOU'D BE INTERESTED IN TEACHING THAT?
WELL, IT DOESN'T LOOK LIKE I HAVE MUCH CHOICE.
WHAT IT ALSO LOOKS LIKE IS THE FIRST STEP IN A GRADUAL PHASING OUT OF THE CLASSICS DEPARTMENT.
IT'S TRUE. I'M SORRY.
WOW! THIS IS JUICY!
BUT I'M NOT SUPPOSED TO BE HEARING THIS. I THINK I'LL SLINK AROUND THE CORNER SO I'M NOT SEEN.
I REALLY FEEL AS THOUGH I DON'T HAVE A CHOICE IN THE MATTER. ENROLLMENT IS DOWN YEAR AFTER YEAR, AND BUDGET CONSTRAINTS BEING WHAT THEY ARE...
I UNDERSTAND.
≷SIGH≶ I COULD USE A SMOKE.
I'LL JOIN YOU.
WE SHOULD GO AROUND THE CORNER, THOUGH, SO THE SMOKE DOESN'T GO THROUGH THE DOORWAY.
!

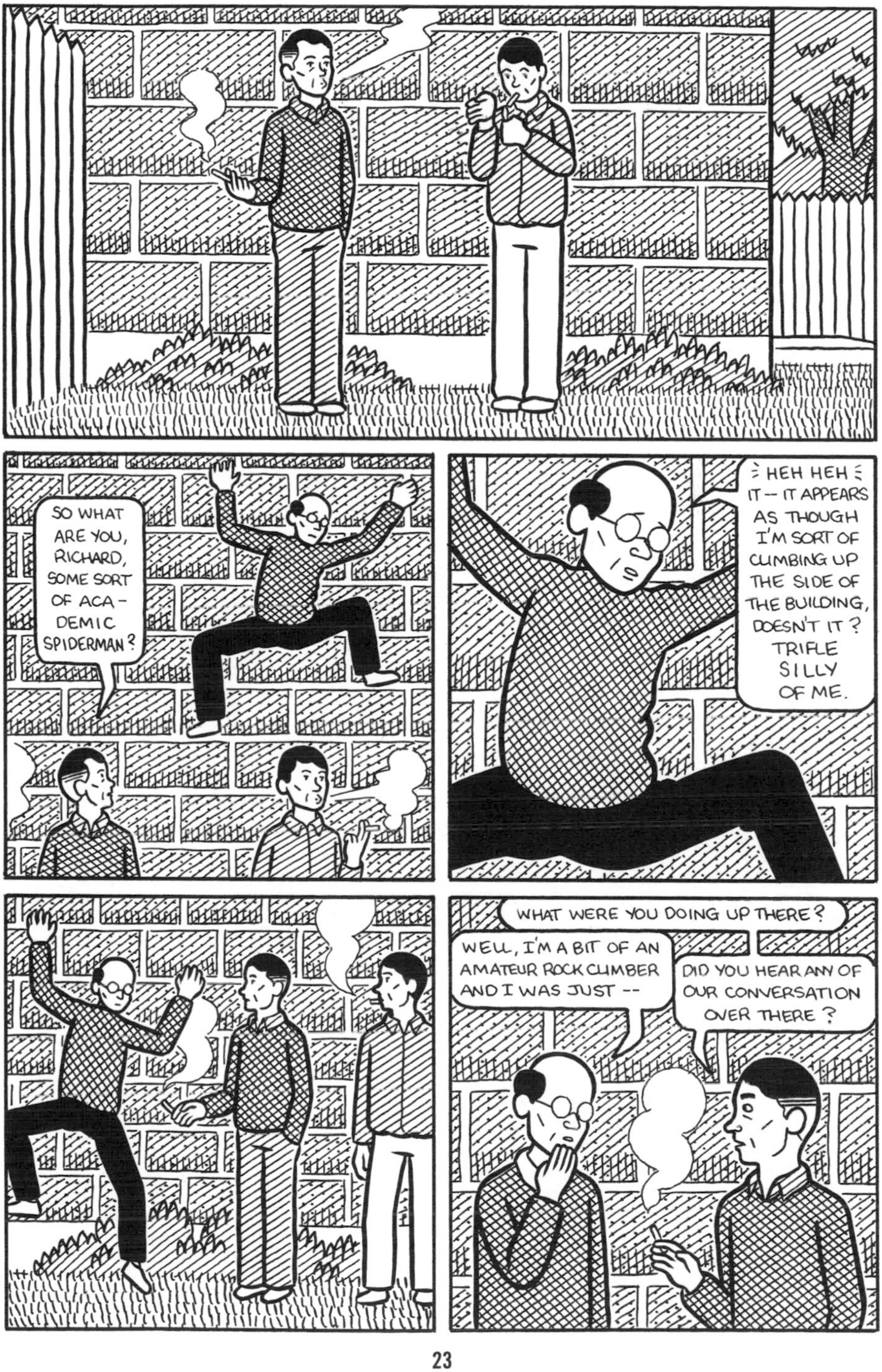
SO WHAT ARE YOU, RICHARD, SOME SORT OF ACA-DEMIC SPIDERMAN?
HEH HEH IT-- IT APPEARS AS THOUGH I'M SORT OF CLIMBING UP THE SIDE OF THE BUILDING, DOESN'T IT? TRIFLE SILLY OF ME.
WHAT WERE YOU DOING UP THERE?
WELL, I'M A BIT OF AN AMATEUR ROCK CLIMBER AND I WAS JUST --
DID YOU HEAR ANY OF OUR CONVERSATION OVER THERE?

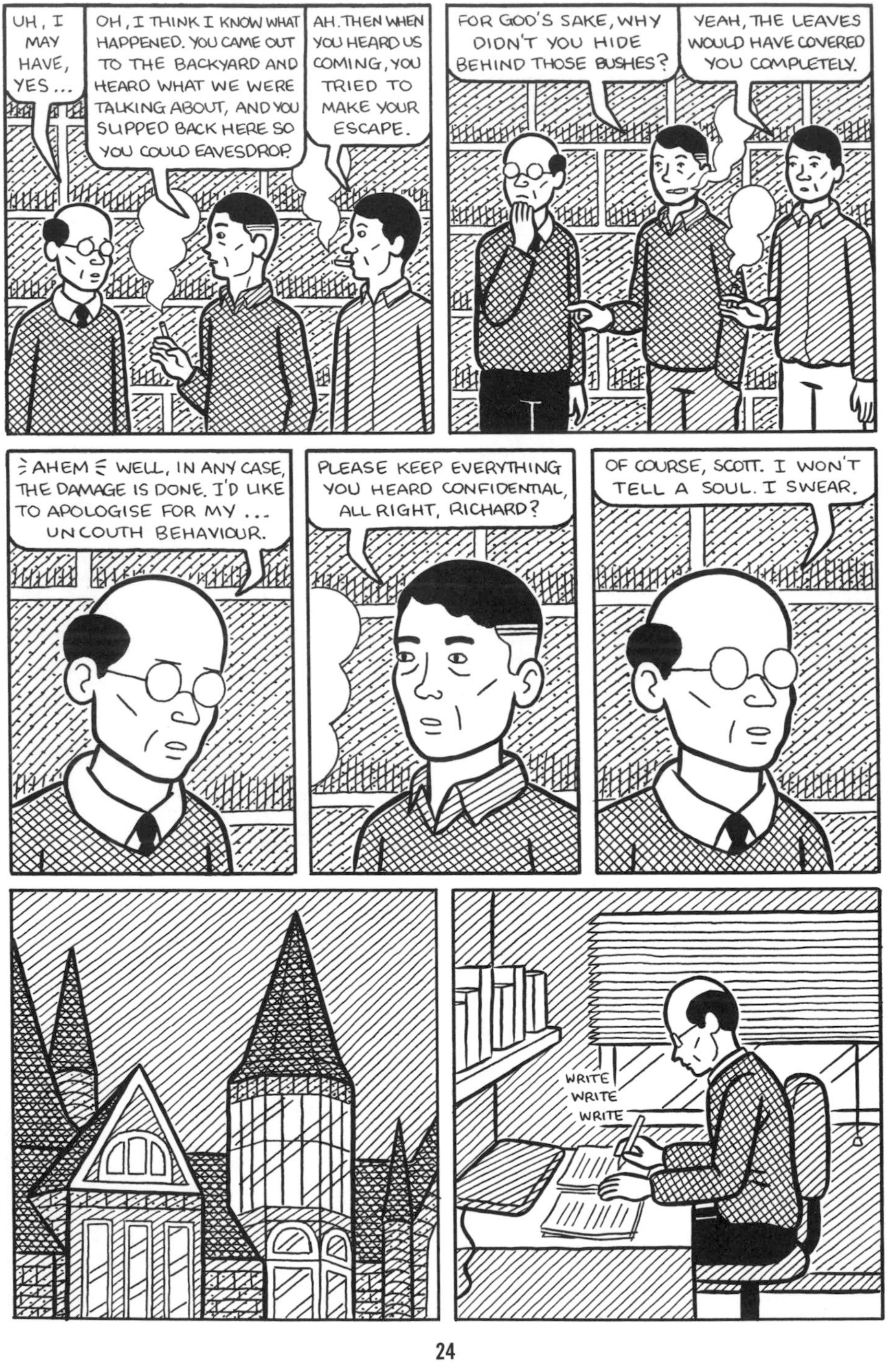
UH, I MAY HAVE, YES...
OH, I THINK I KNOW WHAT HAPPENED. YOU CAME OUT TO THE BACKYARD AND HEARD WHAT WE WERE TALKING ABOUT, AND YOU SLIPPED BACK HERE SO YOU COULD EAVESDROP.
AH. THEN WHEN YOU HEARD US COMING, YOU TRIED TO MAKE YOUR ESCAPE.
FOR GOD'S SAKE, WHY DIDN'T YOU HIDE BEHIND THOSE BUSHES?
YEAH, THE LEAVES WOULD HAVE COVERED YOU COMPLETELY.
AHEM WELL, IN ANY CASE, THE DAMAGE IS DONE. I'D LIKE TO APOLOGISE FOR MY ... UNCOUTH BEHAVIOUR.
PLEASE KEEP EVERYTHING YOU HEARD CONFIDENTIAL, ALL RIGHT, RICHARD?
OF COURSE, SCOTT. I WON'T TELL A SOUL. I SWEAR.
WRITE WRITE WRITE

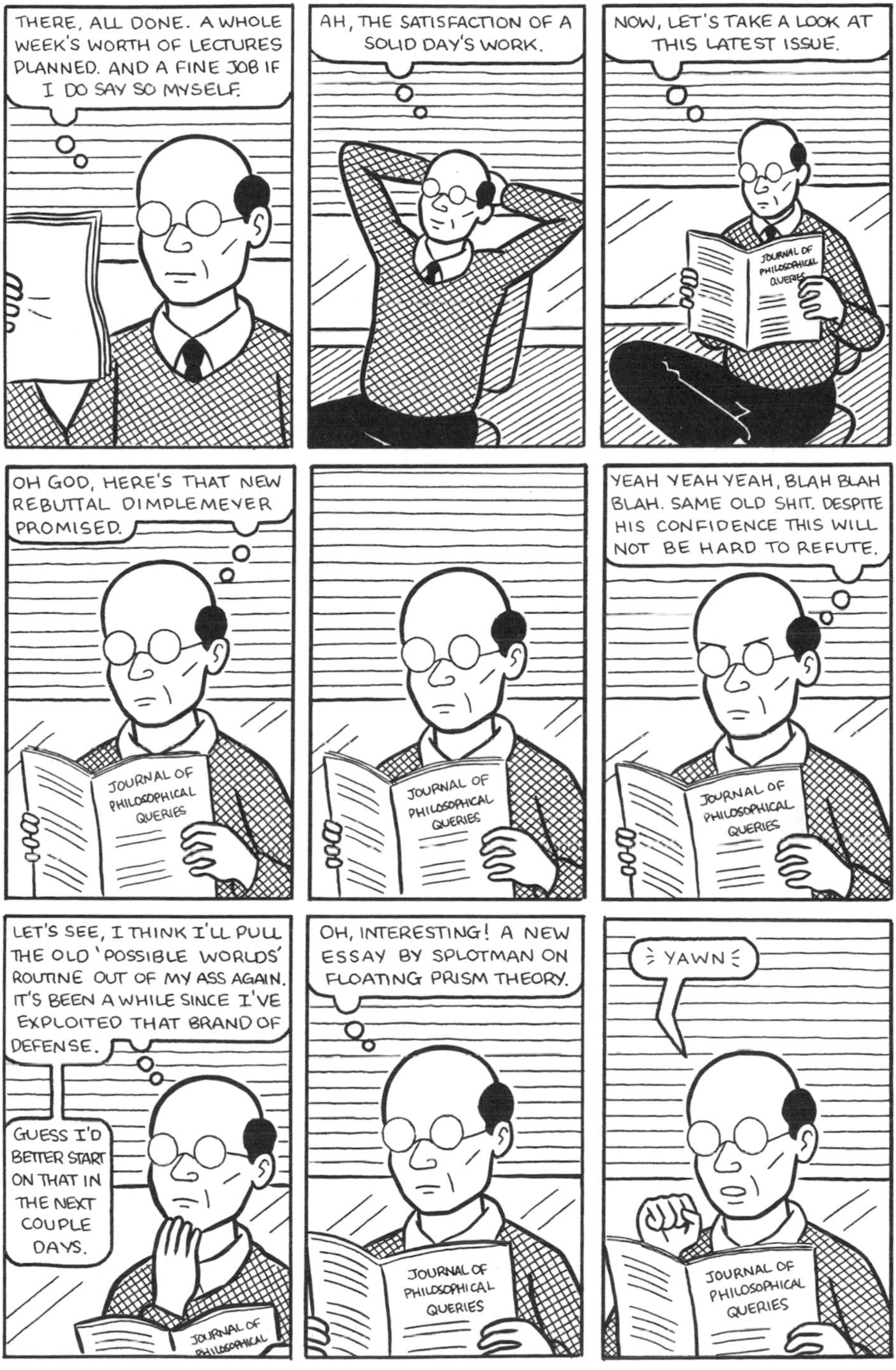
THERE, ALL DONE. A WHOLE WEEK'S WORTH OF LECTURES PLANNED. AND A FINE JOB IF I DO SAY SO MYSELF.
AH, THE SATISFACTION OF A SOLID DAY'S WORK.
NOW, LET'S TAKE A LOOK AT THIS LATEST ISSUE.
JOURNAL OF PHILOSOPHICAL QUERIES
OH GOD, HERE'S THAT NEW REBUTTAL DIMPLEMEYER PROMISED.
JOURNAL OF PHILOSOPHICAL QUERIES
JOURNAL OF PHILOSOPHICAL QUERIES
YEAH YEAH YEAH, BLAH BLAH BLAH. SAME OLD SHIT. DESPITE HIS CONFIDENCE THIS WILL NOT BE HARD TO REFUTE.
JOURNAL OF PHILOSOPHICAL QUERIES
LET'S SEE, I THINK I'LL PULL THE OLD 'POSSIBLE WORLDS' ROUTINE OUT OF MY ASS AGAIN. IT'S BEEN A WHILE SINCE I'VE EXPLOITED THAT BRAND OF DEFENSE.
GUESS I'D BETTER START ON THAT IN THE NEXT COUPLE DAYS.
JOURNAL OF PHILOSOPHICAL
OH, INTERESTING! A NEW ESSAY BY SPLOTMAN ON FLOATING PRISM THEORY.
JOURNAL OF PHILOSOPHICAL QUERIES
YAWN
JOURNAL OF PHILOSOPHICAL QUERIES

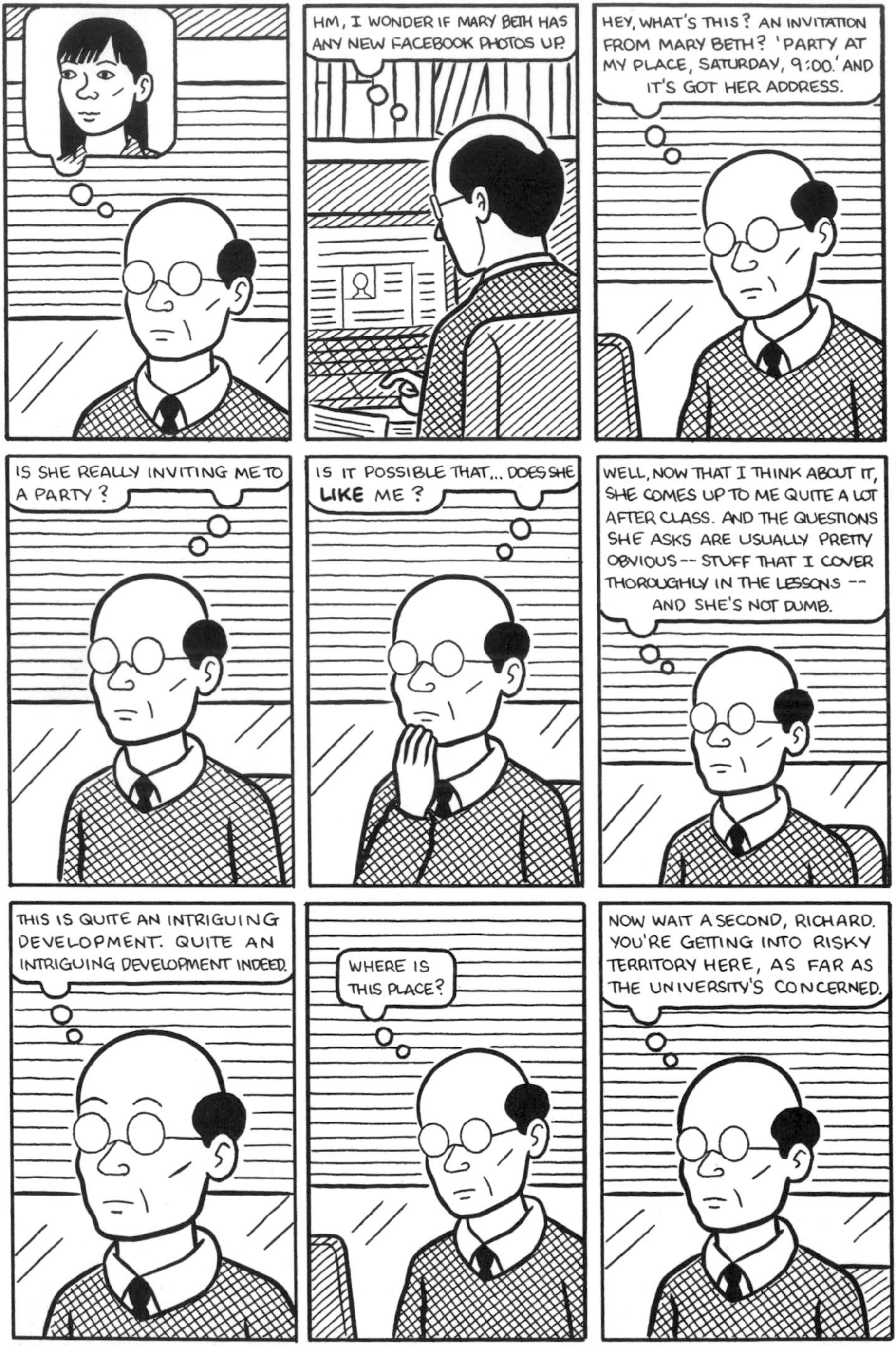
HM, I WONDER IF MARY BETH HAS ANY NEW FACEBOOK PHOTOS UP.
HEY, WHAT'S THIS? AN INVITATION FROM MARY BETH? 'PARTY AT MY PLACE, SATURDAY, 9:00.' AND IT'S GOT HER ADDRESS.
IS SHE REALLY INVITING ME TO A PARTY?
IS IT POSSIBLE THAT... DOES SHE **LIKE** ME?
WELL, NOW THAT I THINK ABOUT IT, SHE COMES UP TO ME QUITE A LOT AFTER CLASS. AND THE QUESTIONS SHE ASKS ARE USUALLY PRETTY OBVIOUS -- STUFF THAT I COVER THOROUGHLY IN THE LESSONS -- AND SHE'S NOT DUMB.
THIS IS QUITE AN INTRIGUING DEVELOPMENT. QUITE AN INTRIGUING DEVELOPMENT INDEED.
WHERE IS THIS PLACE?
NOW WAIT A SECOND, RICHARD. YOU'RE GETTING INTO RISKY TERRITORY HERE, AS FAR AS THE UNIVERSITY'S CONCERNED.

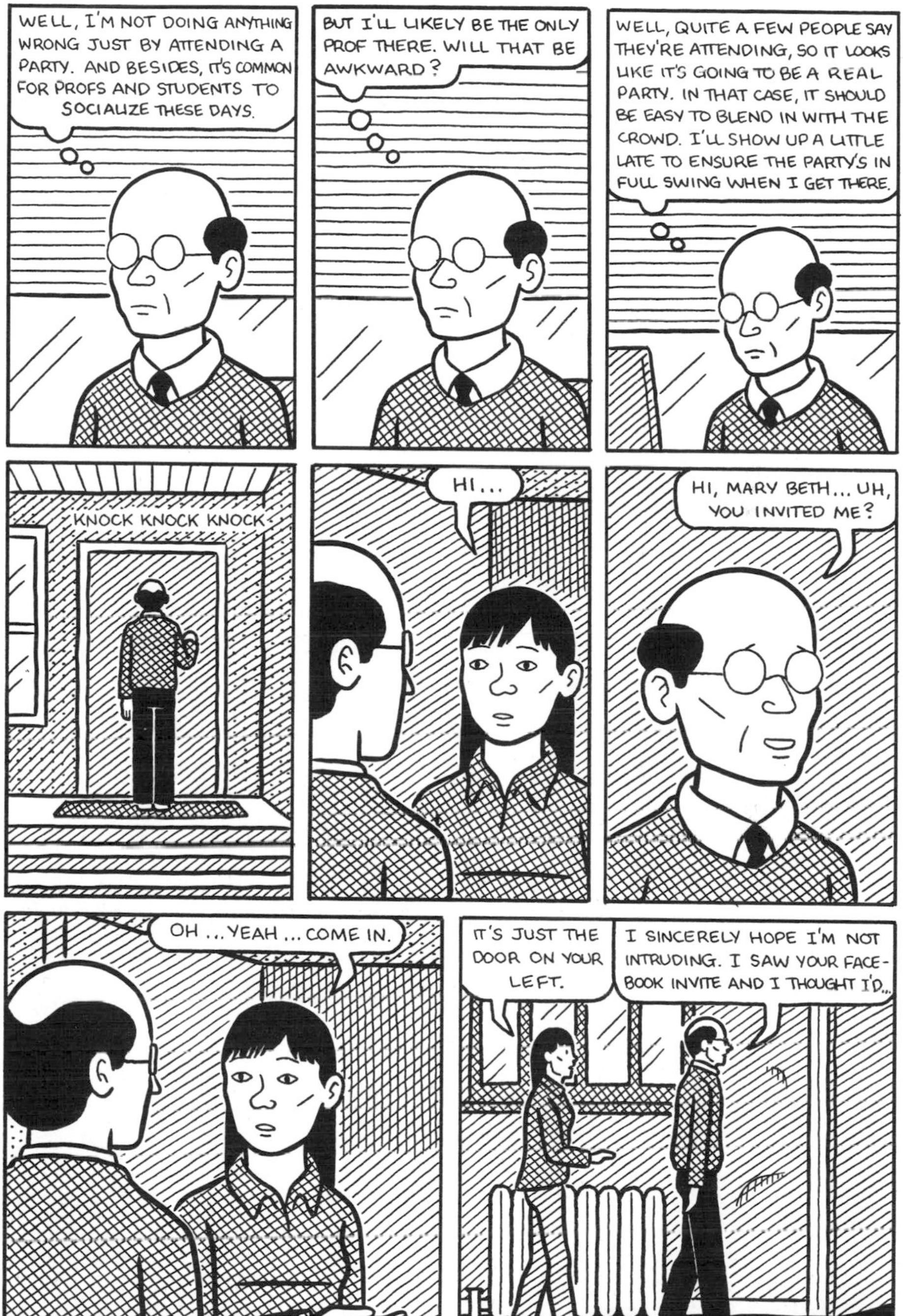
WELL, I'M NOT DOING ANYTHING WRONG JUST BY ATTENDING A PARTY. AND BESIDES, IT'S COMMON FOR PROFS AND STUDENTS TO SOCIALIZE THESE DAYS.
BUT I'LL LIKELY BE THE ONLY PROF THERE. WILL THAT BE AWKWARD?
WELL, QUITE A FEW PEOPLE SAY THEY'RE ATTENDING, SO IT LOOKS LIKE IT'S GOING TO BE A REAL PARTY. IN THAT CASE, IT SHOULD BE EASY TO BLEND IN WITH THE CROWD. I'LL SHOW UP A LITTLE LATE TO ENSURE THE PARTY'S IN FULL SWING WHEN I GET THERE.
KNOCK KNOCK KNOCK
HI...
HI, MARY BETH... UH, YOU INVITED ME?
OH ... YEAH ... COME IN.
IT'S JUST THE DOOR ON YOUR LEFT.
I SINCERELY HOPE I'M NOT INTRUDING. I SAW YOUR FACE-BOOK INVITE AND I THOUGHT I'D...

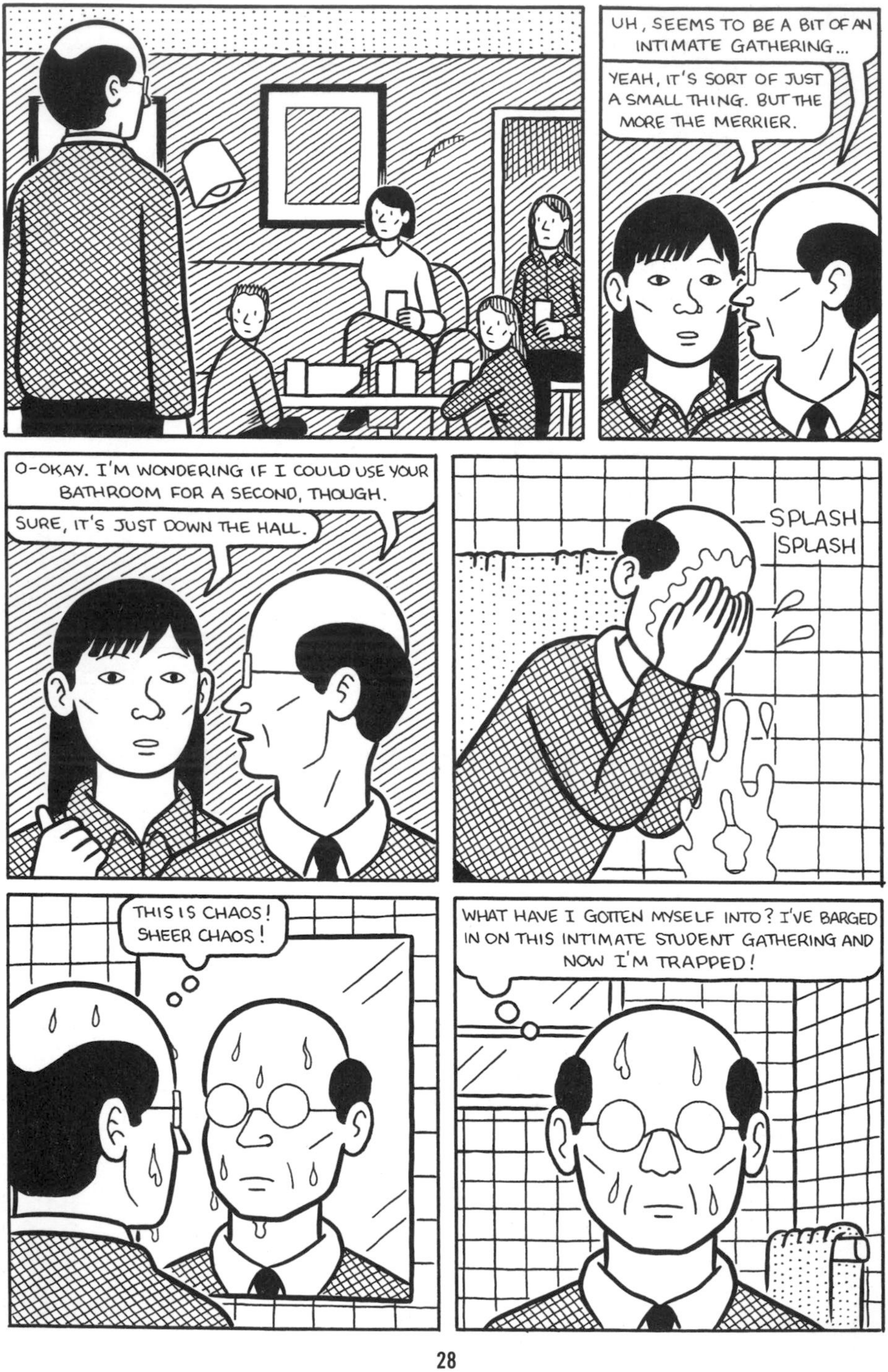
UH, SEEMS TO BE A BIT OF AN INTIMATE GATHERING...
YEAH, IT'S SORT OF JUST A SMALL THING. BUT THE MORE THE MERRIER.
O-OKAY. I'M WONDERING IF I COULD USE YOUR BATHROOM FOR A SECOND, THOUGH.
SURE, IT'S JUST DOWN THE HALL.
SPLASH
SPLASH
THIS IS CHAOS! SHEER CHAOS!
WHAT HAVE I GOTTEN MYSELF INTO? I'VE BARGED IN ON THIS INTIMATE STUDENT GATHERING AND NOW I'M TRAPPED!

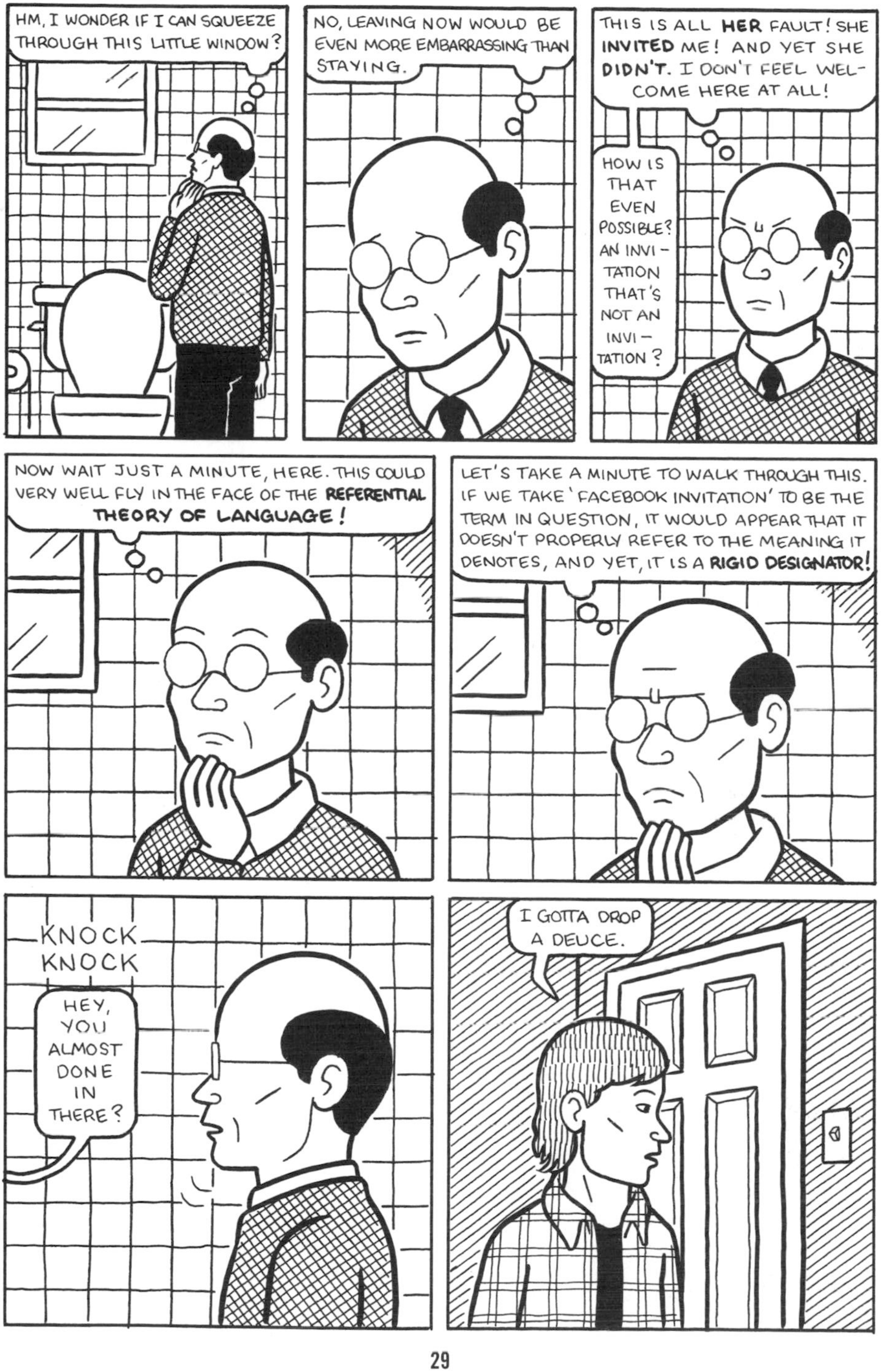
HM, I WONDER IF I CAN SQUEEZE THROUGH THIS LITTLE WINDOW?
NO, LEAVING NOW WOULD BE EVEN MORE EMBARRASSING THAN STAYING.
THIS IS ALL **HER** FAULT! SHE **INVITED** ME! AND YET SHE **DIDN'T**. I DON'T FEEL WEL-COME HERE AT ALL!
HOW IS THAT EVEN POSSIBLE? AN INVI-TATION THAT'S NOT AN INVI-TATION?
NOW WAIT JUST A MINUTE, HERE. THIS COULD VERY WELL FLY IN THE FACE OF THE **REFERENTIAL THEORY OF LANGUAGE**!
LET'S TAKE A MINUTE TO WALK THROUGH THIS. IF WE TAKE 'FACEBOOK INVITATION' TO BE THE TERM IN QUESTION, IT WOULD APPEAR THAT IT DOESN'T PROPERLY REFER TO THE MEANING IT DENOTES, AND YET, IT IS A **RIGID DESIGNATOR**!
KNOCK KNOCK
HEY, YOU ALMOST DONE IN THERE?
I GOTTA DROP A DEUCE.

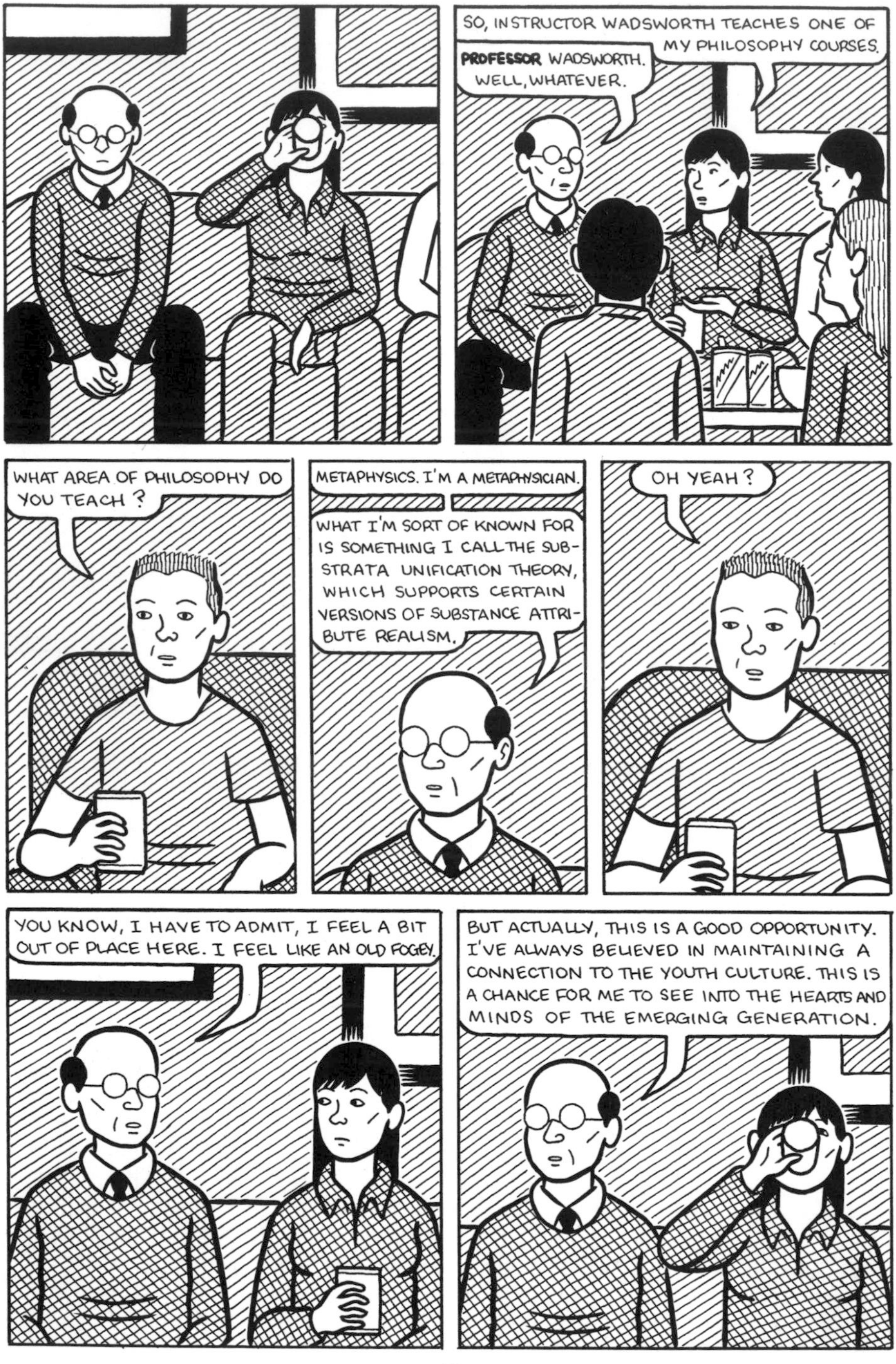
SO, INSTRUCTOR WADSWORTH TEACHES ONE OF MY PHILOSOPHY COURSES.
PROFESSOR WADSWORTH. WELL, WHATEVER.
WHAT AREA OF PHILOSOPHY DO YOU TEACH?
METAPHYSICS. I'M A METAPHYSICIAN.
WHAT I'M SORT OF KNOWN FOR IS SOMETHING I CALL THE SUB-STRATA UNIFICATION THEORY, WHICH SUPPORTS CERTAIN VERSIONS OF SUBSTANCE ATTRI-BUTE REALISM.
OH YEAH?
YOU KNOW, I HAVE TO ADMIT, I FEEL A BIT OUT OF PLACE HERE. I FEEL LIKE AN OLD FOGEY.
BUT ACTUALLY, THIS IS A GOOD OPPORTUNITY. I'VE ALWAYS BELIEVED IN MAINTAINING A CONNECTION TO THE YOUTH CULTURE. THIS IS A CHANCE FOR ME TO SEE INTO THE HEARTS AND MINDS OF THE EMERGING GENERATION.

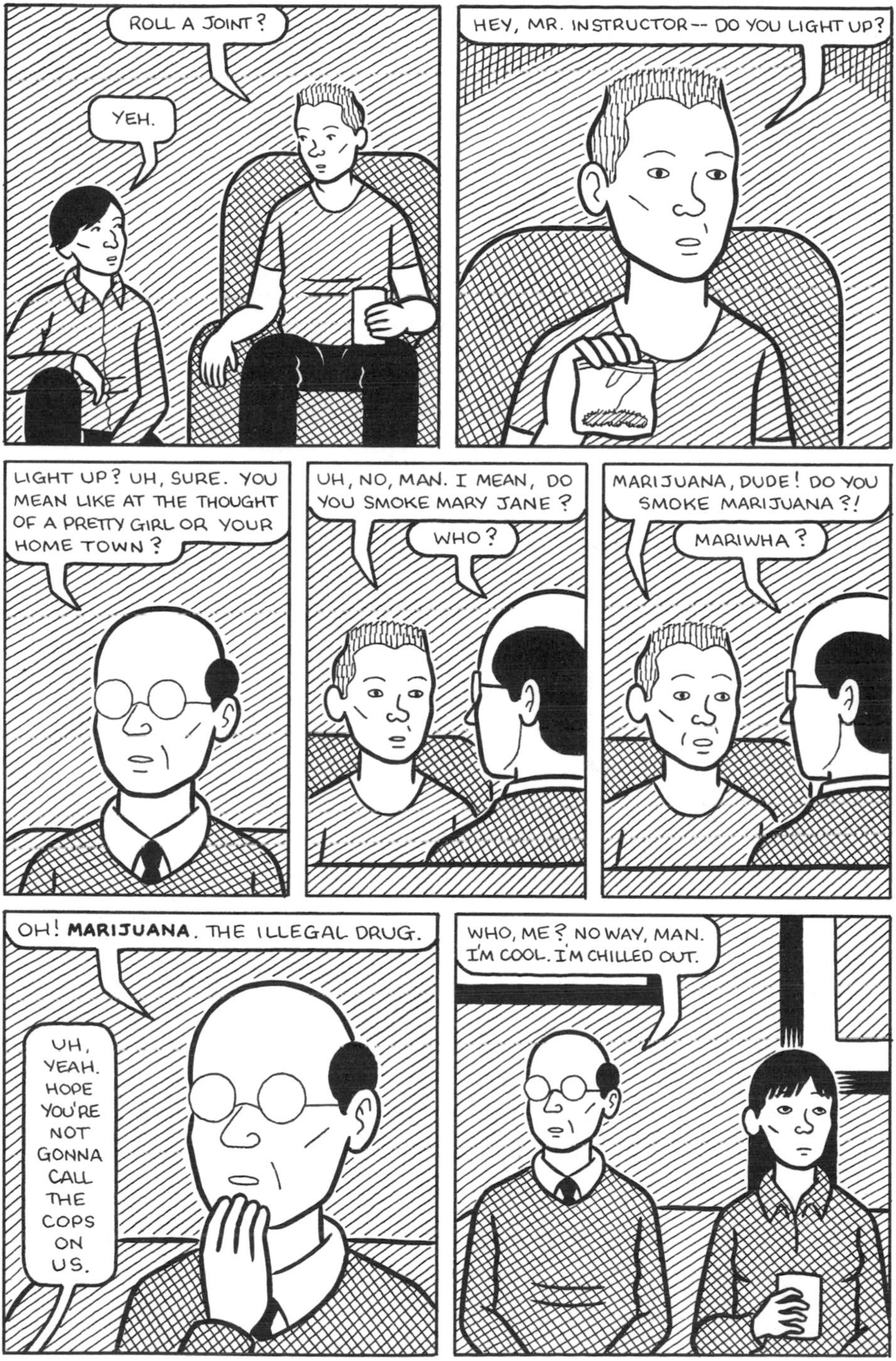
ROLL A JOINT?
YEH.
HEY, MR. INSTRUCTOR-- DO YOU LIGHT UP?
LIGHT UP? UH, SURE. YOU MEAN LIKE AT THE THOUGHT OF A PRETTY GIRL OR YOUR HOME TOWN?
UH, NO, MAN. I MEAN, DO YOU SMOKE MARY JANE?
WHO?
MARIJUANA, DUDE! DO YOU SMOKE MARIJUANA?!
MARIWHA?
OH! **MARIJUANA**. THE ILLEGAL DRUG.
UH, YEAH. HOPE YOU'RE NOT GONNA CALL THE COPS ON US.
WHO, ME? NO WAY, MAN. I'M COOL. I'M CHILLED OUT.

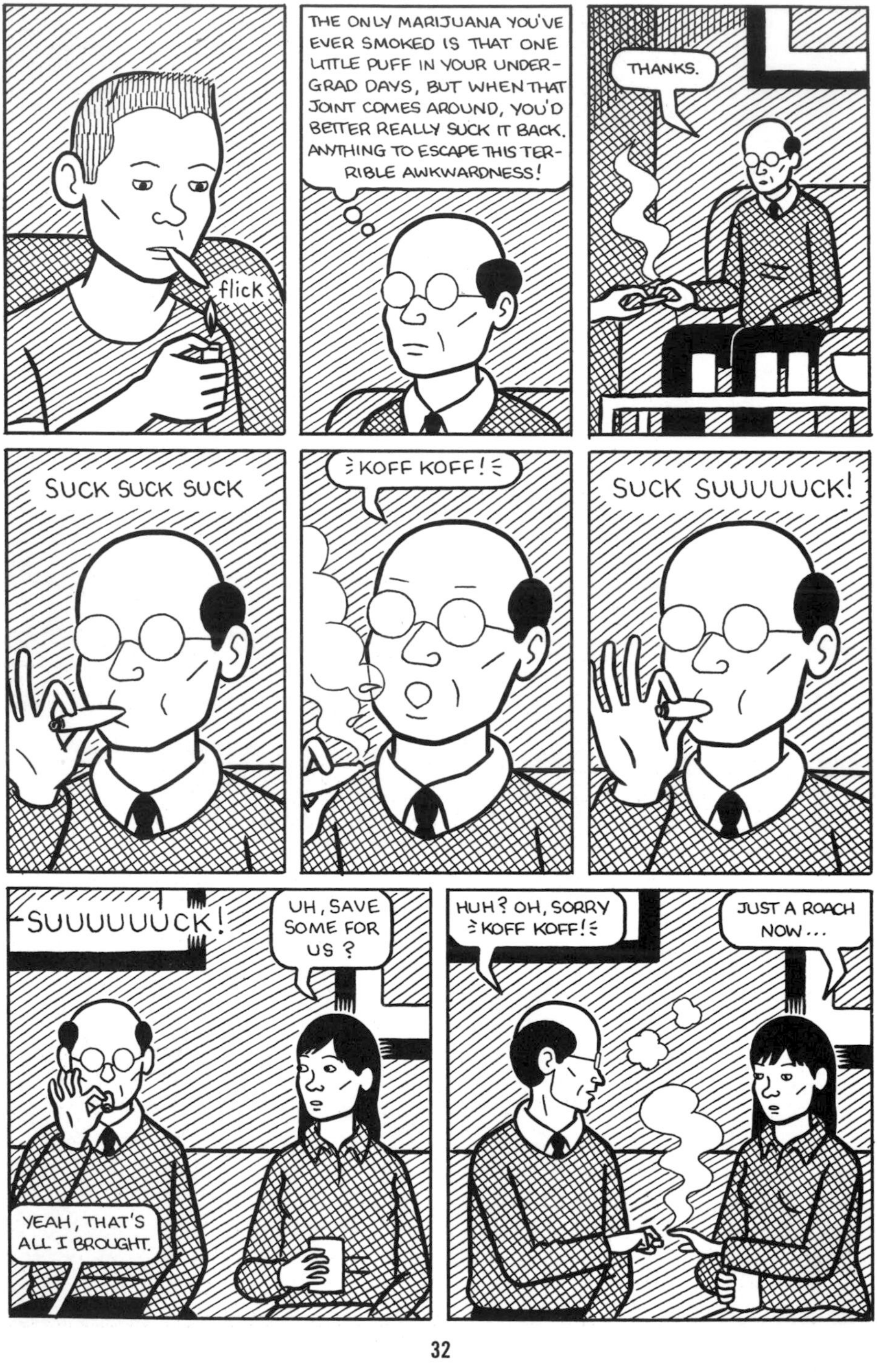
flick
THE ONLY MARIJUANA YOU'VE EVER SMOKED IS THAT ONE LITTLE PUFF IN YOUR UNDERGRAD DAYS, BUT WHEN THAT JOINT COMES AROUND, YOU'D BETTER REALLY SUCK IT BACK. ANYTHING TO ESCAPE THIS TERRIBLE AWKWARDNESS!
THANKS.
SUCK SUCK SUCK
KOFF KOFF!
SUCK SUUUUUCK!
SUUUUUUCK!
UH, SAVE SOME FOR US ?
YEAH, THAT'S ALL I BROUGHT.
HUH ? OH, SORRY KOFF KOFF!
JUST A ROACH NOW...

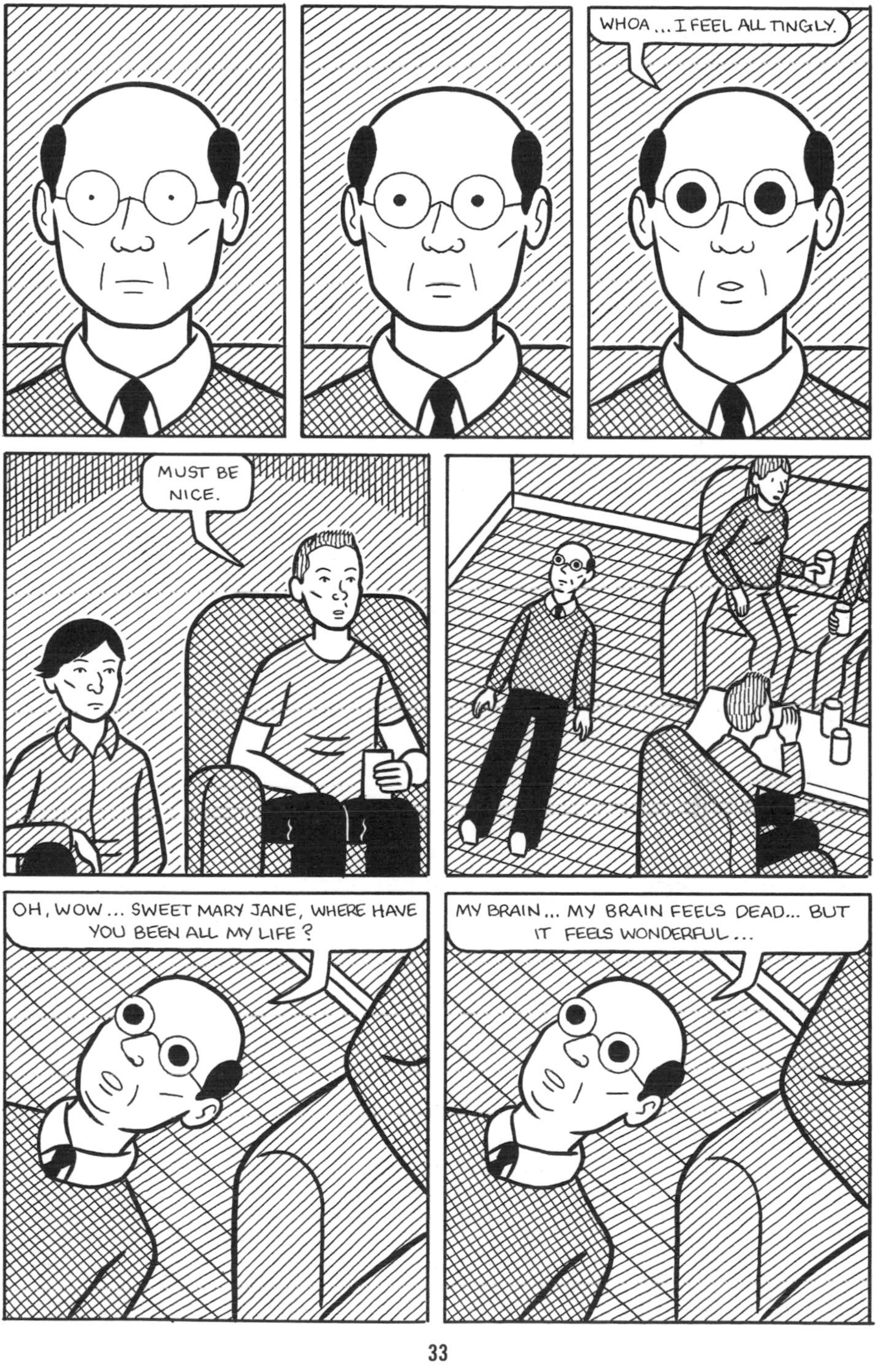
WHOA ... I FEEL ALL TINGLY.
MUST BE NICE.
OH, WOW ... SWEET MARY JANE, WHERE HAVE YOU BEEN ALL MY LIFE?
MY BRAIN... MY BRAIN FEELS DEAD... BUT IT FEELS WONDERFUL...

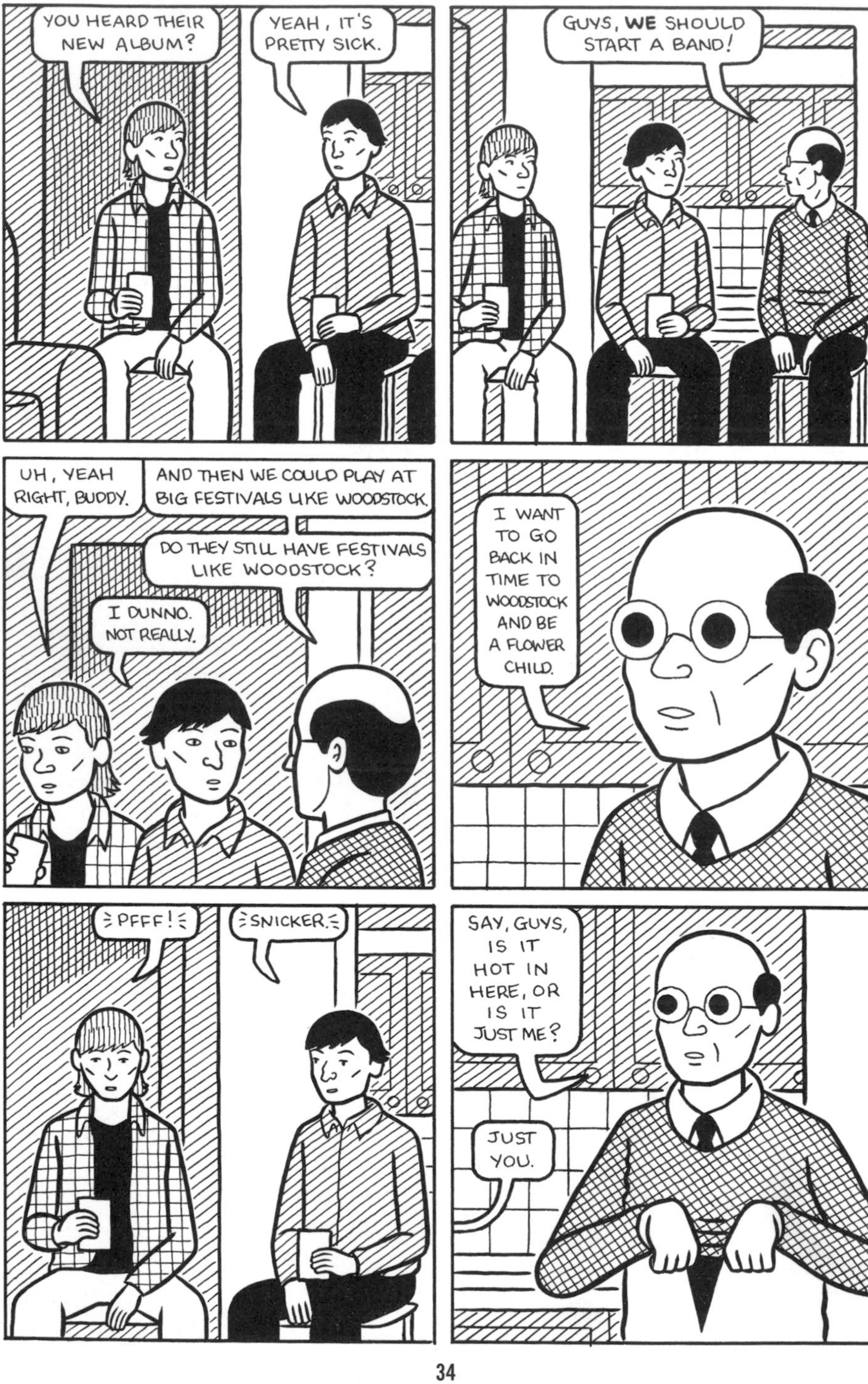
YOU HEARD THEIR NEW ALBUM?
YEAH, IT'S PRETTY SICK.
GUYS, **WE** SHOULD START A BAND!
UH, YEAH RIGHT, BUDDY.
AND THEN WE COULD PLAY AT BIG FESTIVALS LIKE WOODSTOCK.
DO THEY STILL HAVE FESTIVALS LIKE WOODSTOCK?
I DUNNO. NOT REALLY.
I WANT TO GO BACK IN TIME TO WOODSTOCK AND BE A FLOWER CHILD.
PFFF!
SNICKER.
SAY, GUYS, IS IT HOT IN HERE, OR IS IT JUST ME?
JUST YOU.

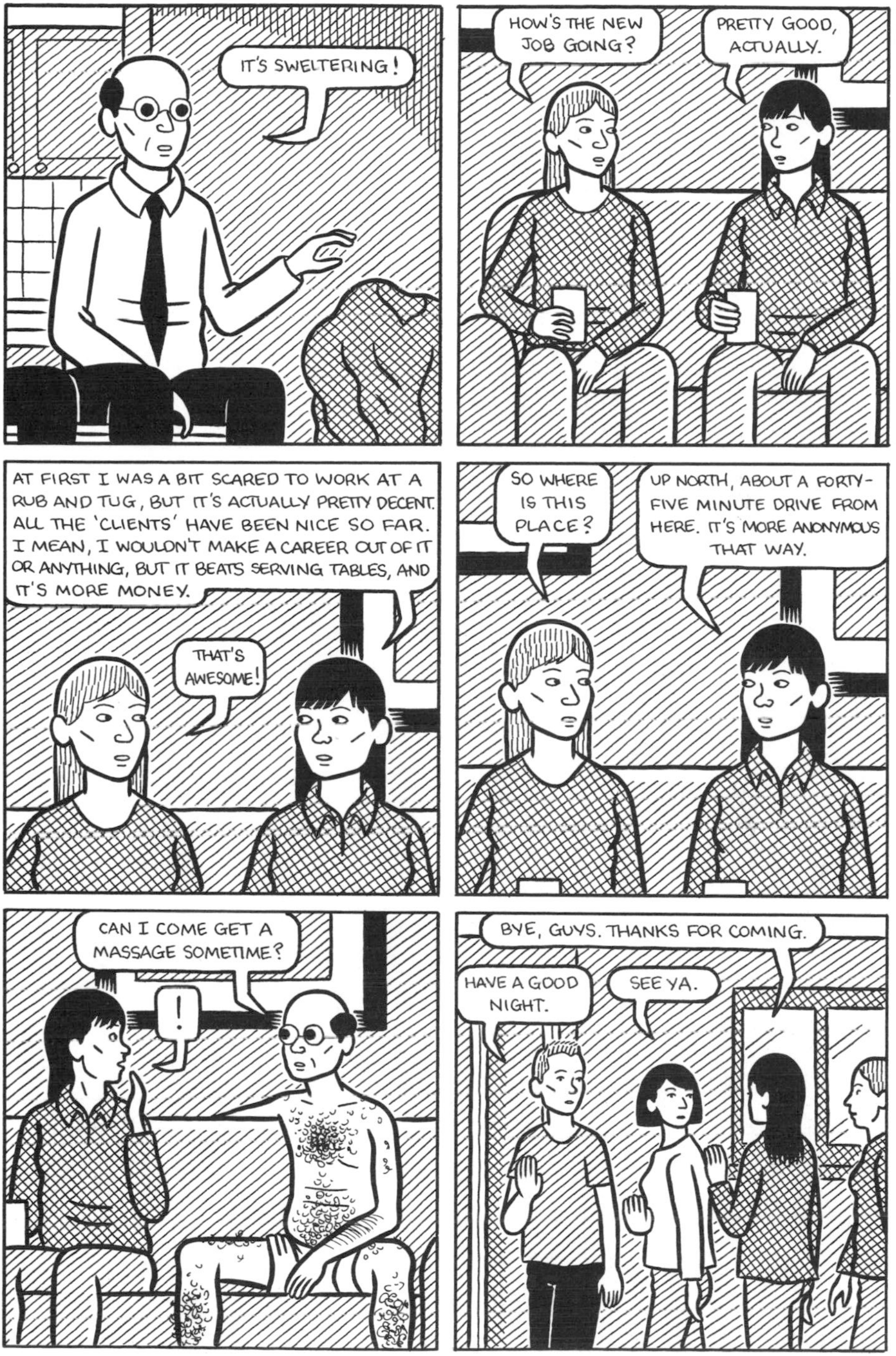
IT'S SWELTERING!
HOW'S THE NEW JOB GOING?
PRETTY GOOD, ACTUALLY.
AT FIRST I WAS A BIT SCARED TO WORK AT A RUB AND TUG, BUT IT'S ACTUALLY PRETTY DECENT. ALL THE 'CLIENTS' HAVE BEEN NICE SO FAR. I MEAN, I WOULDN'T MAKE A CAREER OUT OF IT OR ANYTHING, BUT IT BEATS SERVING TABLES, AND IT'S MORE MONEY.
THAT'S AWESOME!
SO WHERE IS THIS PLACE?
UP NORTH, ABOUT A FORTY-FIVE MINUTE DRIVE FROM HERE. IT'S MORE ANONYMOUS THAT WAY.
CAN I COME GET A MASSAGE SOMETIME?
!
BYE, GUYS. THANKS FOR COMING.
HAVE A GOOD NIGHT.
SEE YA.

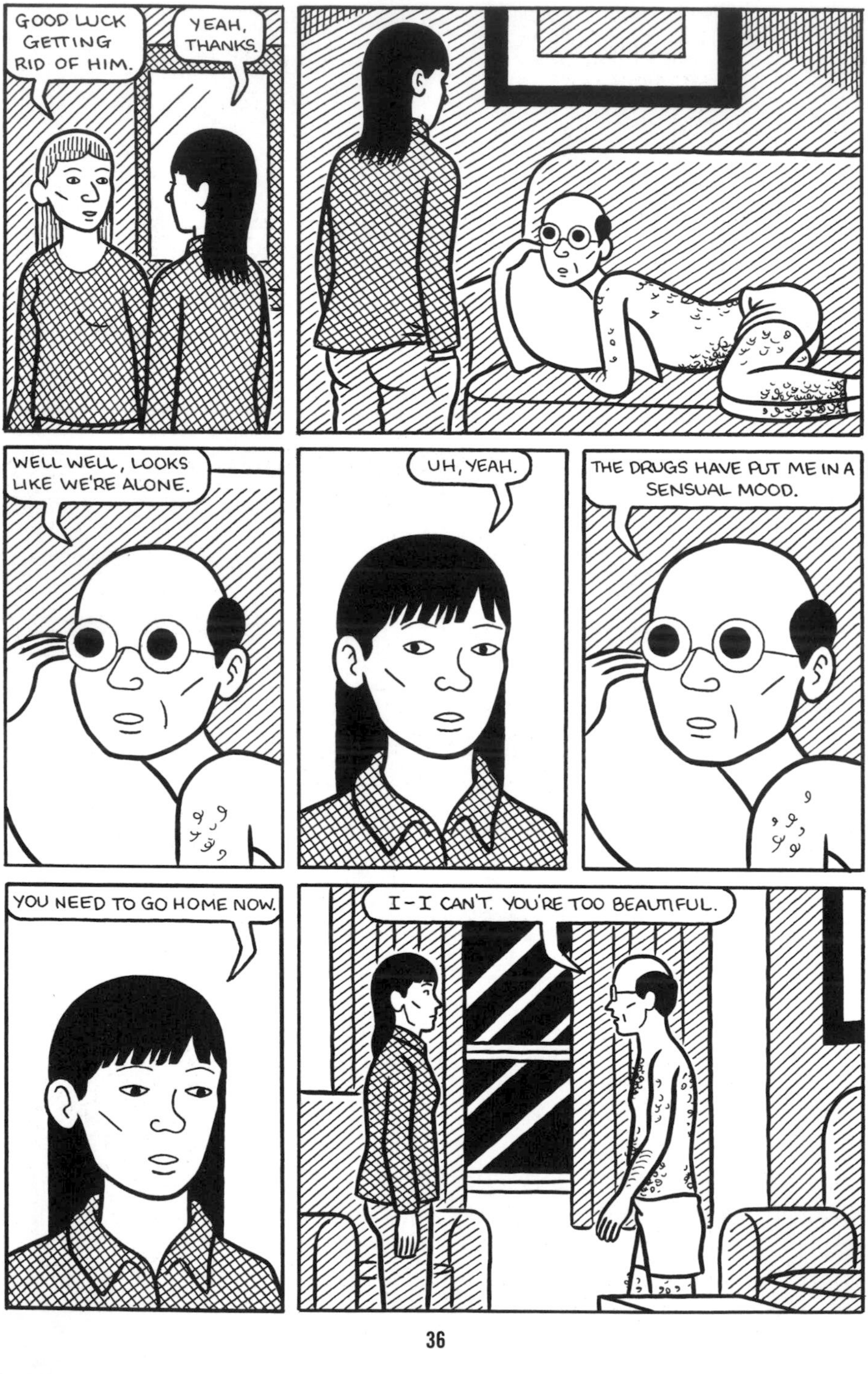
GOOD LUCK GETTING RID OF HIM.
YEAH, THANKS.
WELL WELL, LOOKS LIKE WE'RE ALONE.
UH, YEAH.
THE DRUGS HAVE PUT ME IN A SENSUAL MOOD.
YOU NEED TO GO HOME NOW.
I-I CAN'T. YOU'RE TOO BEAUTIFUL.

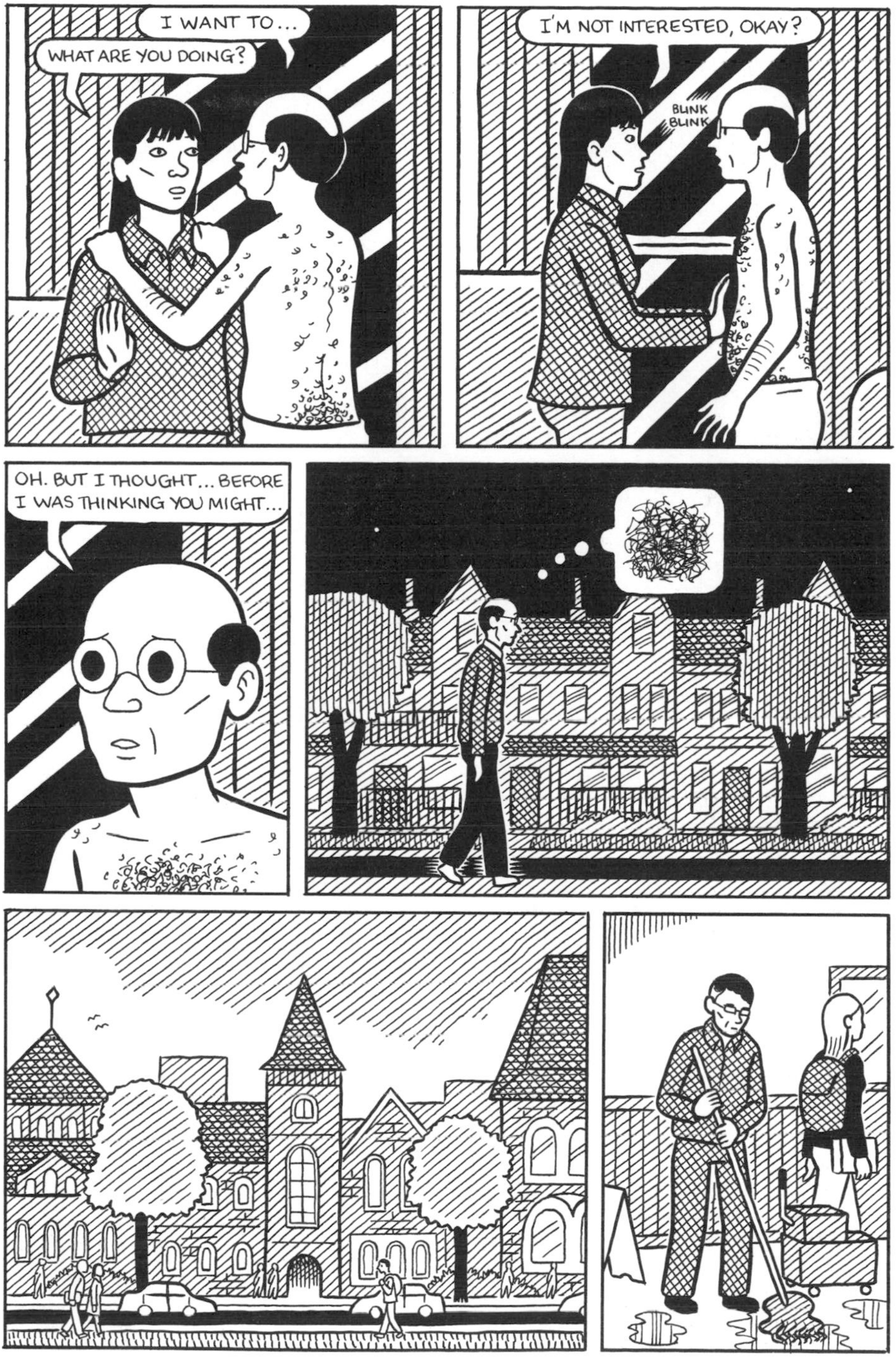
WHAT ARE YOU DOING?
I WANT TO...
I'M NOT INTERESTED, OKAY?
BLINK BLINK
OH. BUT I THOUGHT... BEFORE I WAS THINKING YOU MIGHT...

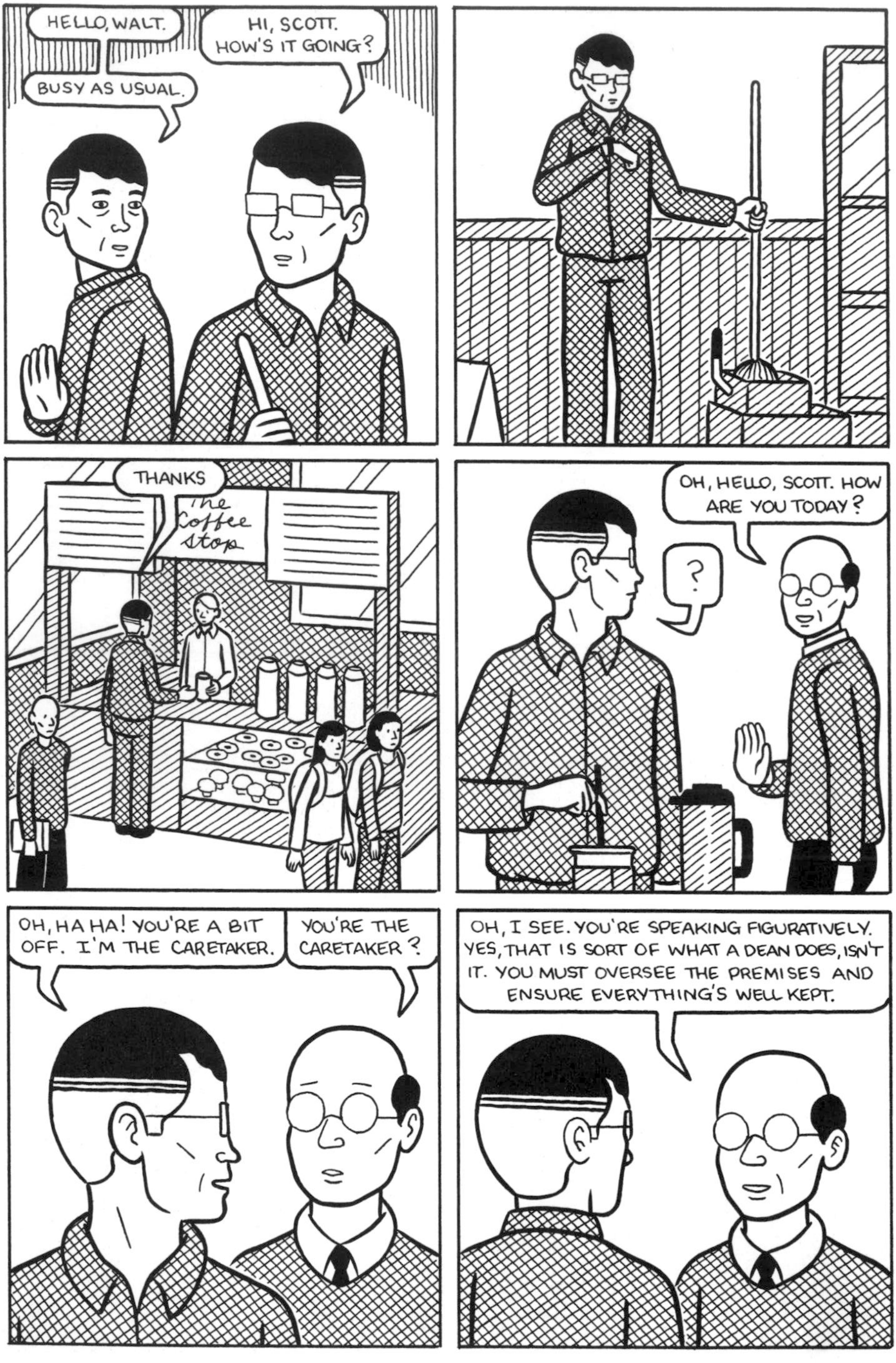
HELLO, WALT.
HI, SCOTT. HOW'S IT GOING?
BUSY AS USUAL.
THANKS
The Coffee Stop
OH, HELLO, SCOTT. HOW ARE YOU TODAY?
?
OH, HA HA! YOU'RE A BIT OFF. I'M THE CARETAKER.
YOU'RE THE CARETAKER?
OH, I SEE. YOU'RE SPEAKING FIGURATIVELY. YES, THAT IS SORT OF WHAT A DEAN DOES, ISN'T IT. YOU MUST OVERSEE THE PREMISES AND ENSURE EVERYTHING'S WELL KEPT.

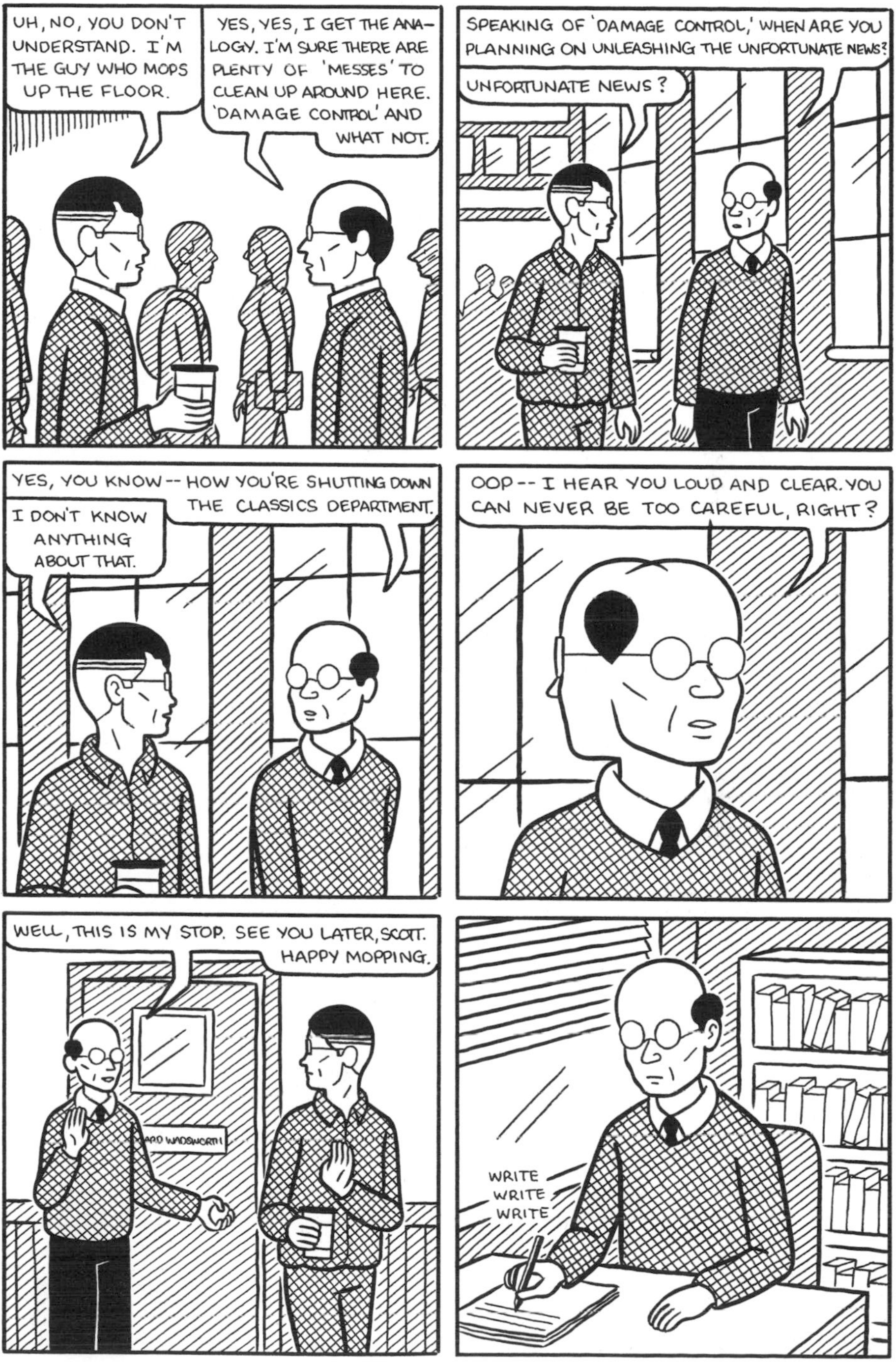

UH, NO, YOU DON'T UNDERSTAND. I'M THE GUY WHO MOPS UP THE FLOOR.
YES, YES, I GET THE ANALOGY. I'M SURE THERE ARE PLENTY OF 'MESSES' TO CLEAN UP AROUND HERE. 'DAMAGE CONTROL' AND WHAT NOT.
SPEAKING OF 'DAMAGE CONTROL,' WHEN ARE YOU PLANNING ON UNLEASHING THE UNFORTUNATE NEWS?
UNFORTUNATE NEWS?
YES, YOU KNOW -- HOW YOU'RE SHUTTING DOWN THE CLASSICS DEPARTMENT.
I DON'T KNOW ANYTHING ABOUT THAT.
OOP -- I HEAR YOU LOUD AND CLEAR. YOU CAN NEVER BE TOO CAREFUL, RIGHT?
WELL, THIS IS MY STOP. SEE YOU LATER, SCOTT. HAPPY MOPPING.
ARD WADSWORTH
WRITE
WRITE
WRITE

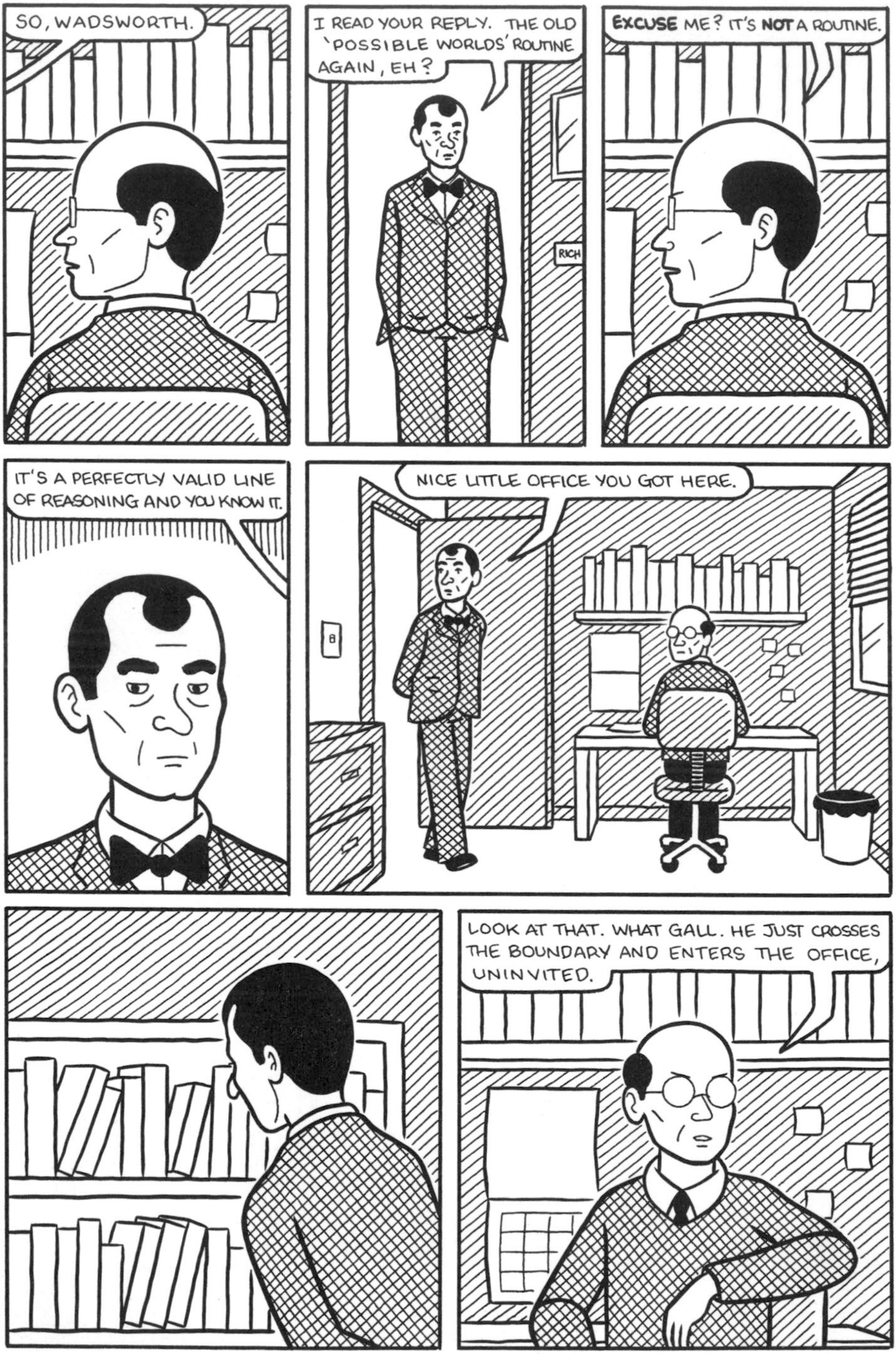
SO, WADSWORTH.
I READ YOUR REPLY. THE OLD 'POSSIBLE WORLDS' ROUTINE AGAIN, EH?
RICH
EXCUSE ME? IT'S **NOT** A ROUTINE.
IT'S A PERFECTLY VALID LINE OF REASONING AND YOU KNOW IT.
NICE LITTLE OFFICE YOU GOT HERE.
LOOK AT THAT. WHAT GALL. HE JUST CROSSES THE BOUNDARY AND ENTERS THE OFFICE, UNINVITED.

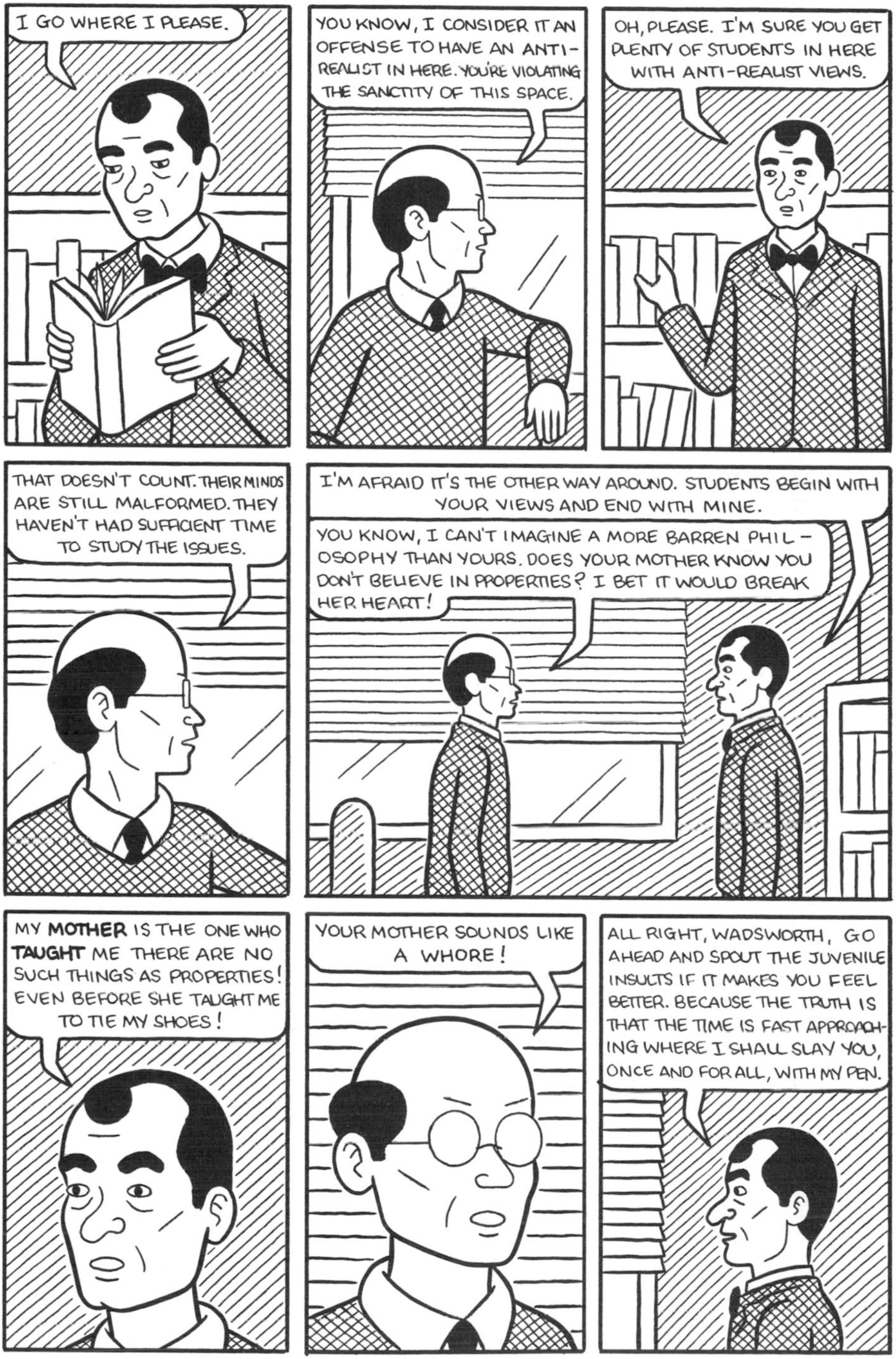
I GO WHERE I PLEASE.
YOU KNOW, I CONSIDER IT AN OFFENSE TO HAVE AN ANTI-REALIST IN HERE. YOU'RE VIOLATING THE SANCTITY OF THIS SPACE.
OH, PLEASE. I'M SURE YOU GET PLENTY OF STUDENTS IN HERE WITH ANTI-REALIST VIEWS.
THAT DOESN'T COUNT. THEIR MINDS ARE STILL MALFORMED. THEY HAVEN'T HAD SUFFICIENT TIME TO STUDY THE ISSUES.
I'M AFRAID IT'S THE OTHER WAY AROUND. STUDENTS BEGIN WITH YOUR VIEWS AND END WITH MINE.
YOU KNOW, I CAN'T IMAGINE A MORE BARREN PHIL-OSOPHY THAN YOURS. DOES YOUR MOTHER KNOW YOU DON'T BELIEVE IN PROPERTIES? I BET IT WOULD BREAK HER HEART!
MY **MOTHER** IS THE ONE WHO **TAUGHT** ME THERE ARE NO SUCH THINGS AS PROPERTIES! EVEN BEFORE SHE TAUGHT ME TO TIE MY SHOES!
YOUR MOTHER SOUNDS LIKE A WHORE!
ALL RIGHT, WADSWORTH, GO AHEAD AND SPOUT THE JUVENILE INSULTS IF IT MAKES YOU FEEL BETTER. BECAUSE THE TRUTH IS THAT THE TIME IS FAST APPROACH-ING WHERE I SHALL SLAY YOU, ONCE AND FOR ALL, WITH MY PEN.

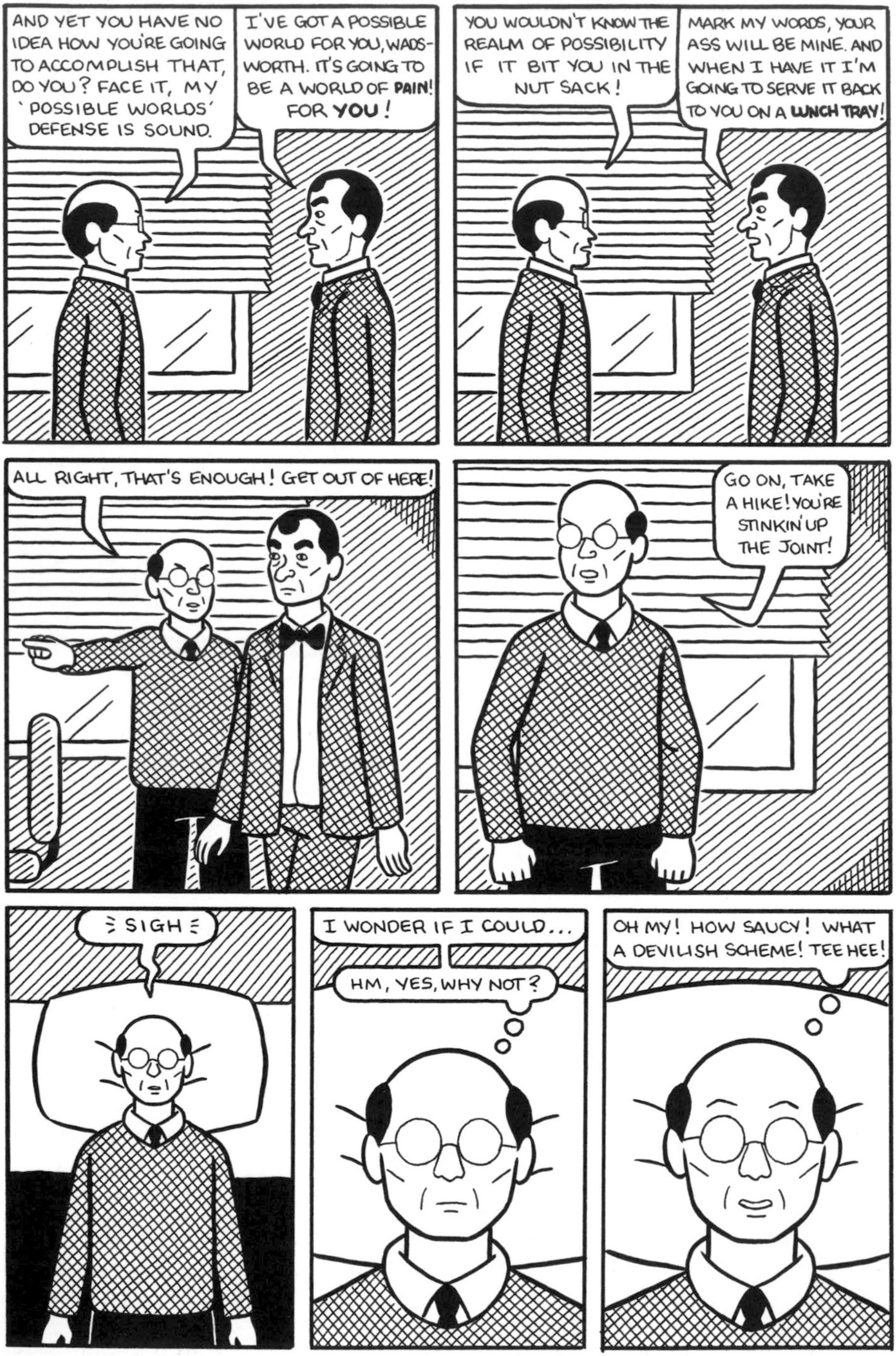
AND YET YOU HAVE NO IDEA HOW YOU'RE GOING TO ACCOMPLISH THAT, DO YOU? FACE IT, MY 'POSSIBLE WORLDS' DEFENSE IS SOUND.
I'VE GOT A POSSIBLE WORLD FOR YOU, WADSWORTH. IT'S GOING TO BE A WORLD OF **PAIN**! FOR **YOU**!
YOU WOULDN'T KNOW THE REALM OF POSSIBILITY IF IT BIT YOU IN THE NUT SACK!
MARK MY WORDS, YOUR ASS WILL BE MINE. AND WHEN I HAVE IT I'M GOING TO SERVE IT BACK TO YOU ON A **LUNCH TRAY**!
ALL RIGHT, THAT'S ENOUGH! GET OUT OF HERE!
GO ON, TAKE A HIKE! YOU'RE STINKIN' UP THE JOINT!
SIGH
I WONDER IF I COULD...
HM, YES, WHY NOT?
OH MY! HOW SAUCY! WHAT A DEVILISH SCHEME! TEE HEE!

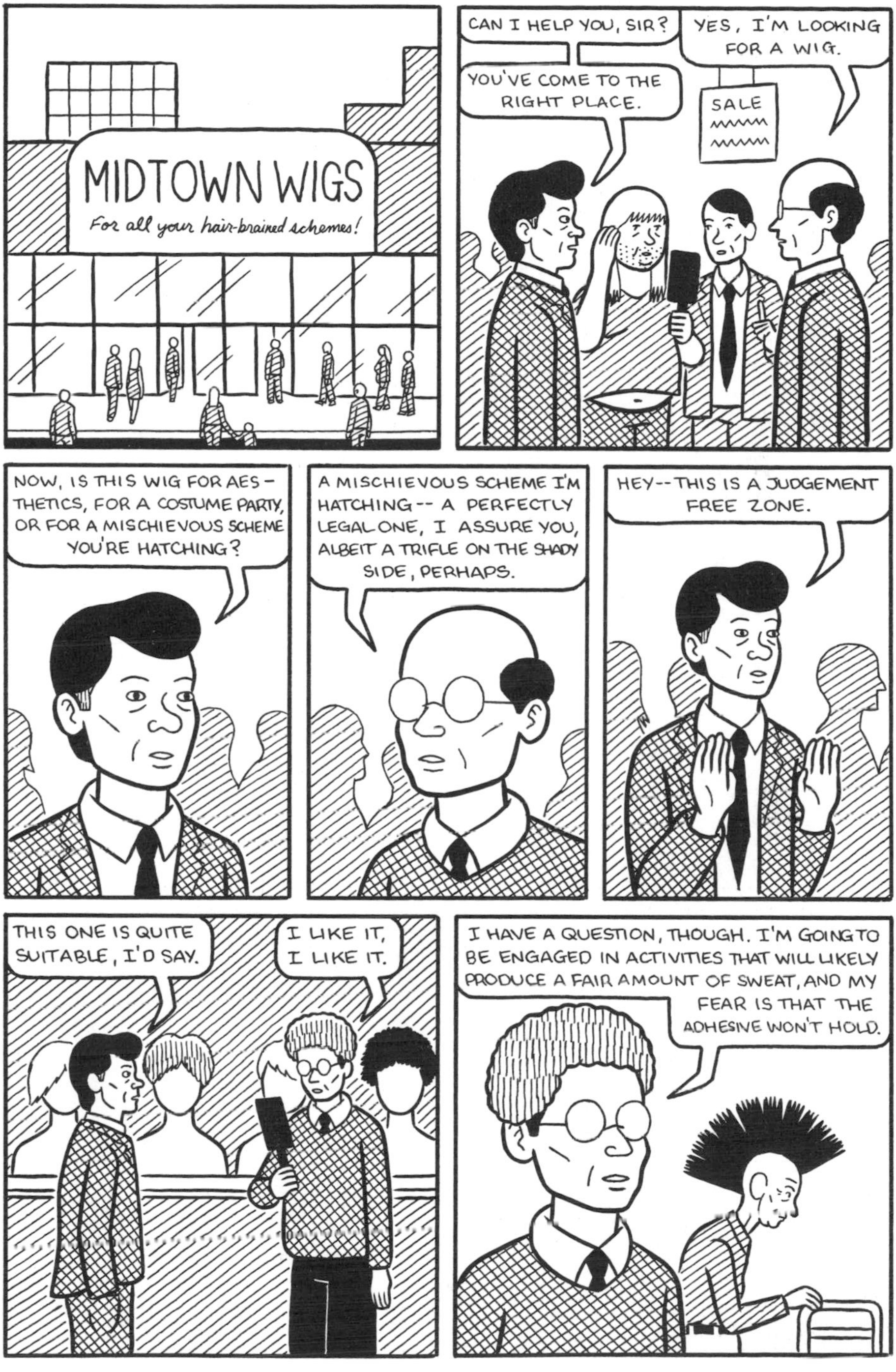
MIDTOWN WIGS
For all your hair-brained schemes!
CAN I HELP YOU, SIR?
YOU'VE COME TO THE RIGHT PLACE.
YES, I'M LOOKING FOR A WIG.
SALE
NOW, IS THIS WIG FOR AES-THETICS, FOR A COSTUME PARTY, OR FOR A MISCHIEVOUS SCHEME YOU'RE HATCHING?
A MISCHIEVOUS SCHEME I'M HATCHING -- A PERFECTLY LEGAL ONE, I ASSURE YOU, ALBEIT A TRIFLE ON THE SHADY SIDE, PERHAPS.
HEY -- THIS IS A JUDGEMENT FREE ZONE.
THIS ONE IS QUITE SUITABLE, I'D SAY.
I LIKE IT, I LIKE IT.
I HAVE A QUESTION, THOUGH. I'M GOING TO BE ENGAGED IN ACTIVITIES THAT WILL LIKELY PRODUCE A FAIR AMOUNT OF SWEAT, AND MY FEAR IS THAT THE ADHESIVE WON'T HOLD.

SURE, WE'VE ALL BEEN THERE. I CAN ASSURE YOU FROM PERSONAL EXPERIENCE THAT THIS WIG ADHESIVE CAN WITHSTAND ENORMOUS QUANTITIES OF SWEAT.

WELL GOOD, THAT EASES MY MIND A BIT.

I THINK I'M INTERESTED IN A MUSTACHE AS WELL.

OUR MUSTACHE DEPARTMENT WILL BE HAPPY TO HELP YOU.

THIS MUST BE THE PLACE.

I MUST PROCEED WITH THE UTMOST CAUTION ON THIS MISSION, BUT I THINK I HAVE MY BASES COVERED. I GUESS IT'S POSSIBLE SHE'LL SEE THROUGH MY DISGUISE, BUT IT'S A RISK I'M WILLING TO TAKE.

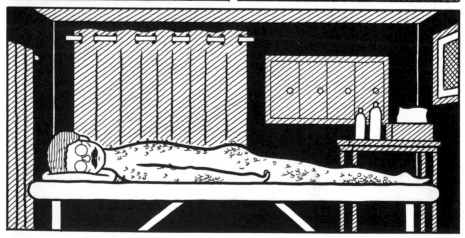

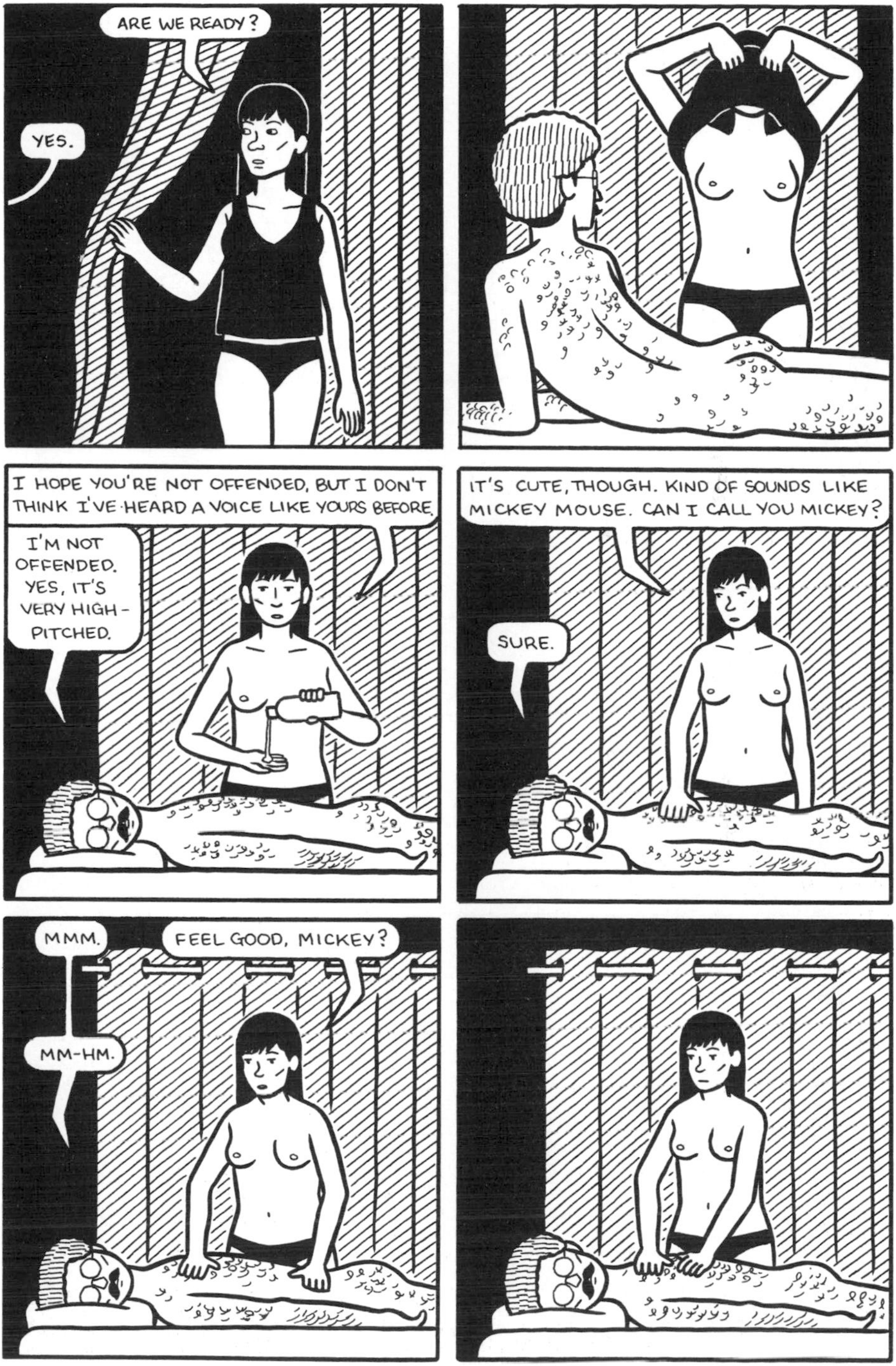
ARE WE READY?
YES.
I HOPE YOU'RE NOT OFFENDED, BUT I DON'T THINK I'VE HEARD A VOICE LIKE YOURS BEFORE.
I'M NOT OFFENDED. YES, IT'S VERY HIGH-PITCHED.
IT'S CUTE, THOUGH. KIND OF SOUNDS LIKE MICKEY MOUSE. CAN I CALL YOU MICKEY?
SURE.
MMM.
FEEL GOOD, MICKEY?
MM-HM.

READY TO TURN OVER?

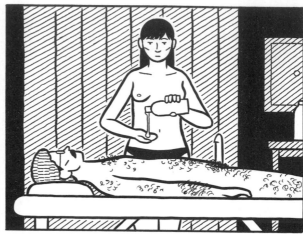

YOU KNOW, YOU LOOK A LITTLE FAMILIAR. DO I KNOW YOU FROM SOMEWHERE?

I-I DON'T KNOW WHAT YOU'RE TALKING ABOUT. WHERE DO YOU THINK YOU KNOW ME FROM?

HM, I DON'T KNOW. I GUESS I'M JUST BEING PARANOID. NEVER MIND.

HEH, WELL, IT HAPPENS. THESE FUNNY BRAINS OF OURS...

WAIT — I KNOW WHERE I KNOW YOU FROM!

HUH? WH-WHERE?

AREN'T YOU DOCTOR FLEMING, MY DENTIST FROM HIGH SCHOOL?

D-DENTIST? NO! I'M A DRY CLEANER! I INHERITED MY FATHER'S DRY CLEANING BUSINESS IN 2003. I'VE BEEN A DRY CLEANER EVER SINCE.

OH YEAH, NO, YOU'RE TOTALLY RIGHT. I'M SORRY. DOCTOR FLEMING HAD BROWN HAIR.

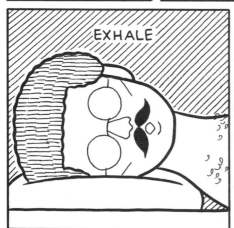

EXHALE

AH, WE'RE BACK, I SEE.

OHHHHHHH.

Cupid Mass

THAT'S IT, MICKEY. YOU LIKE IT, DON'T YOU?

OH, YES I DO!

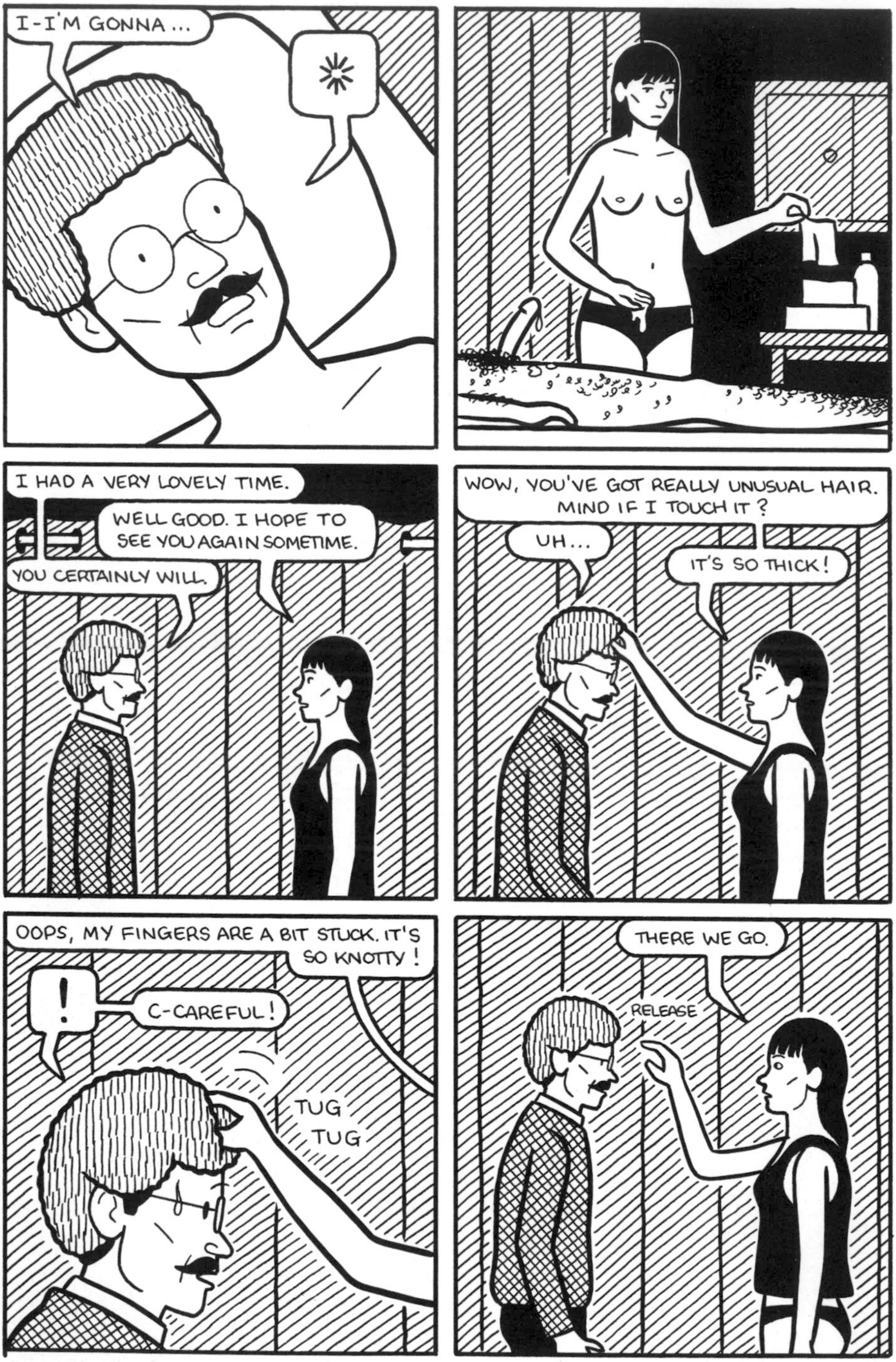
I-I'M GONNA...
I HAD A VERY LOVELY TIME.
WELL GOOD. I HOPE TO SEE YOU AGAIN SOMETIME.
YOU CERTAINLY WILL.
WOW, YOU'VE GOT REALLY UNUSUAL HAIR. MIND IF I TOUCH IT?
UH...
IT'S SO THICK!
OOPS, MY FINGERS ARE A BIT STUCK. IT'S SO KNOTTY!
!
C-CAREFUL!
TUG
TUG
THERE WE GO.
RELEASE

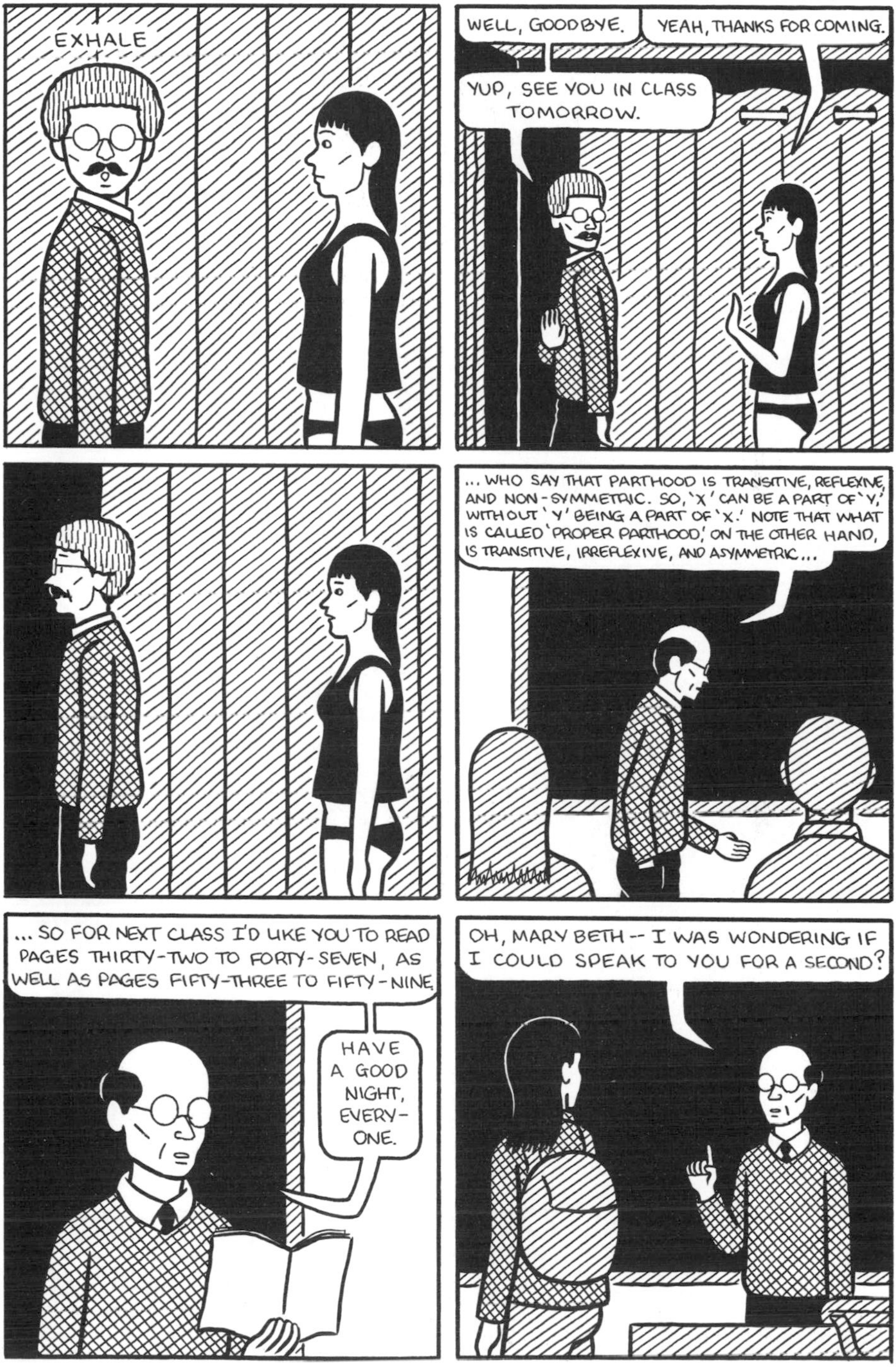
EXHALE
WELL, GOODBYE.
YEAH, THANKS FOR COMING.
YUP, SEE YOU IN CLASS TOMORROW.
... WHO SAY THAT PARTHOOD IS TRANSITIVE, REFLEXIVE, AND NON-SYMMETRIC. SO, 'X' CAN BE A PART OF 'Y,' WITHOUT 'Y' BEING A PART OF 'X.' NOTE THAT WHAT IS CALLED 'PROPER PARTHOOD,' ON THE OTHER HAND, IS TRANSITIVE, IRREFLEXIVE, AND ASYMMETRIC...
... SO FOR NEXT CLASS I'D LIKE YOU TO READ PAGES THIRTY-TWO TO FORTY-SEVEN, AS WELL AS PAGES FIFTY-THREE TO FIFTY-NINE.
HAVE A GOOD NIGHT, EVERY-ONE.
OH, MARY BETH -- I WAS WONDERING IF I COULD SPEAK TO YOU FOR A SECOND?

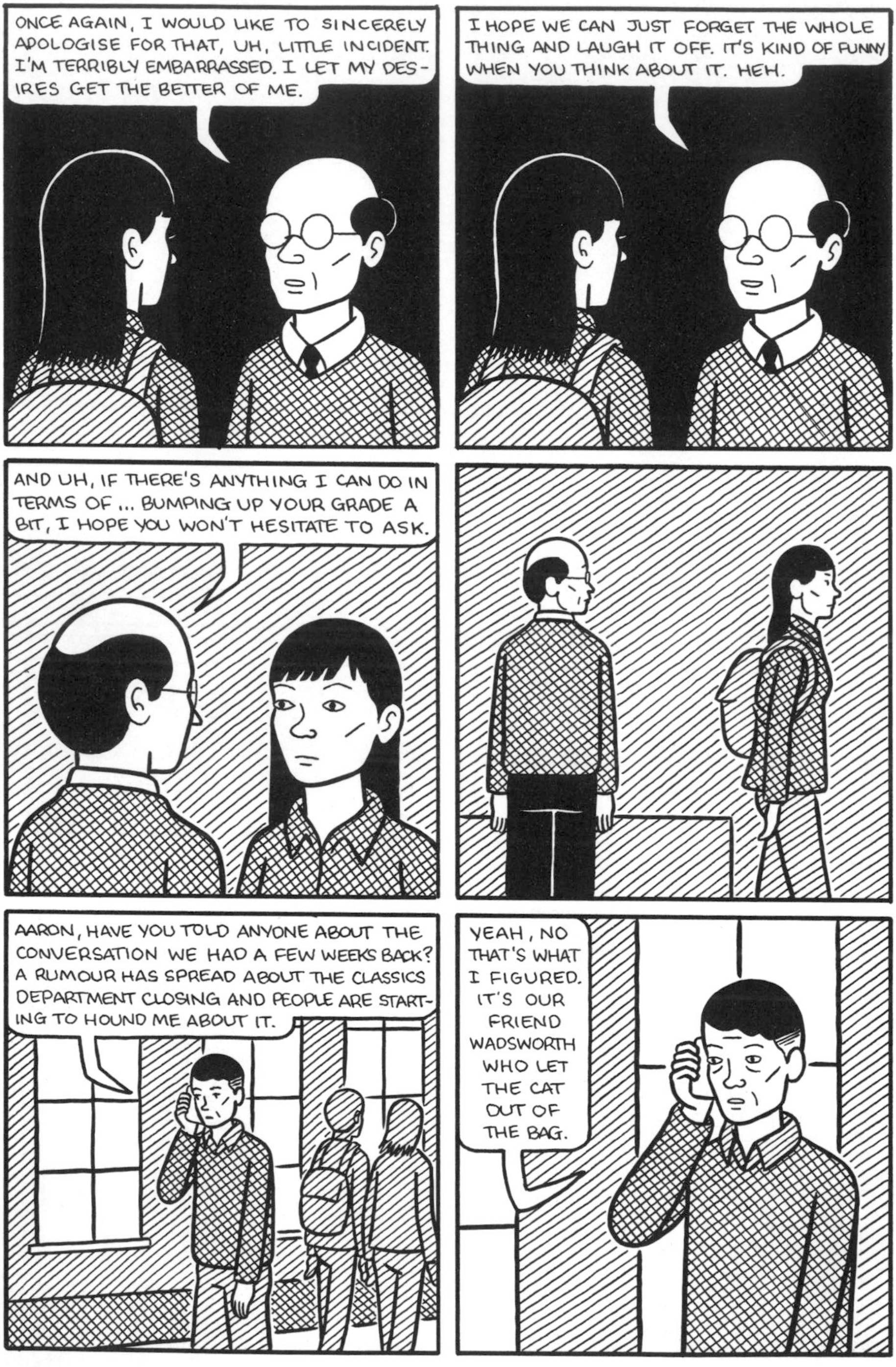
ONCE AGAIN, I WOULD LIKE TO SINCERELY APOLOGISE FOR THAT, UH, LITTLE INCIDENT. I'M TERRIBLY EMBARRASSED. I LET MY DESIRES GET THE BETTER OF ME.
I HOPE WE CAN JUST FORGET THE WHOLE THING AND LAUGH IT OFF. IT'S KIND OF FUNNY WHEN YOU THINK ABOUT IT. HEH.
AND UH, IF THERE'S ANYTHING I CAN DO IN TERMS OF ... BUMPING UP YOUR GRADE A BIT, I HOPE YOU WON'T HESITATE TO ASK.
AARON, HAVE YOU TOLD ANYONE ABOUT THE CONVERSATION WE HAD A FEW WEEKS BACK? A RUMOUR HAS SPREAD ABOUT THE CLASSICS DEPARTMENT CLOSING AND PEOPLE ARE STARTING TO HOUND ME ABOUT IT.
YEAH, NO THAT'S WHAT I FIGURED. IT'S OUR FRIEND WADSWORTH WHO LET THE CAT OUT OF THE BAG.

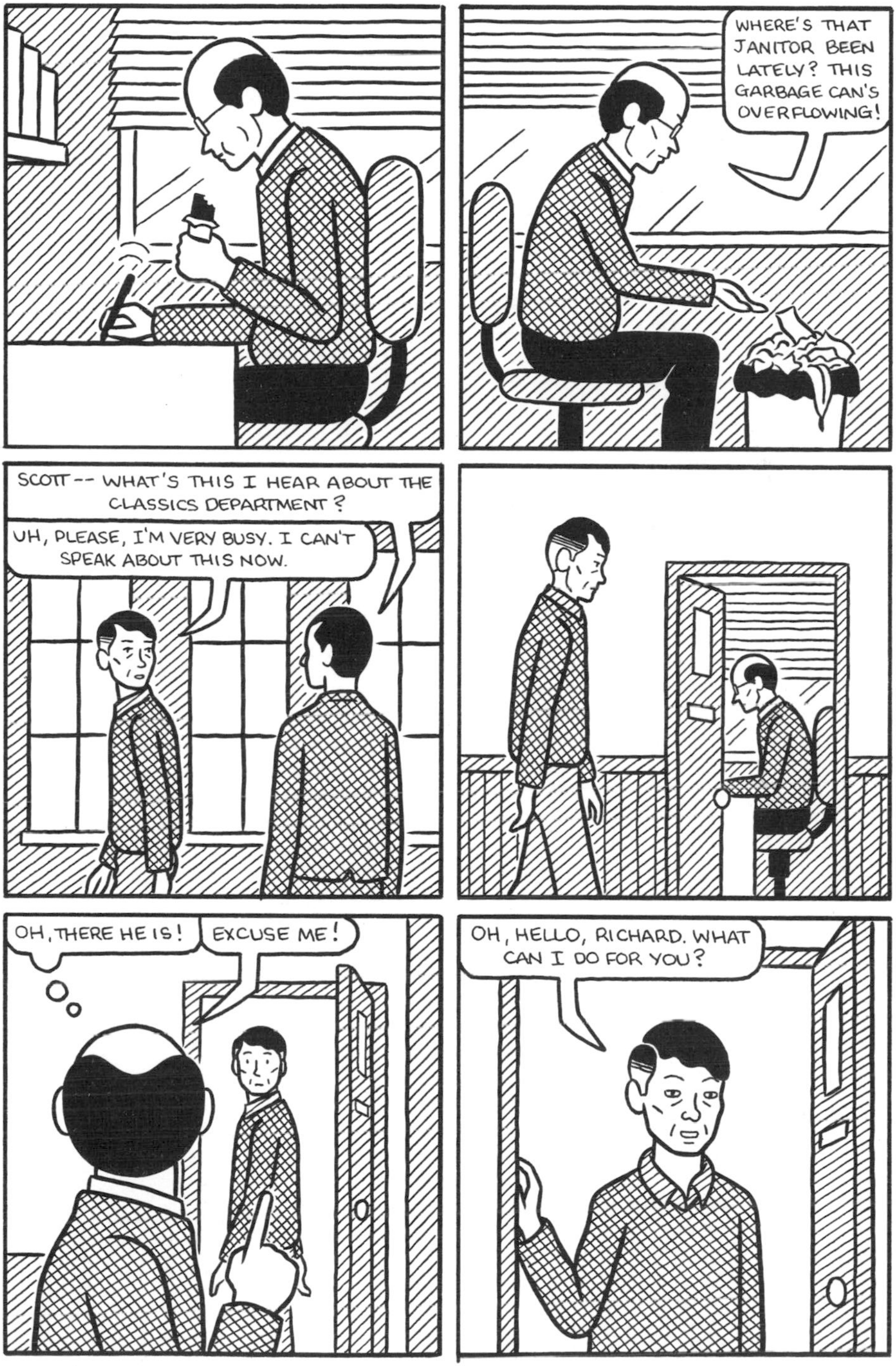
WHERE'S THAT JANITOR BEEN LATELY? THIS GARBAGE CAN'S OVERFLOWING!
SCOTT -- WHAT'S THIS I HEAR ABOUT THE CLASSICS DEPARTMENT?
UH, PLEASE, I'M VERY BUSY. I CAN'T SPEAK ABOUT THIS NOW.
OH, THERE HE IS!
EXCUSE ME!
OH, HELLO, RICHARD. WHAT CAN I DO FOR YOU?

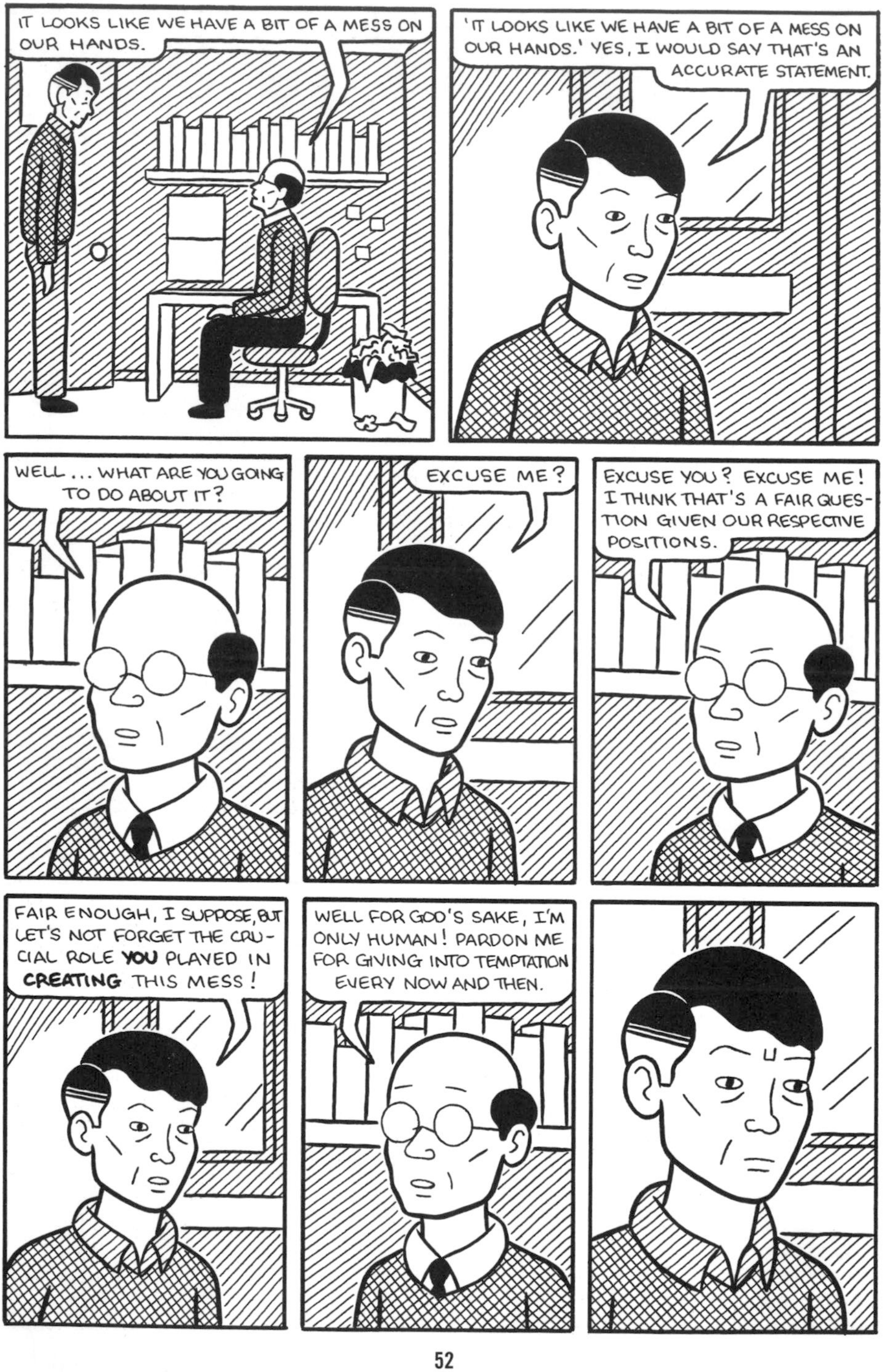
IT LOOKS LIKE WE HAVE A BIT OF A MESS ON OUR HANDS.
'IT LOOKS LIKE WE HAVE A BIT OF A MESS ON OUR HANDS.' YES, I WOULD SAY THAT'S AN ACCURATE STATEMENT.
WELL... WHAT ARE YOU GOING TO DO ABOUT IT?
EXCUSE ME?
EXCUSE YOU? EXCUSE ME! I THINK THAT'S A FAIR QUESTION GIVEN OUR RESPECTIVE POSITIONS.
FAIR ENOUGH, I SUPPOSE, BUT LET'S NOT FORGET THE CRUCIAL ROLE **YOU** PLAYED IN **CREATING** THIS MESS!
WELL FOR GOD'S SAKE, I'M ONLY HUMAN! PARDON ME FOR GIVING INTO TEMPTATION EVERY NOW AND THEN.

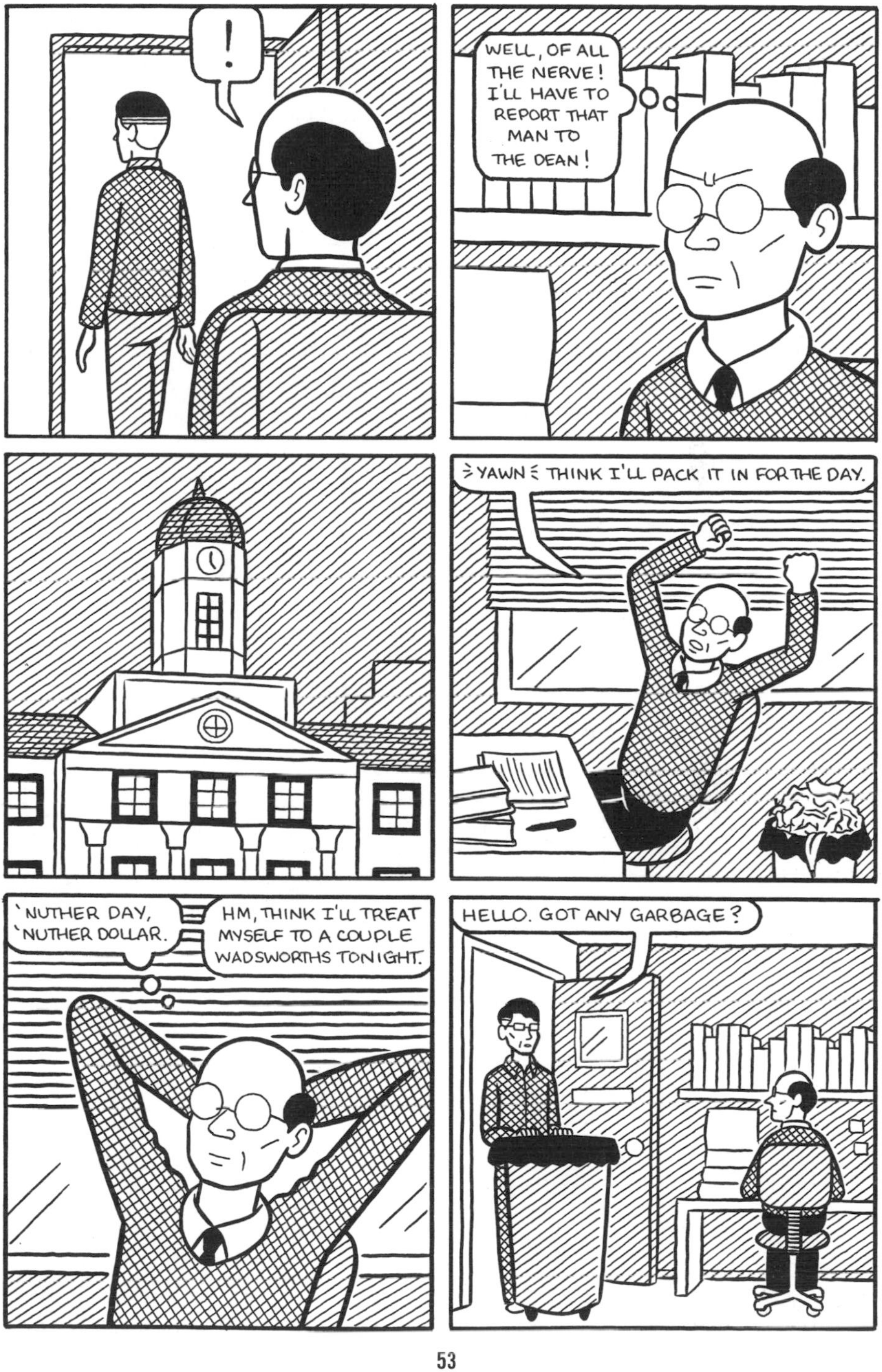
!
WELL, OF ALL THE NERVE! I'LL HAVE TO REPORT THAT MAN TO THE DEAN!
YAWN THINK I'LL PACK IT IN FOR THE DAY.
'NUTHER DAY, 'NUTHER DOLLAR.
HM, THINK I'LL TREAT MYSELF TO A COUPLE WADSWORTHS TONIGHT.
HELLO. GOT ANY GARBAGE?

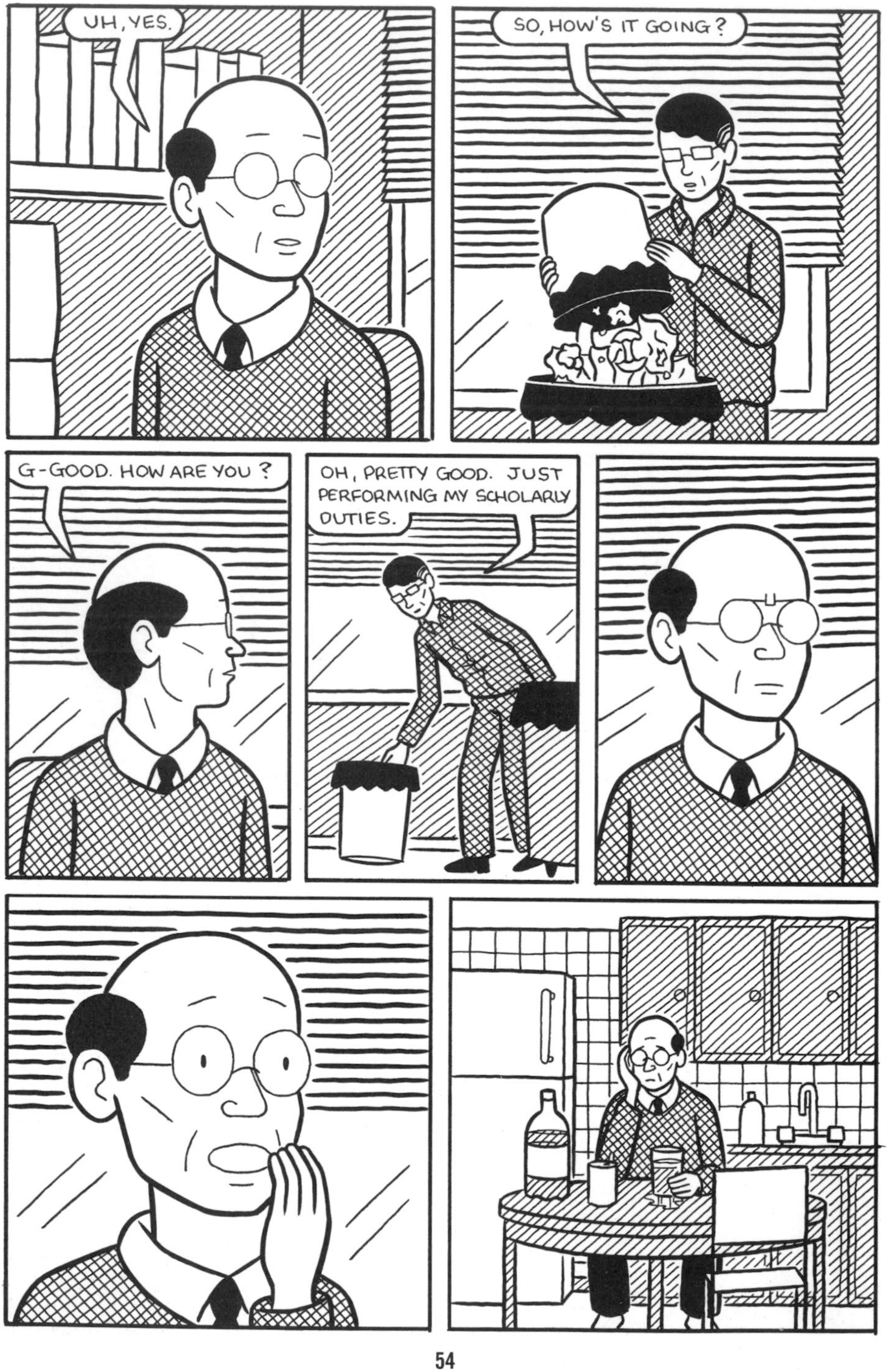
UH, YES.
SO, HOW'S IT GOING?
G-GOOD. HOW ARE YOU?
OH, PRETTY GOOD. JUST PERFORMING MY SCHOLARLY DUTIES.

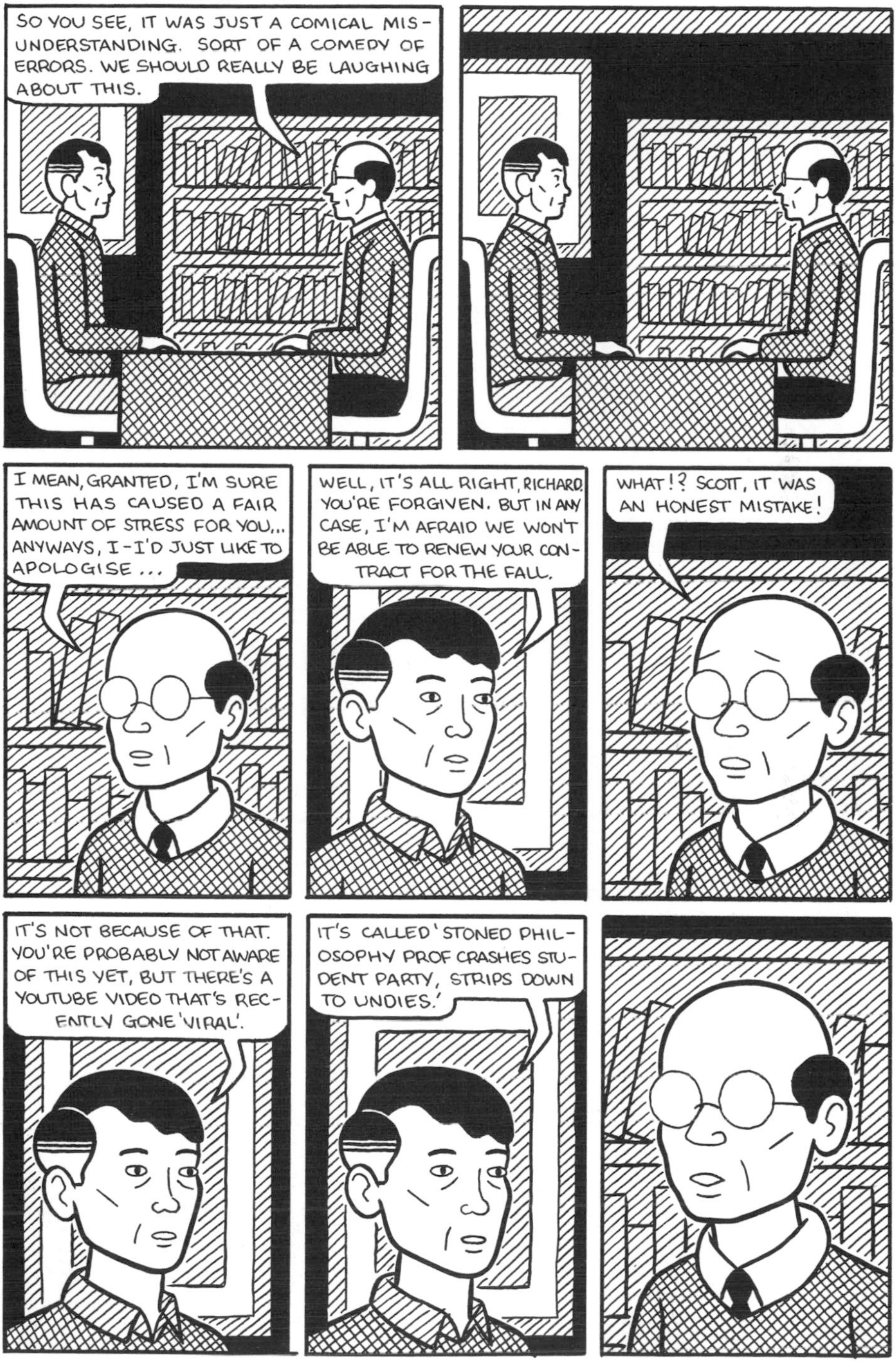
SO YOU SEE, IT WAS JUST A COMICAL MIS-UNDERSTANDING. SORT OF A COMEDY OF ERRORS. WE SHOULD REALLY BE LAUGHING ABOUT THIS.
I MEAN, GRANTED, I'M SURE THIS HAS CAUSED A FAIR AMOUNT OF STRESS FOR YOU,.. ANYWAYS, I-I'D JUST LIKE TO APOLOGISE ...
WELL, IT'S ALL RIGHT, RICHARD. YOU'RE FORGIVEN. BUT IN ANY CASE, I'M AFRAID WE WON'T BE ABLE TO RENEW YOUR CON-TRACT FOR THE FALL.
WHAT!? SCOTT, IT WAS AN HONEST MISTAKE!
IT'S NOT BECAUSE OF THAT. YOU'RE PROBABLY NOT AWARE OF THIS YET, BUT THERE'S A YOUTUBE VIDEO THAT'S REC-ENTLY GONE 'VIRAL'.
IT'S CALLED 'STONED PHIL-OSOPHY PROF CRASHES STU-DENT PARTY, STRIPS DOWN TO UNDIES.'

WE CAN'T HAVE YOU REPRESENTING THE UNIVERSITY IN THIS WAY, RICHARD.

AT LEAST SHE CALLED ME 'PROF.'

YOU'LL HAVE THREE HOURS TO COMPLETE THE EXAM. PLEASE KEEP THE PAPERS FACE DOWN UNTIL I SAY TO BEGIN.

PLEASE ENSURE YOUR CELL PHONES ARE TURNED OFF AND PUT AWAY.

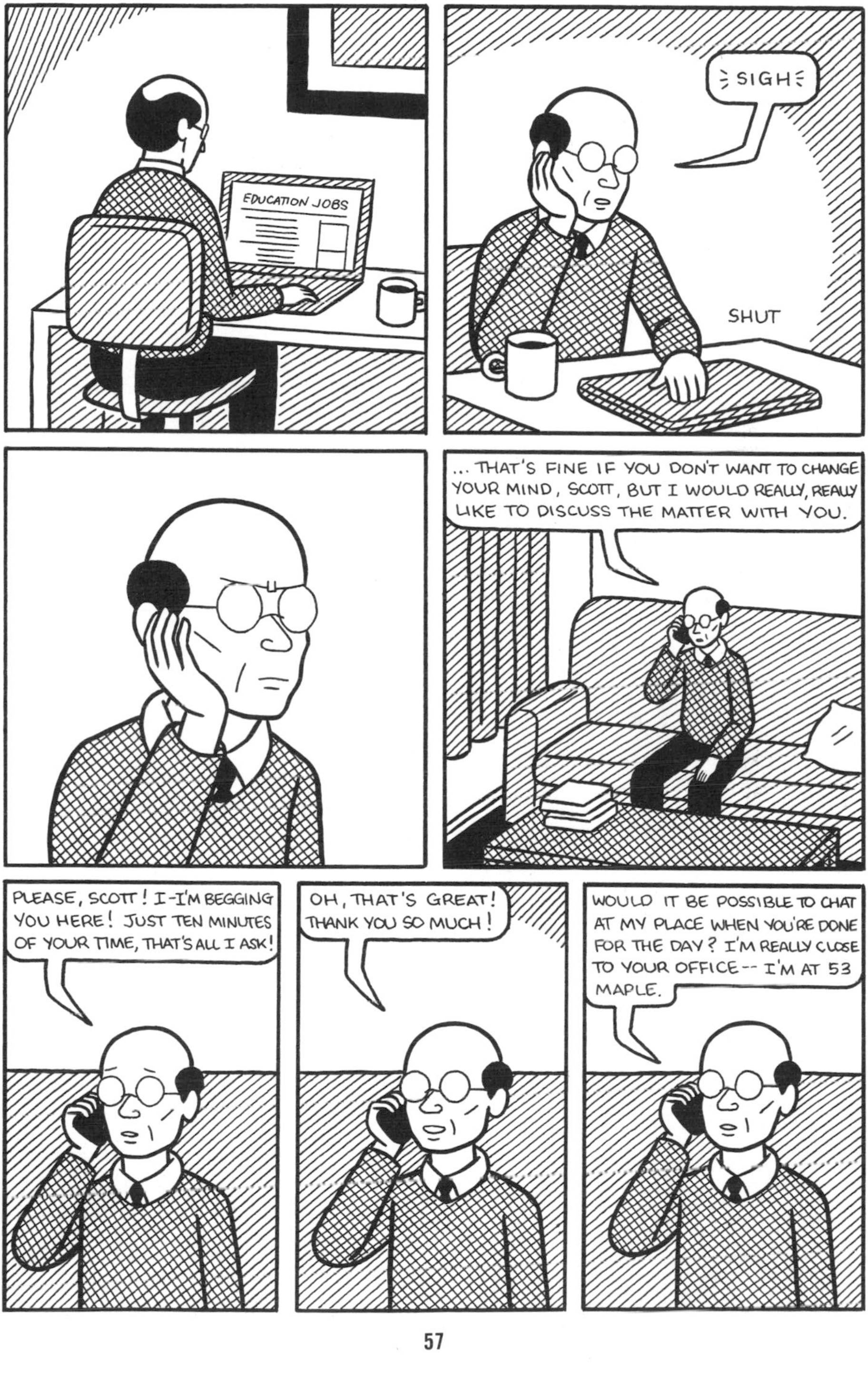
EDUCATION JOBS
SIGH
SHUT
... THAT'S FINE IF YOU DON'T WANT TO CHANGE YOUR MIND, SCOTT, BUT I WOULD REALLY, REALLY LIKE TO DISCUSS THE MATTER WITH YOU.
PLEASE, SCOTT! I-I'M BEGGING YOU HERE! JUST TEN MINUTES OF YOUR TIME, THAT'S ALL I ASK!
OH, THAT'S GREAT! THANK YOU SO MUCH!
WOULD IT BE POSSIBLE TO CHAT AT MY PLACE WHEN YOU'RE DONE FOR THE DAY? I'M REALLY CLOSE TO YOUR OFFICE -- I'M AT 53 MAPLE.

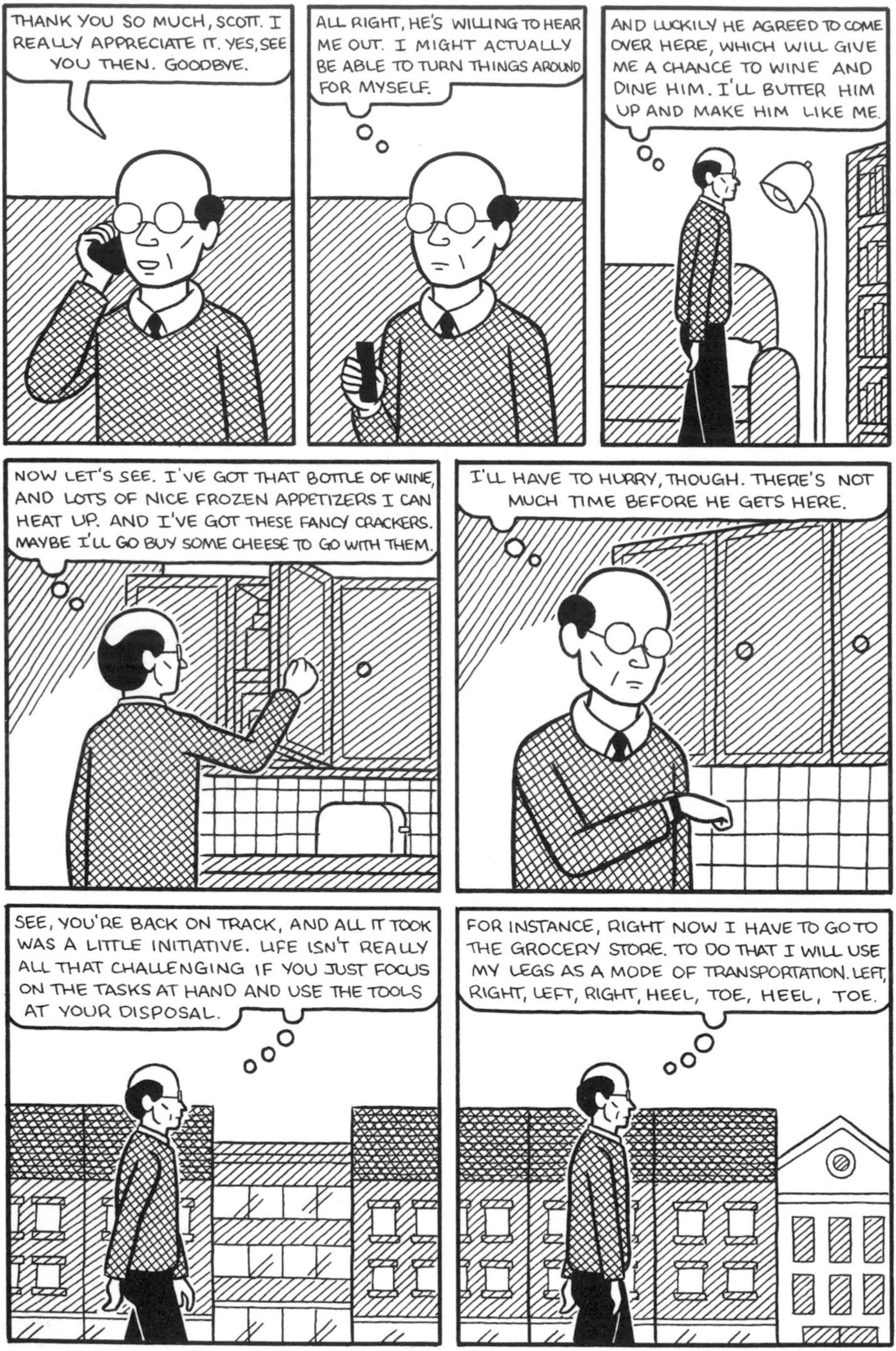
THANK YOU SO MUCH, SCOTT. I REALLY APPRECIATE IT. YES, SEE YOU THEN. GOODBYE.
ALL RIGHT, HE'S WILLING TO HEAR ME OUT. I MIGHT ACTUALLY BE ABLE TO TURN THINGS AROUND FOR MYSELF.
AND LUCKILY HE AGREED TO COME OVER HERE, WHICH WILL GIVE ME A CHANCE TO WINE AND DINE HIM. I'LL BUTTER HIM UP AND MAKE HIM LIKE ME.
NOW LET'S SEE. I'VE GOT THAT BOTTLE OF WINE, AND LOTS OF NICE FROZEN APPETIZERS I CAN HEAT UP. AND I'VE GOT THESE FANCY CRACKERS. MAYBE I'LL GO BUY SOME CHEESE TO GO WITH THEM.
I'LL HAVE TO HURRY, THOUGH. THERE'S NOT MUCH TIME BEFORE HE GETS HERE.
SEE, YOU'RE BACK ON TRACK, AND ALL IT TOOK WAS A LITTLE INITIATIVE. LIFE ISN'T REALLY ALL THAT CHALLENGING IF YOU JUST FOCUS ON THE TASKS AT HAND AND USE THE TOOLS AT YOUR DISPOSAL.
FOR INSTANCE, RIGHT NOW I HAVE TO GO TO THE GROCERY STORE. TO DO THAT I WILL USE MY LEGS AS A MODE OF TRANSPORTATION. LEFT, RIGHT, LEFT, RIGHT, HEEL, TOE, HEEL, TOE.

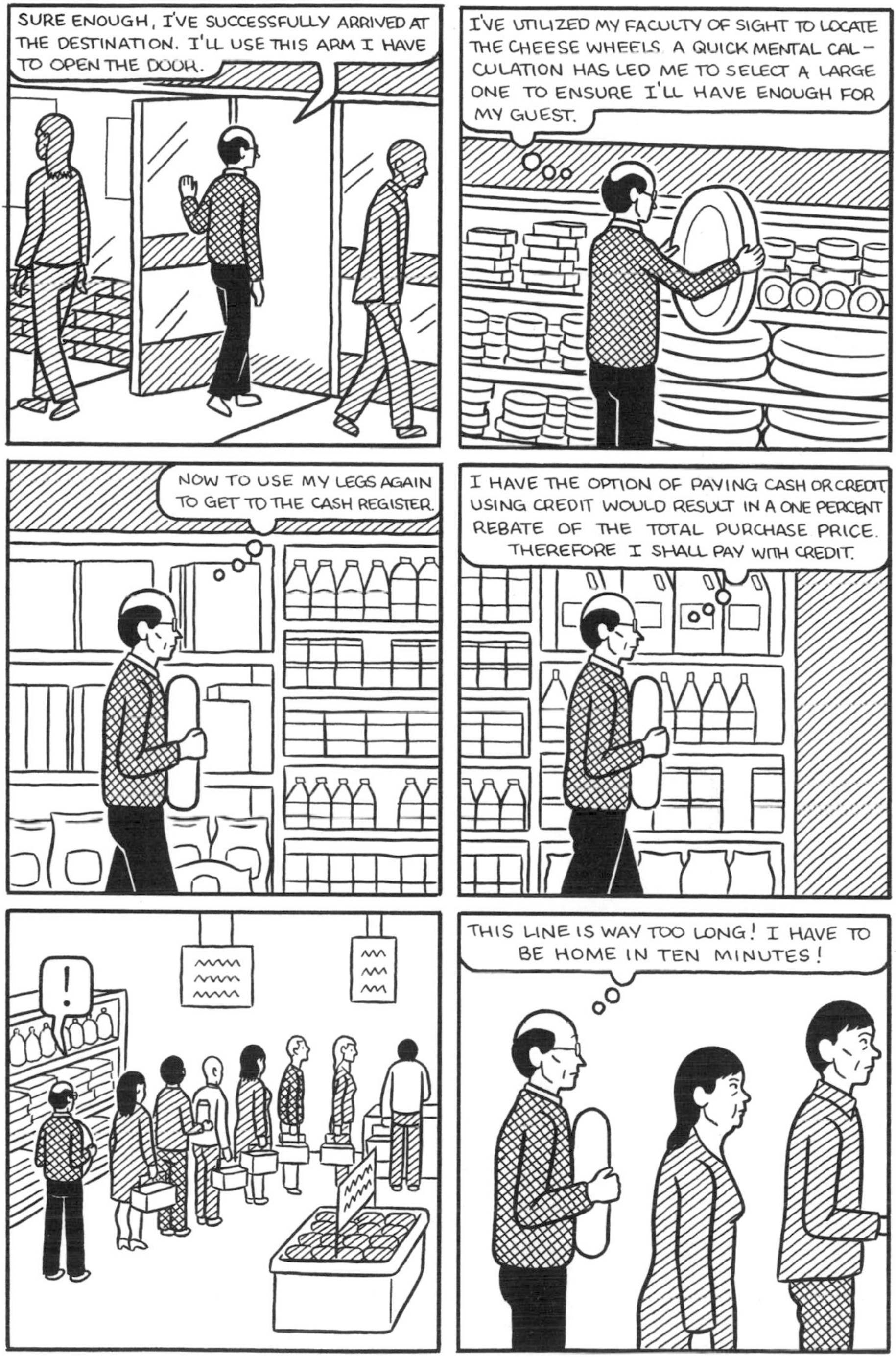
SURE ENOUGH, I'VE SUCCESSFULLY ARRIVED AT THE DESTINATION. I'LL USE THIS ARM I HAVE TO OPEN THE DOOR.
I'VE UTILIZED MY FACULTY OF SIGHT TO LOCATE THE CHEESE WHEELS. A QUICK MENTAL CAL-CULATION HAS LED ME TO SELECT A LARGE ONE TO ENSURE I'LL HAVE ENOUGH FOR MY GUEST.
NOW TO USE MY LEGS AGAIN TO GET TO THE CASH REGISTER.
I HAVE THE OPTION OF PAYING CASH OR CREDIT. USING CREDIT WOULD RESULT IN A ONE PERCENT REBATE OF THE TOTAL PURCHASE PRICE. THEREFORE I SHALL PAY WITH CREDIT.
!
THIS LINE IS WAY TOO LONG! I HAVE TO BE HOME IN TEN MINUTES!

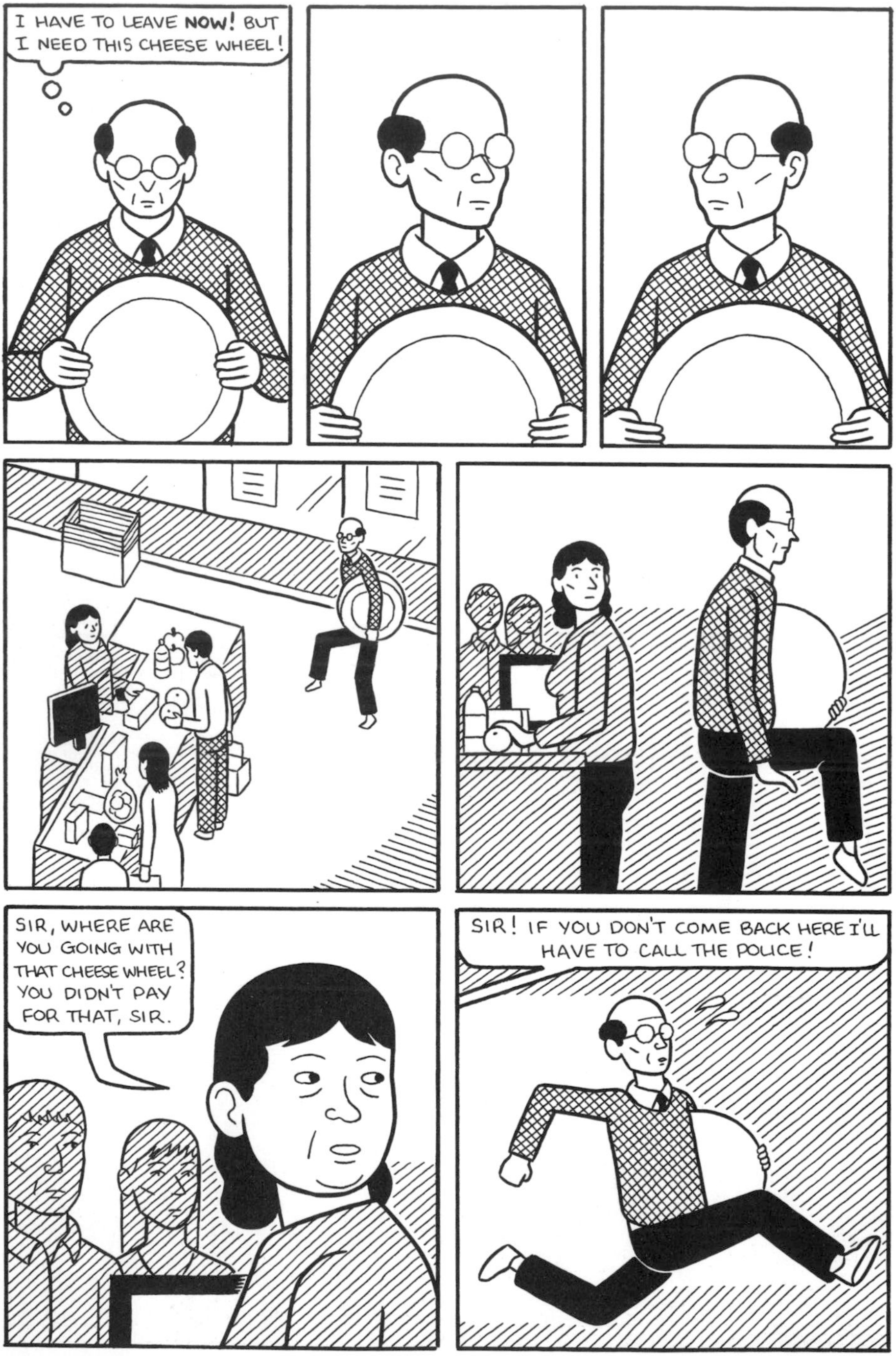
I HAVE TO LEAVE **NOW!** BUT I NEED THIS CHEESE WHEEL!
SIR, WHERE ARE YOU GOING WITH THAT CHEESE WHEEL? YOU DIDN'T PAY FOR THAT, SIR.
SIR! IF YOU DON'T COME BACK HERE I'LL HAVE TO CALL THE POLICE!

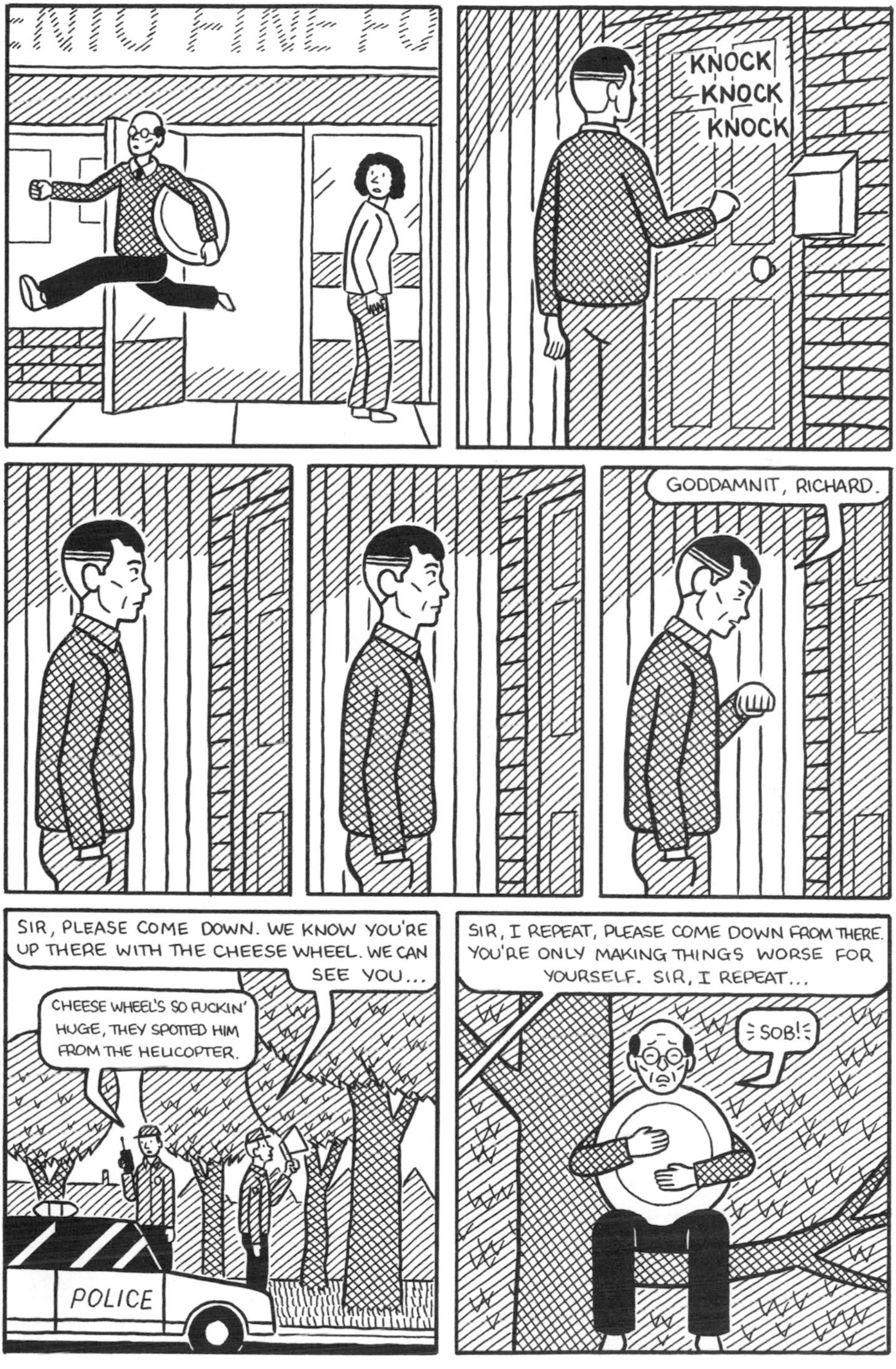
NIO FINE FO
KNOCK
KNOCK
KNOCK
GODDAMNIT, RICHARD.
SIR, PLEASE COME DOWN. WE KNOW YOU'RE UP THERE WITH THE CHEESE WHEEL. WE CAN SEE YOU...
CHEESE WHEEL'S SO FUCKIN' HUGE, THEY SPOTTED HIM FROM THE HELICOPTER.
POLICE
SIR, I REPEAT, PLEASE COME DOWN FROM THERE. YOU'RE ONLY MAKING THINGS WORSE FOR YOURSELF. SIR, I REPEAT...
SOB!

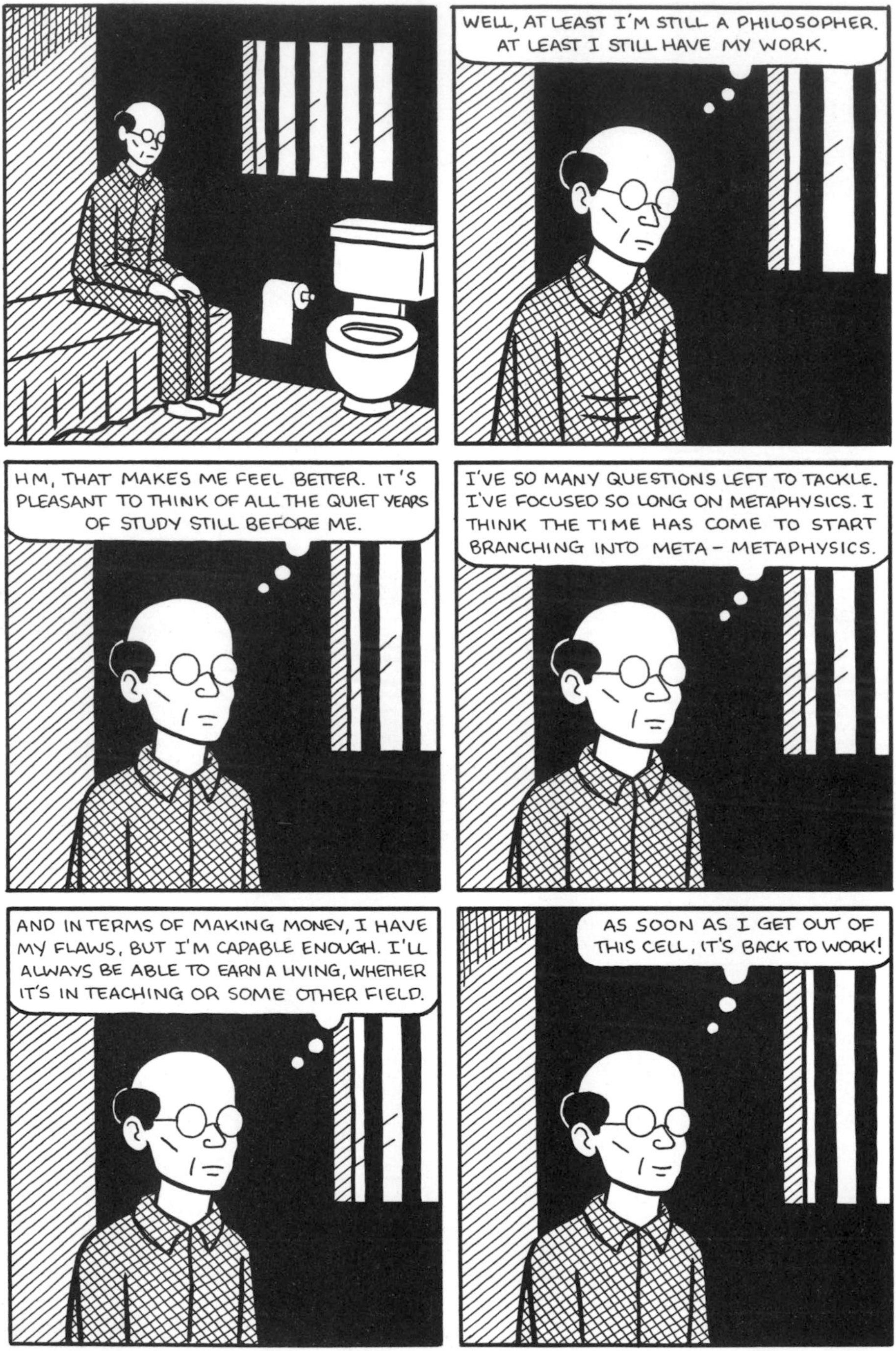
WELL, AT LEAST I'M STILL A PHILOSOPHER. AT LEAST I STILL HAVE MY WORK.
HM, THAT MAKES ME FEEL BETTER. IT'S PLEASANT TO THINK OF ALL THE QUIET YEARS OF STUDY STILL BEFORE ME.
I'VE SO MANY QUESTIONS LEFT TO TACKLE. I'VE FOCUSED SO LONG ON METAPHYSICS. I THINK THE TIME HAS COME TO START BRANCHING INTO META-METAPHYSICS.
AND IN TERMS OF MAKING MONEY, I HAVE MY FLAWS, BUT I'M CAPABLE ENOUGH. I'LL ALWAYS BE ABLE TO EARN A LIVING, WHETHER IT'S IN TEACHING OR SOME OTHER FIELD.
AS SOON AS I GET OUT OF THIS CELL, IT'S BACK TO WORK!

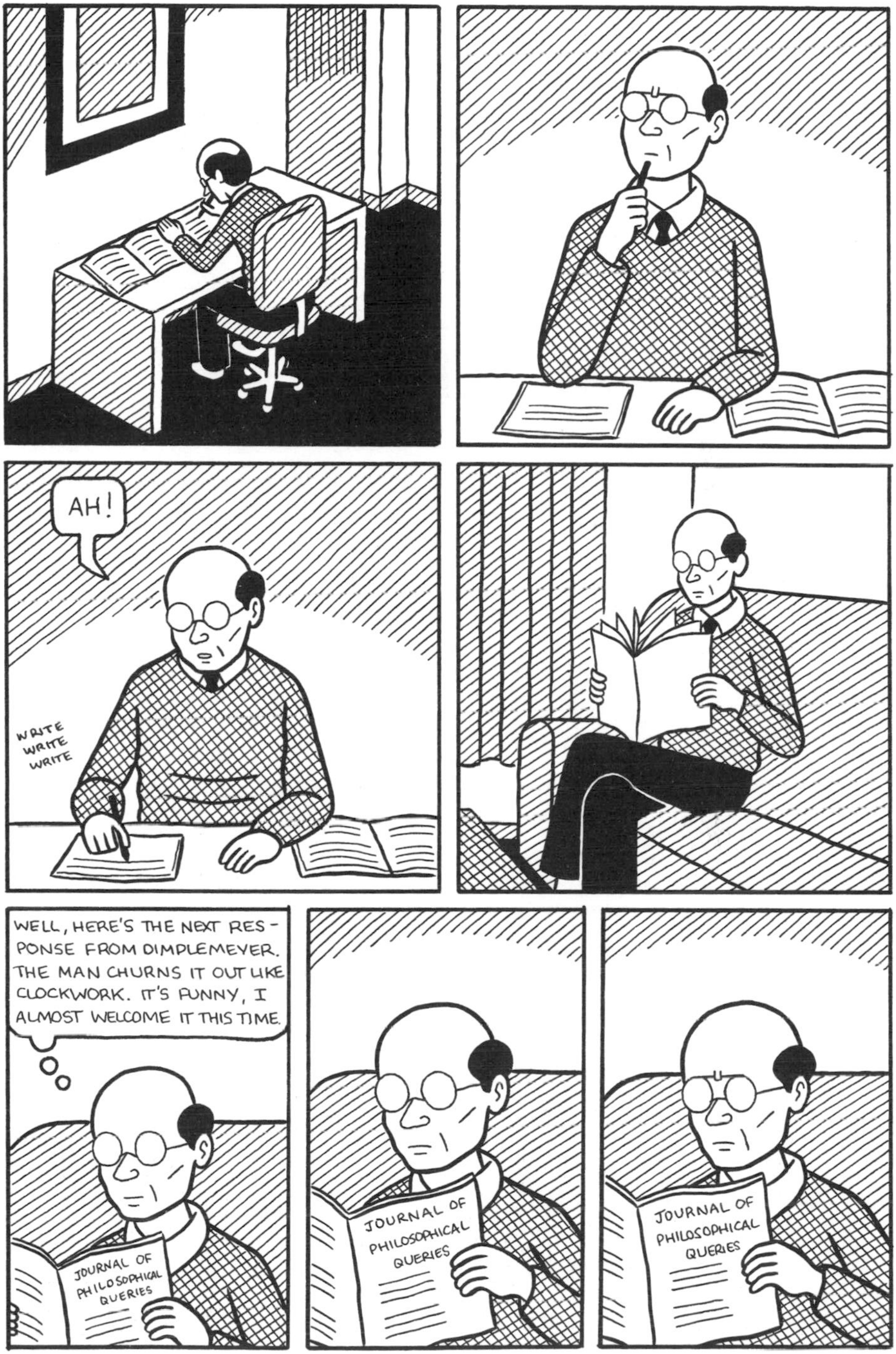
AH!
WRITE WRITE WRITE
WELL, HERE'S THE NEXT RESPONSE FROM DIMPLEMEYER. THE MAN CHURNS IT OUT LIKE CLOCKWORK. IT'S FUNNY, I ALMOST WELCOME IT THIS TIME.
JOURNAL OF PHILOSOPHICAL QUERIES
JOURNAL OF PHILOSOPHICAL QUERIES
JOURNAL OF PHILOSOPHICAL QUERIES

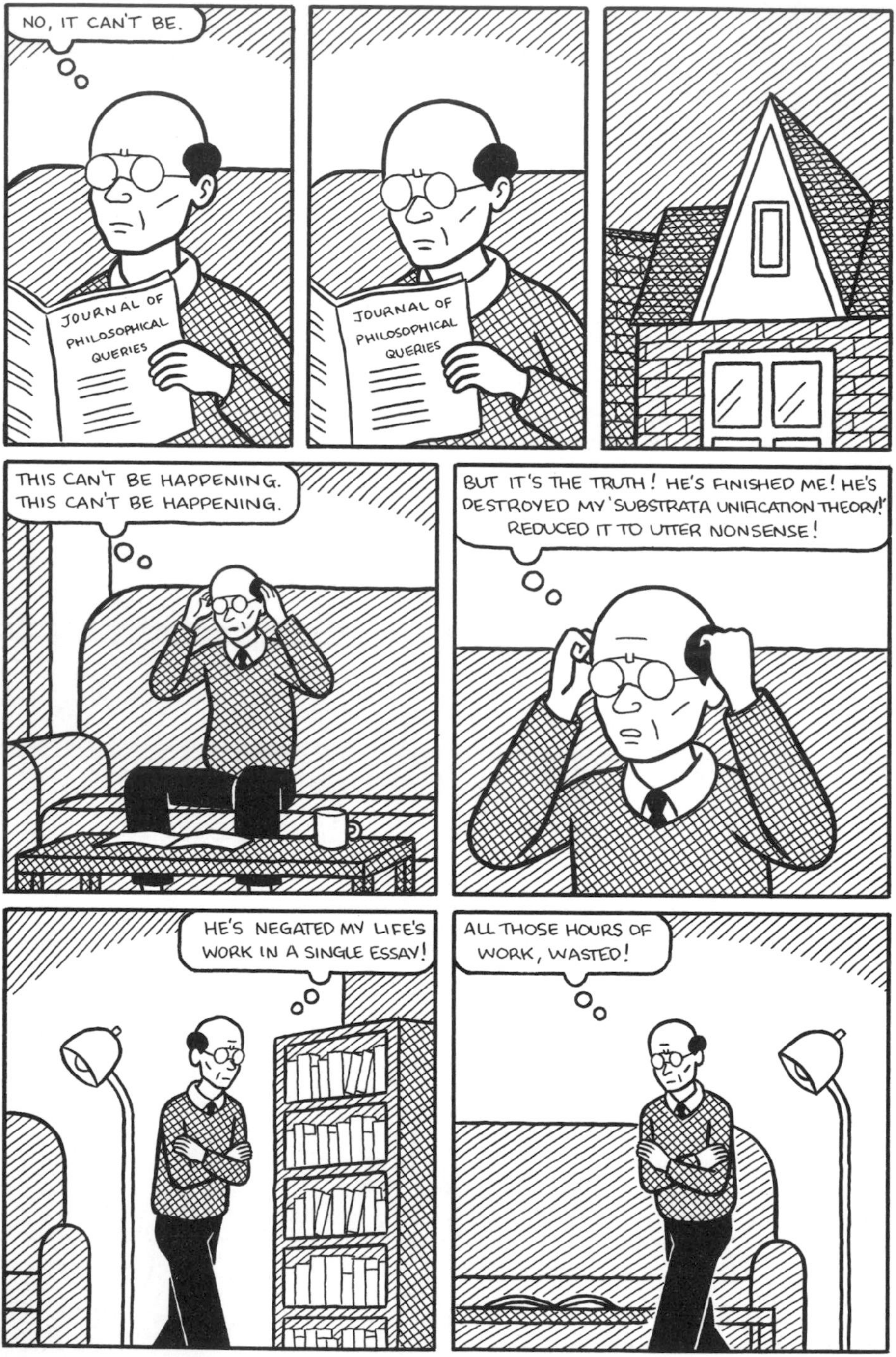
NO, IT CAN'T BE.
JOURNAL OF PHILOSOPHICAL QUERIES
JOURNAL OF PHILOSOPHICAL QUERIES
THIS CAN'T BE HAPPENING. THIS CAN'T BE HAPPENING.
BUT IT'S THE TRUTH! HE'S FINISHED ME! HE'S DESTROYED MY 'SUBSTRATA UNIFICATION THEORY!' REDUCED IT TO UTTER NONSENSE!
HE'S NEGATED MY LIFE'S WORK IN A SINGLE ESSAY!
ALL THOSE HOURS OF WORK, WASTED!

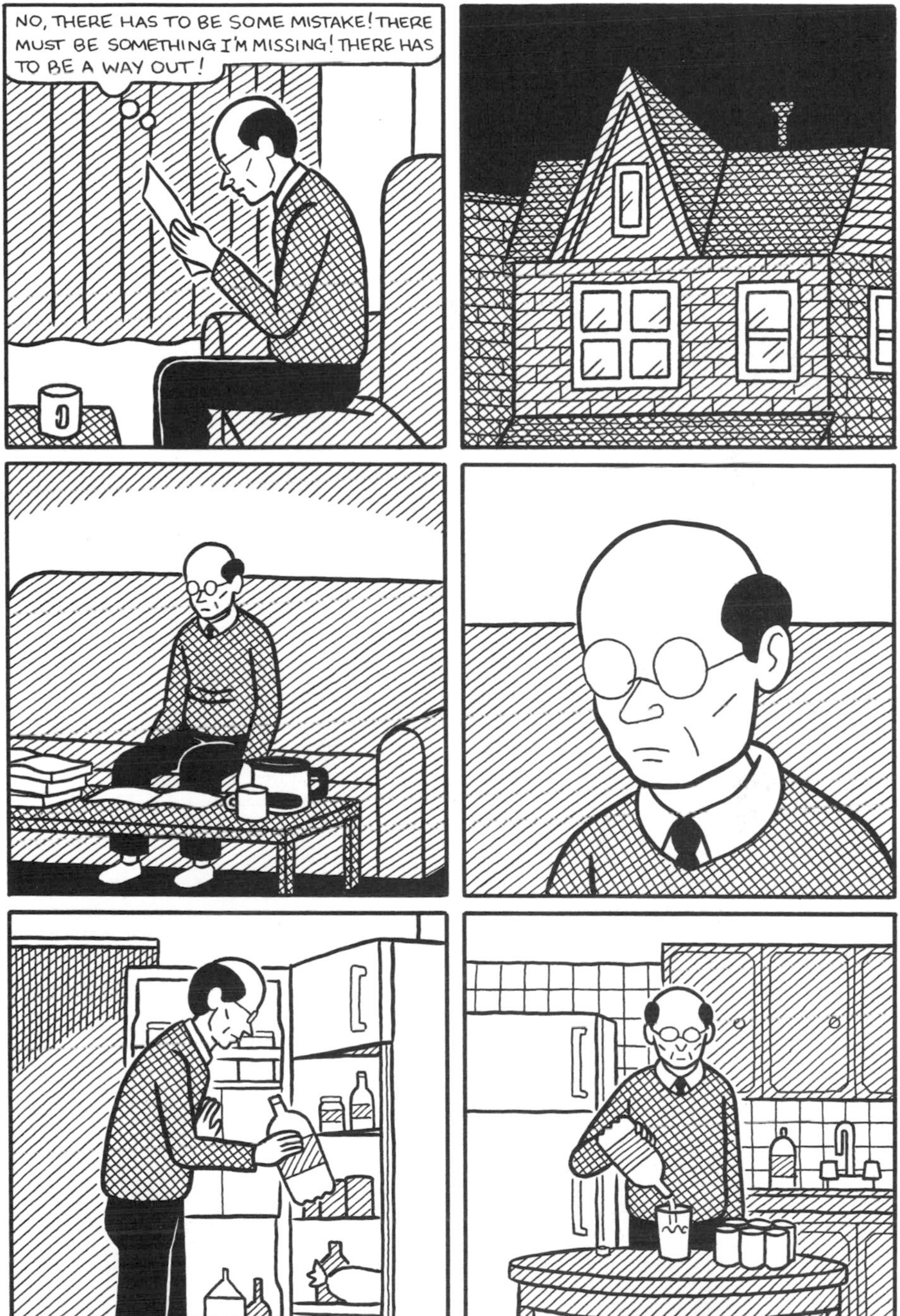
NO, THERE HAS TO BE SOME MISTAKE! THERE MUST BE SOMETHING I'M MISSING! THERE HAS TO BE A WAY OUT!

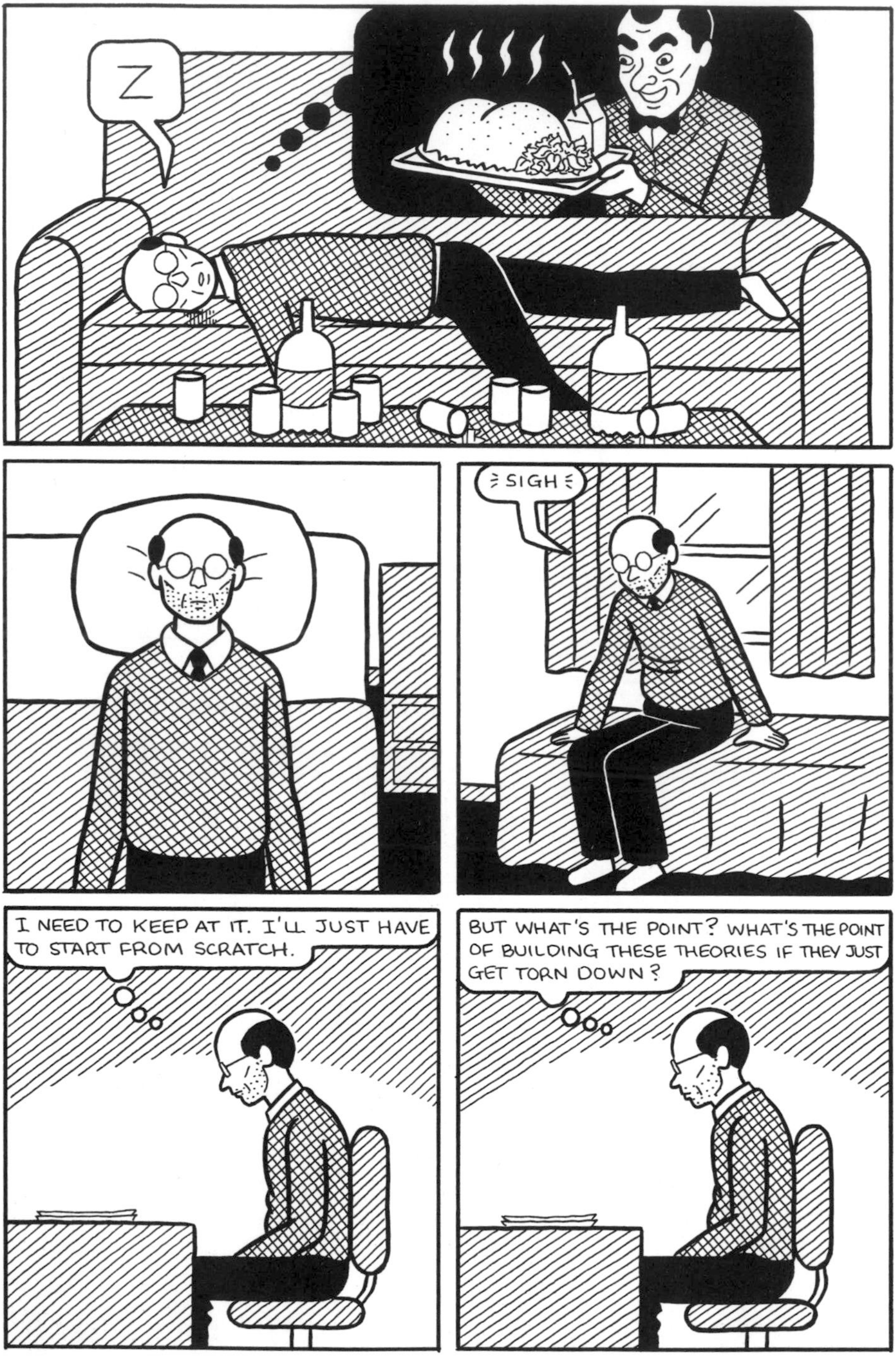
Z
SIGH
I NEED TO KEEP AT IT. I'LL JUST HAVE TO START FROM SCRATCH.
BUT WHAT'S THE POINT? WHAT'S THE POINT OF BUILDING THESE THEORIES IF THEY JUST GET TORN DOWN?

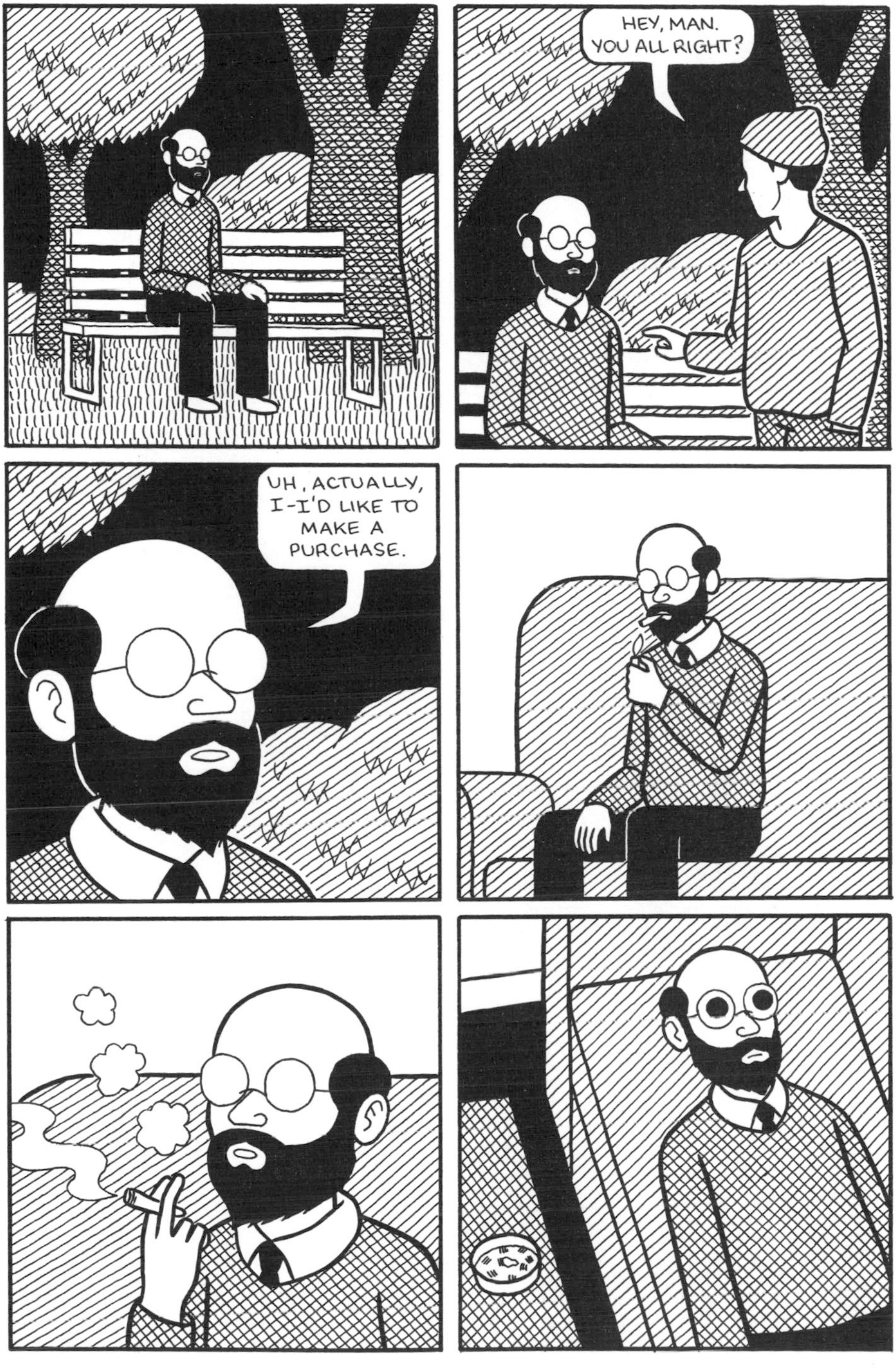
HEY, MAN. YOU ALL RIGHT?
UH, ACTUALLY, I-I'D LIKE TO MAKE A PURCHASE.

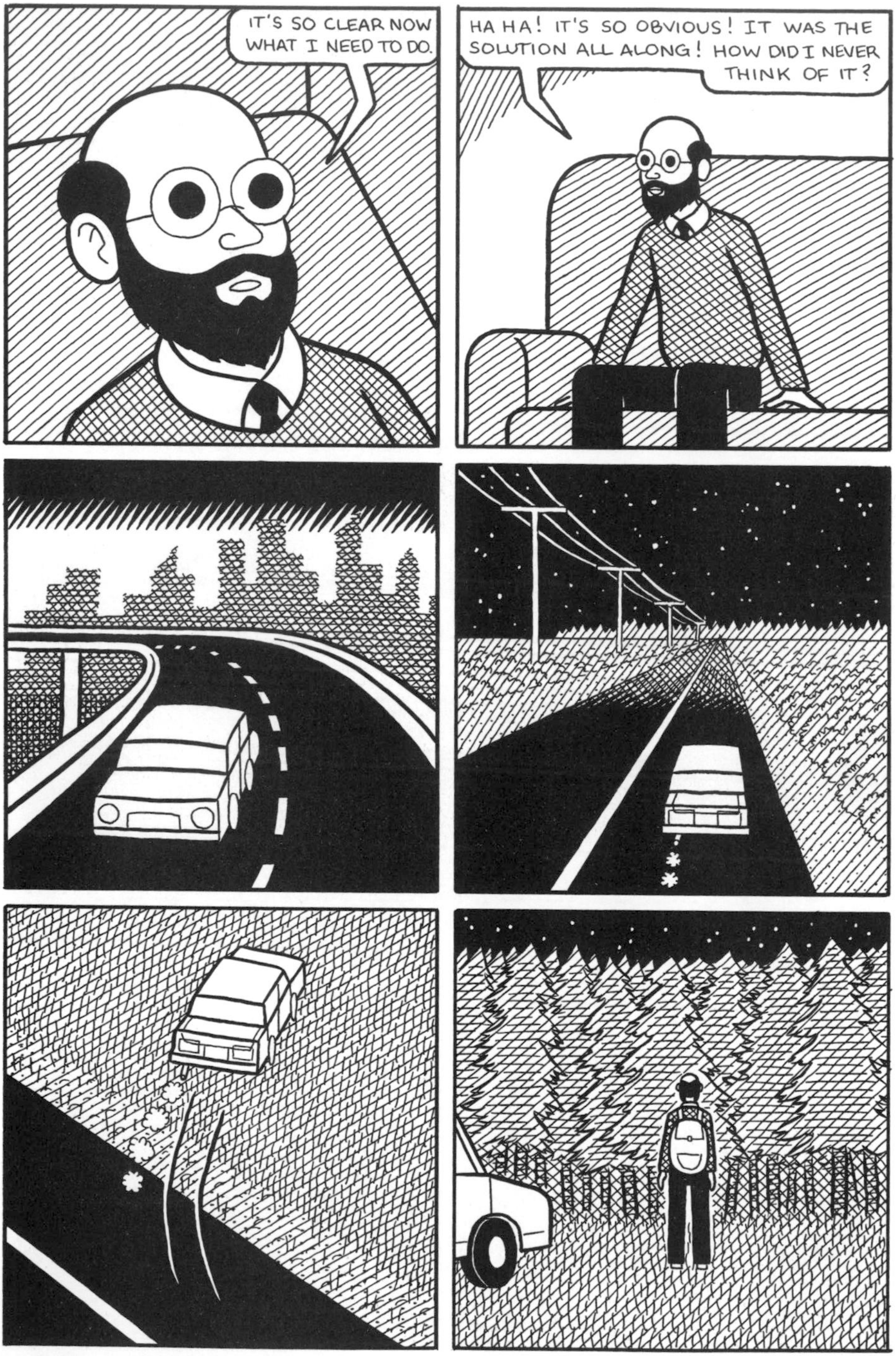
IT'S SO CLEAR NOW WHAT I NEED TO DO.
HA HA! IT'S SO OBVIOUS! IT WAS THE SOLUTION ALL ALONG! HOW DID I NEVER THINK OF IT?

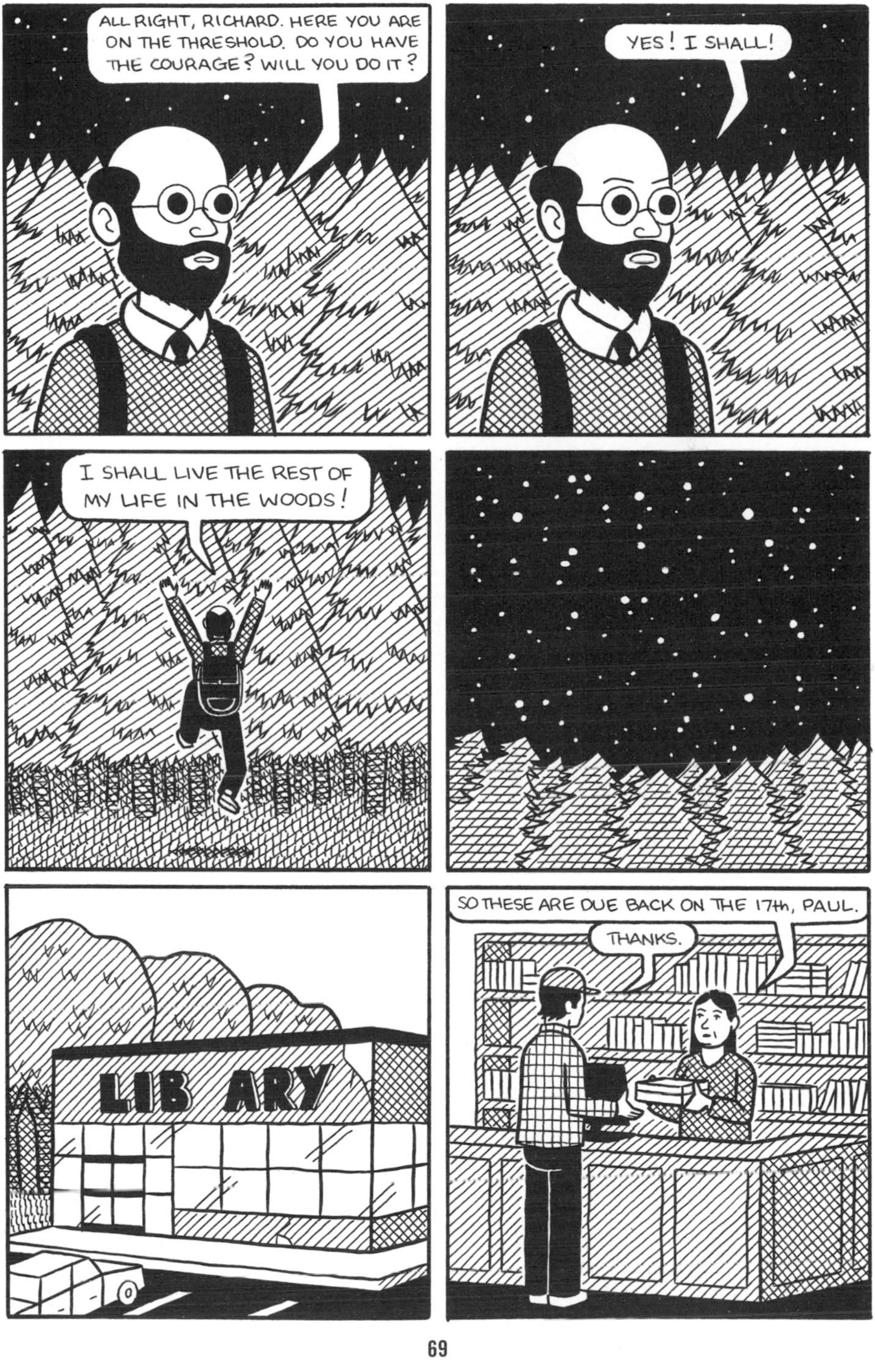
ALL RIGHT, RICHARD. HERE YOU ARE ON THE THRESHOLD. DO YOU HAVE THE COURAGE? WILL YOU DO IT?
YES! I SHALL!
I SHALL LIVE THE REST OF MY LIFE IN THE WOODS!
LIB ARY
SO THESE ARE DUE BACK ON THE 17th, PAUL.
THANKS.

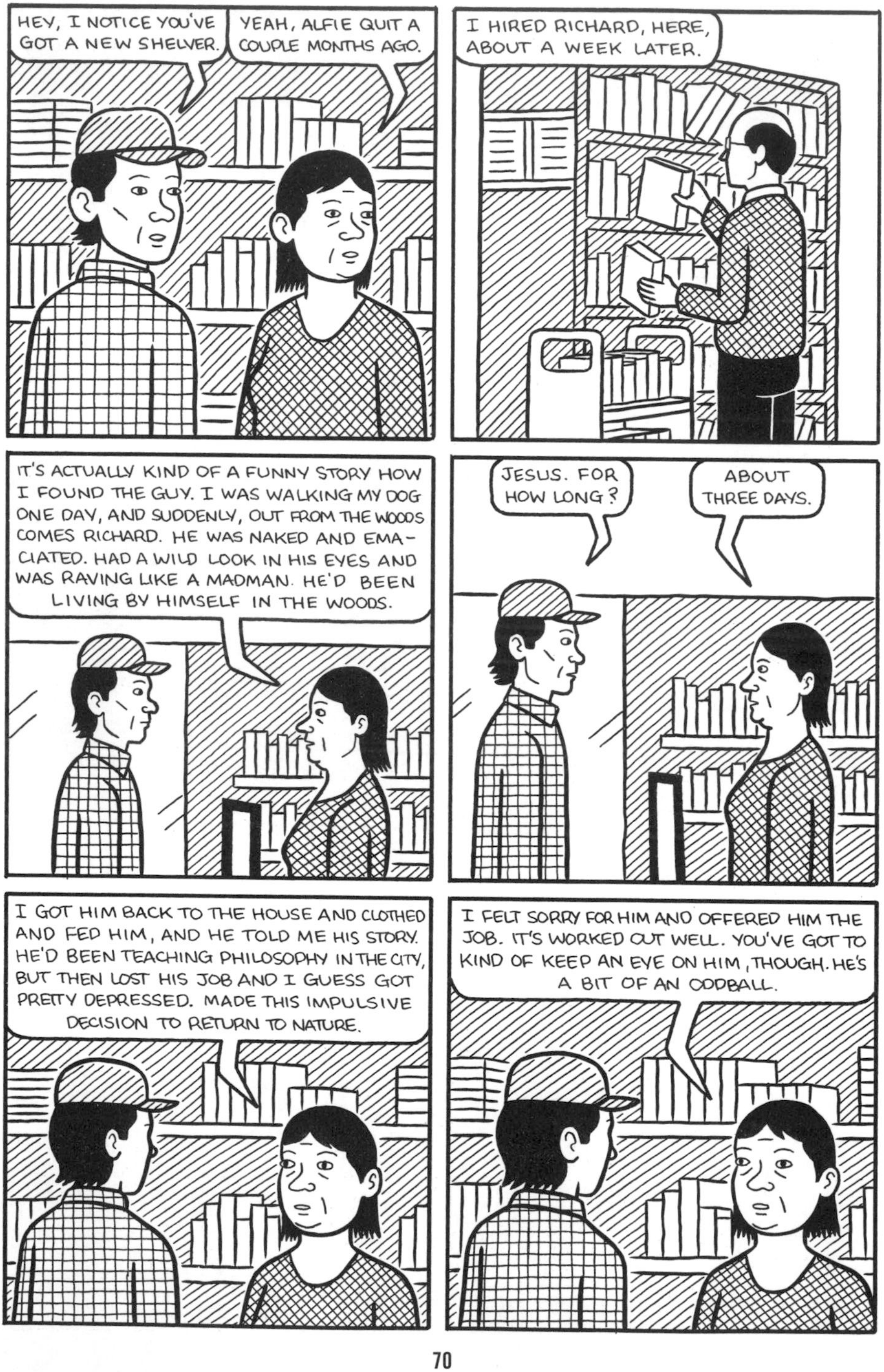
HEY, I NOTICE YOU'VE GOT A NEW SHELVER.
YEAH, ALFIE QUIT A COUPLE MONTHS AGO.
I HIRED RICHARD, HERE, ABOUT A WEEK LATER.
IT'S ACTUALLY KIND OF A FUNNY STORY HOW I FOUND THE GUY. I WAS WALKING MY DOG ONE DAY, AND SUDDENLY, OUT FROM THE WOODS COMES RICHARD. HE WAS NAKED AND EMACIATED. HAD A WILD LOOK IN HIS EYES AND WAS RAVING LIKE A MADMAN. HE'D BEEN LIVING BY HIMSELF IN THE WOODS.
JESUS. FOR HOW LONG?
ABOUT THREE DAYS.
I GOT HIM BACK TO THE HOUSE AND CLOTHED AND FED HIM, AND HE TOLD ME HIS STORY. HE'D BEEN TEACHING PHILOSOPHY IN THE CITY, BUT THEN LOST HIS JOB AND I GUESS GOT PRETTY DEPRESSED. MADE THIS IMPULSIVE DECISION TO RETURN TO NATURE.
I FELT SORRY FOR HIM AND OFFERED HIM THE JOB. IT'S WORKED OUT WELL. YOU'VE GOT TO KIND OF KEEP AN EYE ON HIM, THOUGH. HE'S A BIT OF AN ODDBALL.

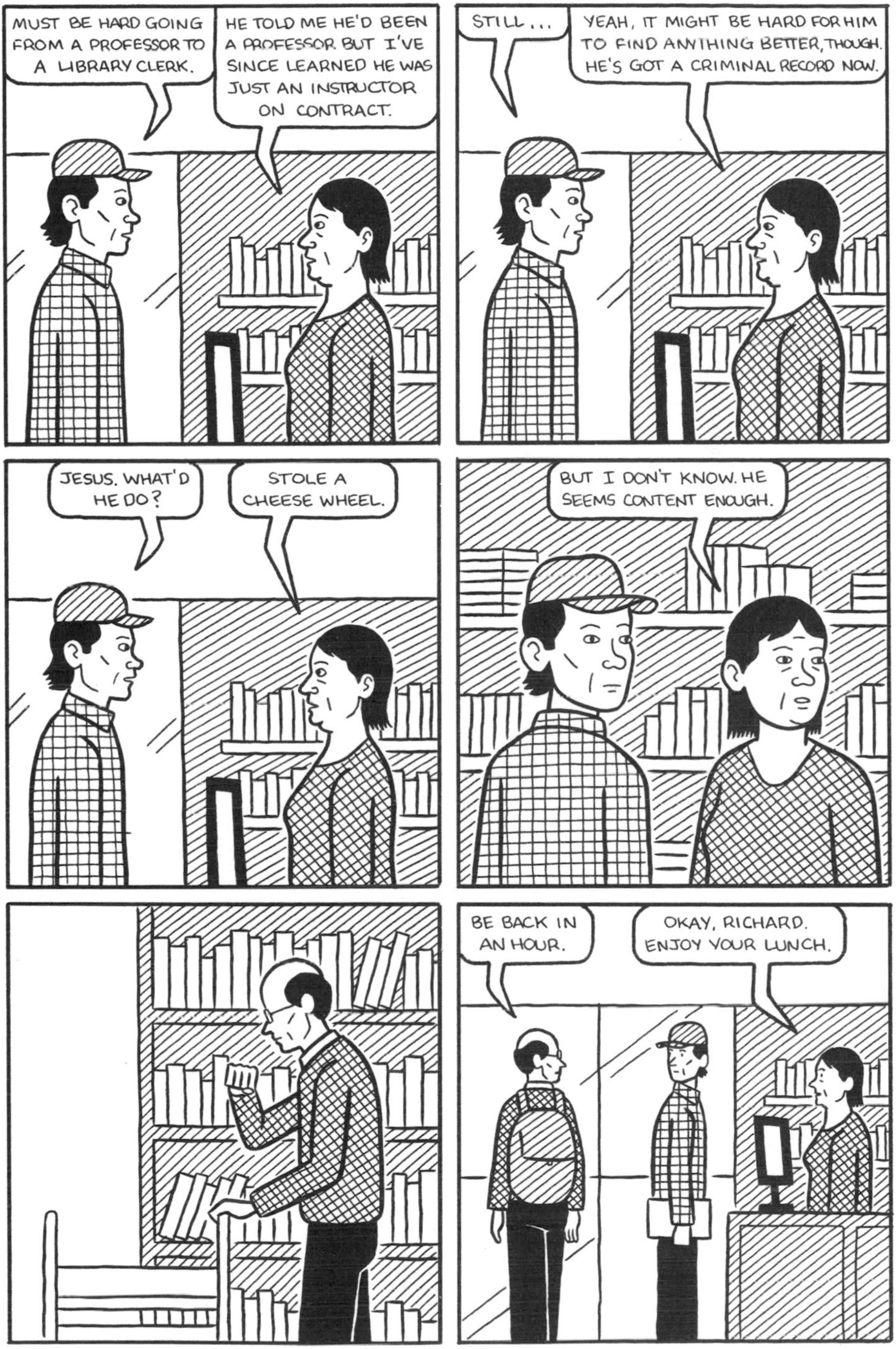
MUST BE HARD GOING FROM A PROFESSOR TO A LIBRARY CLERK.
HE TOLD ME HE'D BEEN A PROFESSOR BUT I'VE SINCE LEARNED HE WAS JUST AN INSTRUCTOR ON CONTRACT.
STILL...
YEAH, IT MIGHT BE HARD FOR HIM TO FIND ANYTHING BETTER, THOUGH. HE'S GOT A CRIMINAL RECORD NOW.
JESUS. WHAT'D HE DO?
STOLE A CHEESE WHEEL.
BUT I DON'T KNOW. HE SEEMS CONTENT ENOUGH.
BE BACK IN AN HOUR.
OKAY, RICHARD. ENJOY YOUR LUNCH.

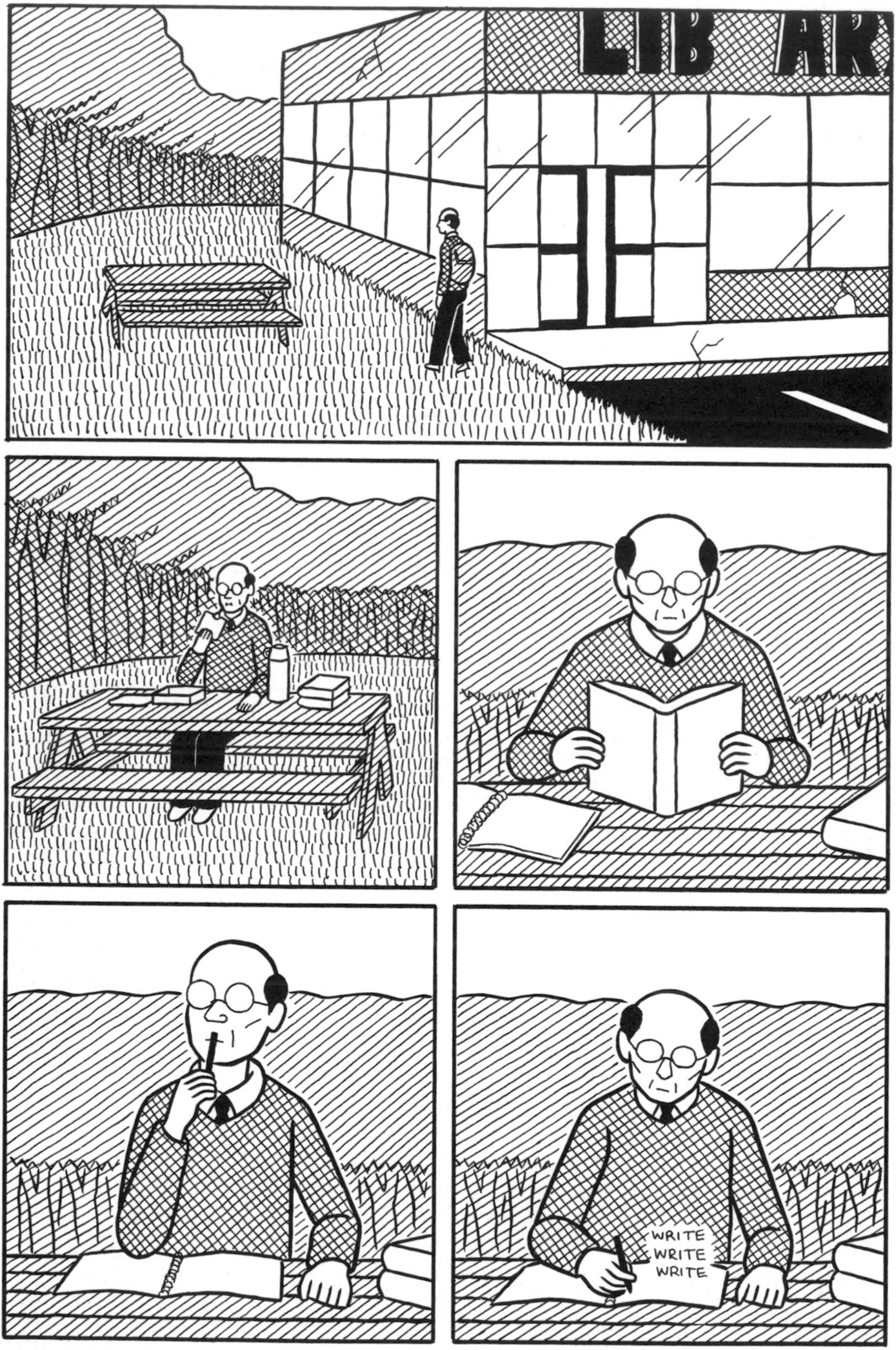
LIB AR
WRITE
WRITE
WRITE

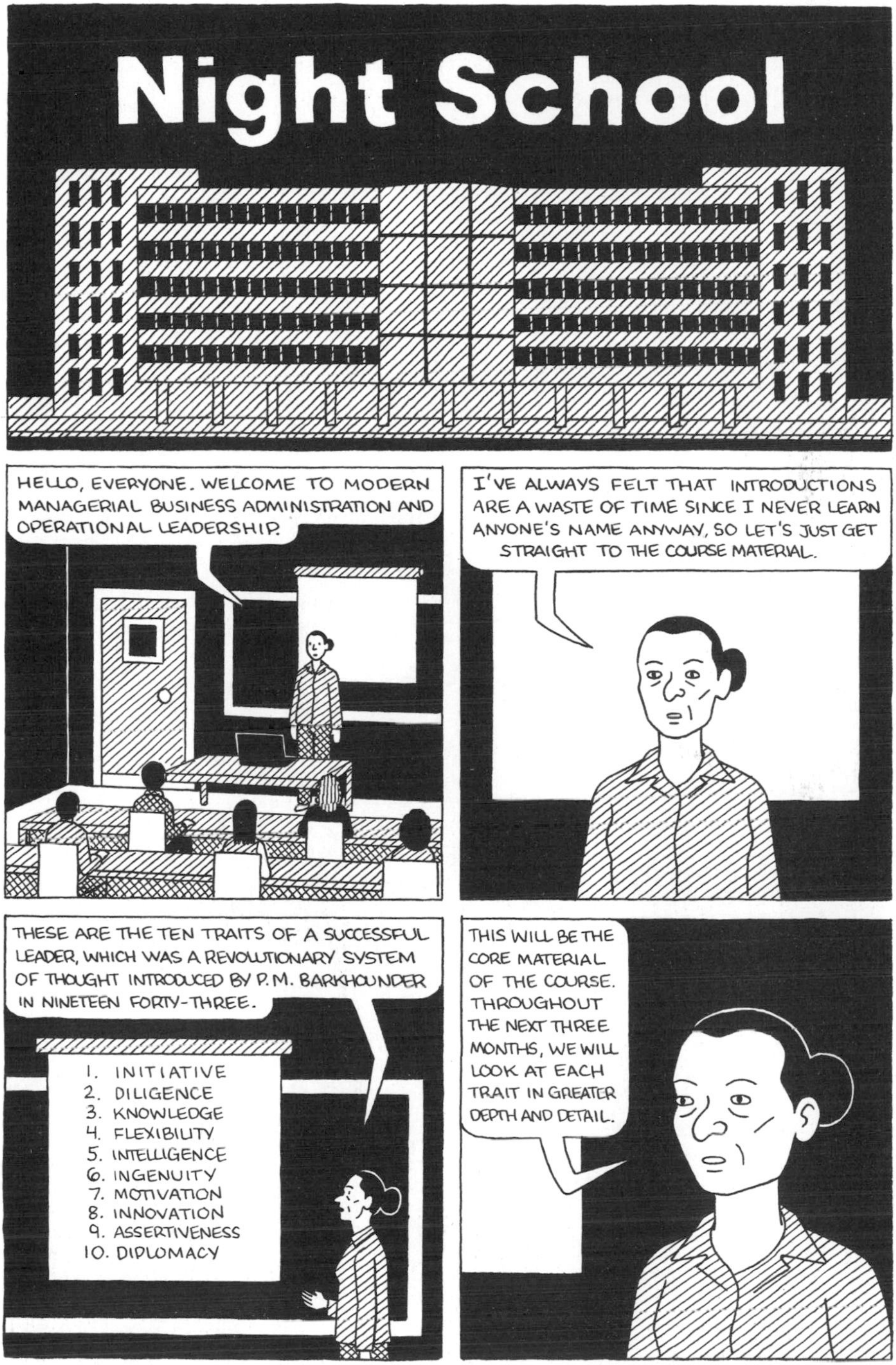
Night School
HELLO, EVERYONE. WELCOME TO MODERN MANAGERIAL BUSINESS ADMINISTRATION AND OPERATIONAL LEADERSHIP.
I'VE ALWAYS FELT THAT INTRODUCTIONS ARE A WASTE OF TIME SINCE I NEVER LEARN ANYONE'S NAME ANYWAY, SO LET'S JUST GET STRAIGHT TO THE COURSE MATERIAL.
THESE ARE THE TEN TRAITS OF A SUCCESSFUL LEADER, WHICH WAS A REVOLUTIONARY SYSTEM OF THOUGHT INTRODUCED BY P.M. BARKHOUNDER IN NINETEEN FORTY-THREE.
1. INITIATIVE
2. DILIGENCE
3. KNOWLEDGE
4. FLEXIBILITY
5. INTELLIGENCE
6. INGENUITY
7. MOTIVATION
8. INNOVATION
9. ASSERTIVENESS
10. DIPLOMACY
THIS WILL BE THE CORE MATERIAL OF THE COURSE. THROUGHOUT THE NEXT THREE MONTHS, WE WILL LOOK AT EACH TRAIT IN GREATER DEPTH AND DETAIL.

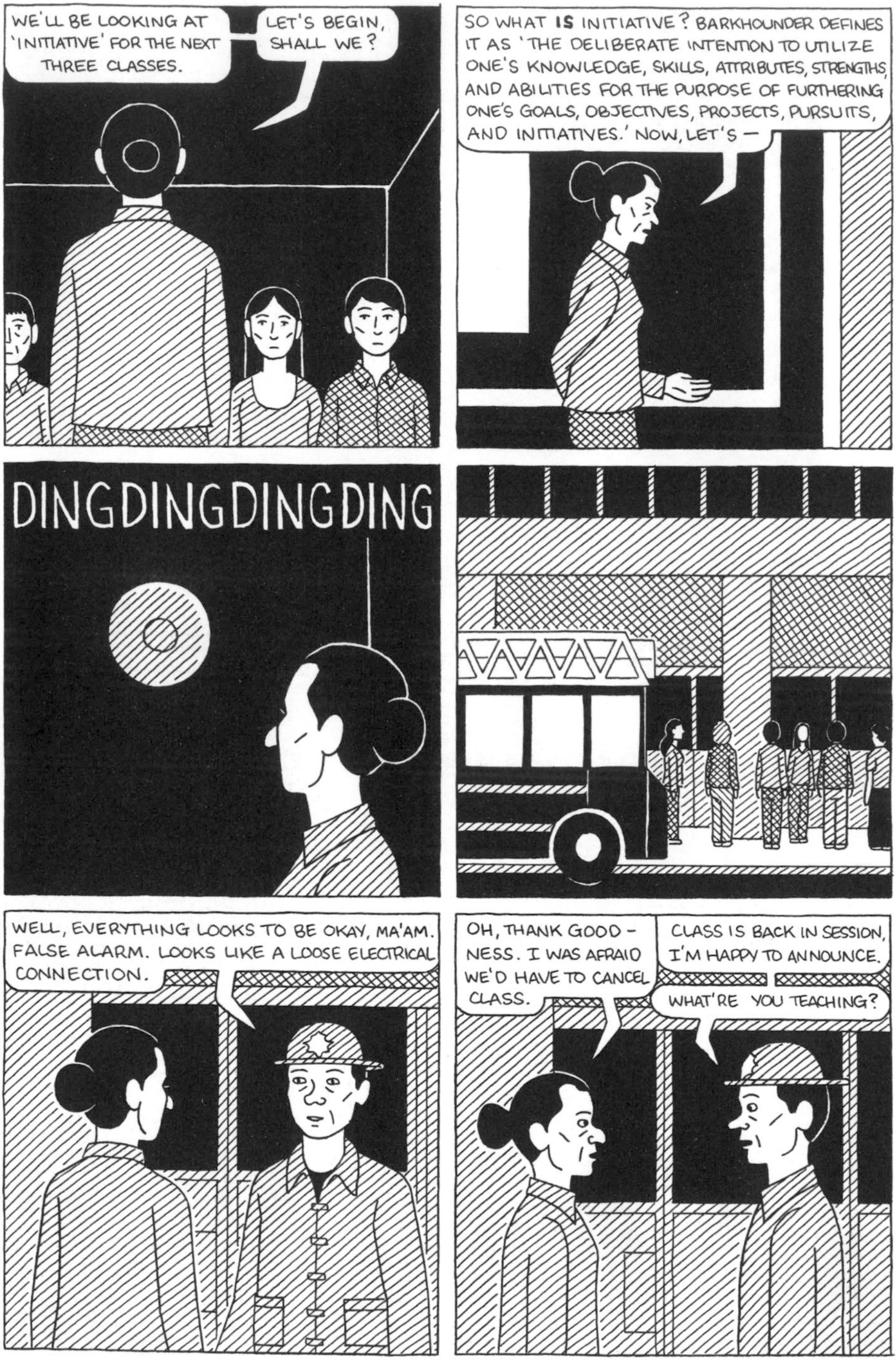

WE'LL BE LOOKING AT 'INITIATIVE' FOR THE NEXT THREE CLASSES.
LET'S BEGIN, SHALL WE?
SO WHAT **IS** INITIATIVE? BARKHOUNDER DEFINES IT AS 'THE DELIBERATE INTENTION TO UTILIZE ONE'S KNOWLEDGE, SKILLS, ATTRIBUTES, STRENGTHS, AND ABILITIES FOR THE PURPOSE OF FURTHERING ONE'S GOALS, OBJECTIVES, PROJECTS, PURSUITS, AND INITIATIVES.' NOW, LET'S —
DINGDINGDINGDING
WELL, EVERYTHING LOOKS TO BE OKAY, MA'AM. FALSE ALARM. LOOKS LIKE A LOOSE ELECTRICAL CONNECTION.
OH, THANK GOOD - NESS. I WAS AFRAID WE'D HAVE TO CANCEL CLASS.
CLASS IS BACK IN SESSION, I'M HAPPY TO ANNOUNCE.
WHAT'RE YOU TEACHING?

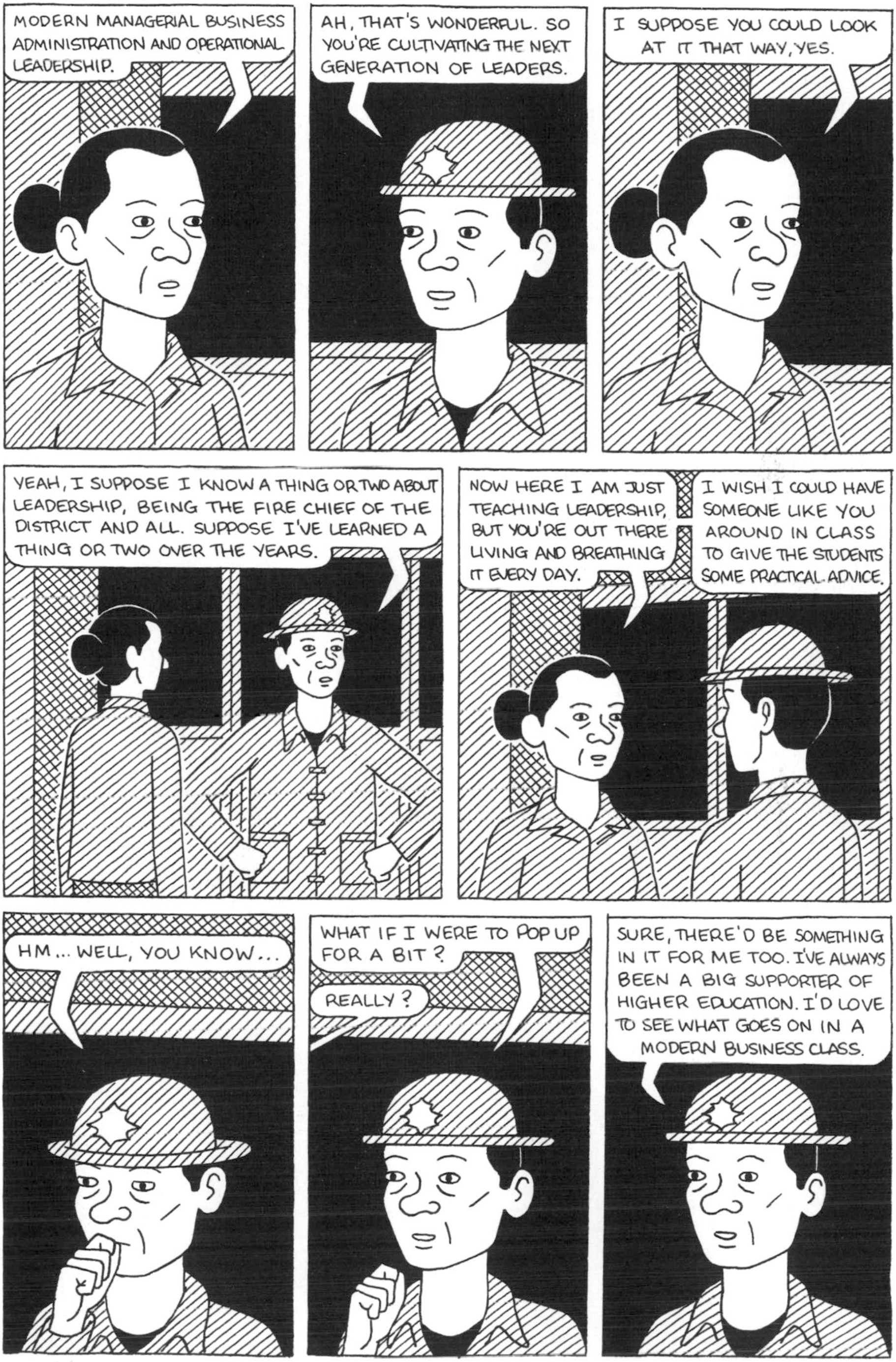
MODERN MANAGERIAL BUSINESS ADMINISTRATION AND OPERATIONAL LEADERSHIP.
AH, THAT'S WONDERFUL. SO YOU'RE CULTIVATING THE NEXT GENERATION OF LEADERS.
I SUPPOSE YOU COULD LOOK AT IT THAT WAY, YES.
YEAH, I SUPPOSE I KNOW A THING OR TWO ABOUT LEADERSHIP, BEING THE FIRE CHIEF OF THE DISTRICT AND ALL. SUPPOSE I'VE LEARNED A THING OR TWO OVER THE YEARS.
NOW HERE I AM JUST TEACHING LEADERSHIP, BUT YOU'RE OUT THERE LIVING AND BREATHING IT EVERY DAY.
I WISH I COULD HAVE SOMEONE LIKE YOU AROUND IN CLASS TO GIVE THE STUDENTS SOME PRACTICAL ADVICE.
HM... WELL, YOU KNOW...
WHAT IF I WERE TO POP UP FOR A BIT?
REALLY?
SURE, THERE'D BE SOMETHING IN IT FOR ME TOO. I'VE ALWAYS BEEN A BIG SUPPORTER OF HIGHER EDUCATION. I'D LOVE TO SEE WHAT GOES ON IN A MODERN BUSINESS CLASS.

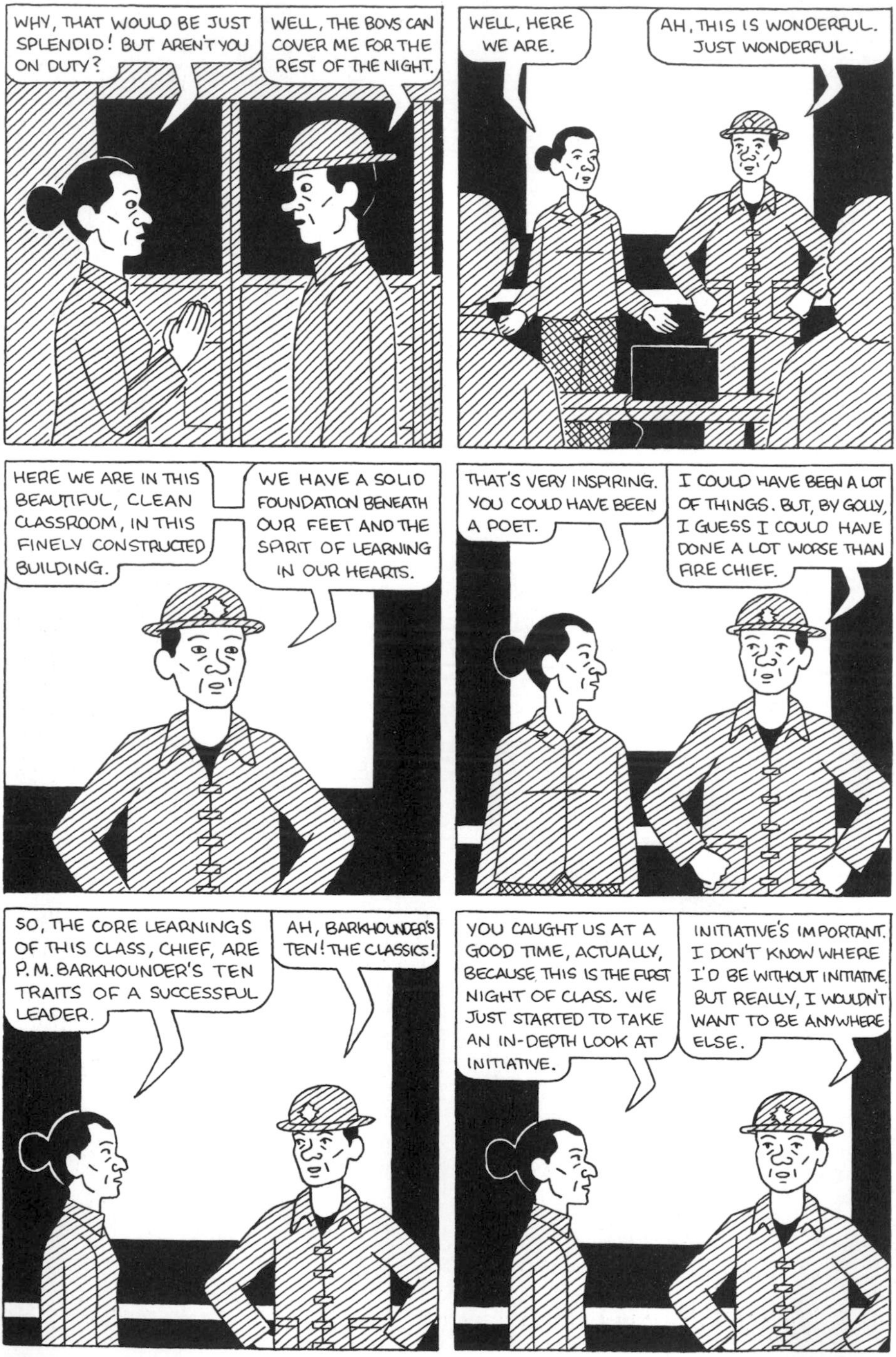
WHY, THAT WOULD BE JUST SPLENDID! BUT AREN'T YOU ON DUTY?
WELL, THE BOYS CAN COVER ME FOR THE REST OF THE NIGHT.
WELL, HERE WE ARE.
AH, THIS IS WONDERFUL. JUST WONDERFUL.
HERE WE ARE IN THIS BEAUTIFUL, CLEAN CLASSROOM, IN THIS FINELY CONSTRUCTED BUILDING.
WE HAVE A SOLID FOUNDATION BENEATH OUR FEET AND THE SPIRIT OF LEARNING IN OUR HEARTS.
THAT'S VERY INSPIRING. YOU COULD HAVE BEEN A POET.
I COULD HAVE BEEN A LOT OF THINGS. BUT, BY GOLLY, I GUESS I COULD HAVE DONE A LOT WORSE THAN FIRE CHIEF.
SO, THE CORE LEARNINGS OF THIS CLASS, CHIEF, ARE P.M. BARKHOUNDER'S TEN TRAITS OF A SUCCESSFUL LEADER.
AH, BARKHOUNDER'S TEN! THE CLASSICS!
YOU CAUGHT US AT A GOOD TIME, ACTUALLY, BECAUSE THIS IS THE FIRST NIGHT OF CLASS. WE JUST STARTED TO TAKE AN IN-DEPTH LOOK AT INITIATIVE.
INITIATIVE'S IMPORTANT. I DON'T KNOW WHERE I'D BE WITHOUT INITIATIVE. BUT REALLY, I WOULDN'T WANT TO BE ANYWHERE ELSE.

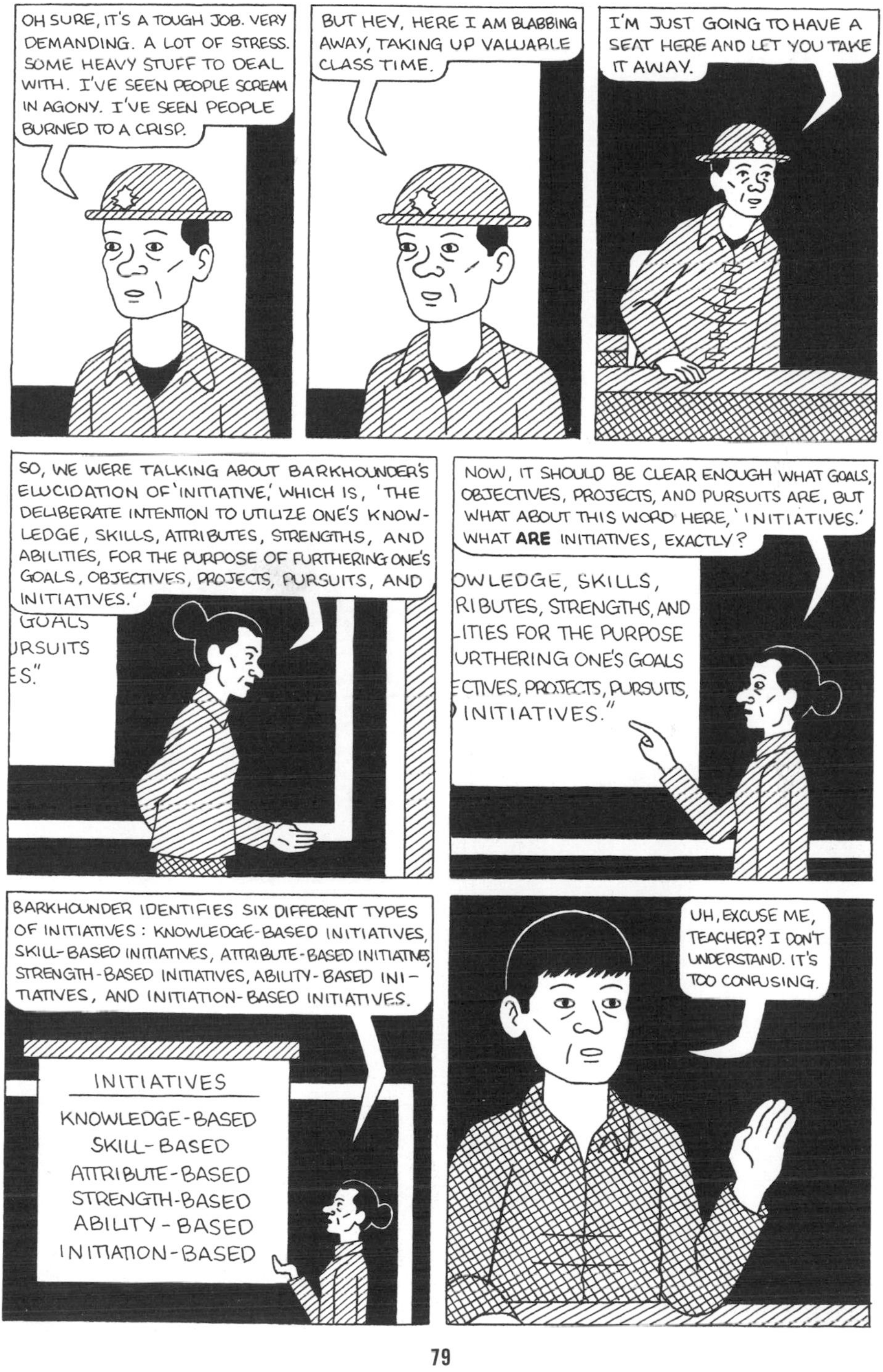
OH SURE, IT'S A TOUGH JOB. VERY DEMANDING. A LOT OF STRESS. SOME HEAVY STUFF TO DEAL WITH. I'VE SEEN PEOPLE SCREAM IN AGONY. I'VE SEEN PEOPLE BURNED TO A CRISP.
BUT HEY, HERE I AM BLABBING AWAY, TAKING UP VALUABLE CLASS TIME.
I'M JUST GOING TO HAVE A SEAT HERE AND LET YOU TAKE IT AWAY.
SO, WE WERE TALKING ABOUT BARKHOUNDER'S ELUCIDATION OF 'INITIATIVE,' WHICH IS, 'THE DELIBERATE INTENTION TO UTILIZE ONE'S KNOWLEDGE, SKILLS, ATTRIBUTES, STRENGTHS, AND ABILITIES, FOR THE PURPOSE OF FURTHERING ONE'S GOALS, OBJECTIVES, PROJECTS, PURSUITS, AND INITIATIVES.'
GOALS
RSUITS
ES."
NOW, IT SHOULD BE CLEAR ENOUGH WHAT GOALS, OBJECTIVES, PROJECTS, AND PURSUITS ARE, BUT WHAT ABOUT THIS WORD HERE, 'INITIATIVES.' WHAT **ARE** INITIATIVES, EXACTLY?
OWLEDGE, SKILLS, RIBUTES, STRENGTHS, AND LITIES FOR THE PURPOSE URTHERING ONE'S GOALS ECTIVES, PROJECTS, PURSUITS, INITIATIVES."
BARKHOUNDER IDENTIFIES SIX DIFFERENT TYPES OF INITIATIVES: KNOWLEDGE-BASED INITIATIVES, SKILL-BASED INITIATIVES, ATTRIBUTE-BASED INITIATIVES, STRENGTH-BASED INITIATIVES, ABILITY-BASED INITIATIVES, AND INITIATION-BASED INITIATIVES.
INITIATIVES
KNOWLEDGE-BASED
SKILL-BASED
ATTRIBUTE-BASED
STRENGTH-BASED
ABILITY-BASED
INITIATION-BASED
UH, EXCUSE ME, TEACHER? I DON'T UNDERSTAND. IT'S TOO CONFUSING.

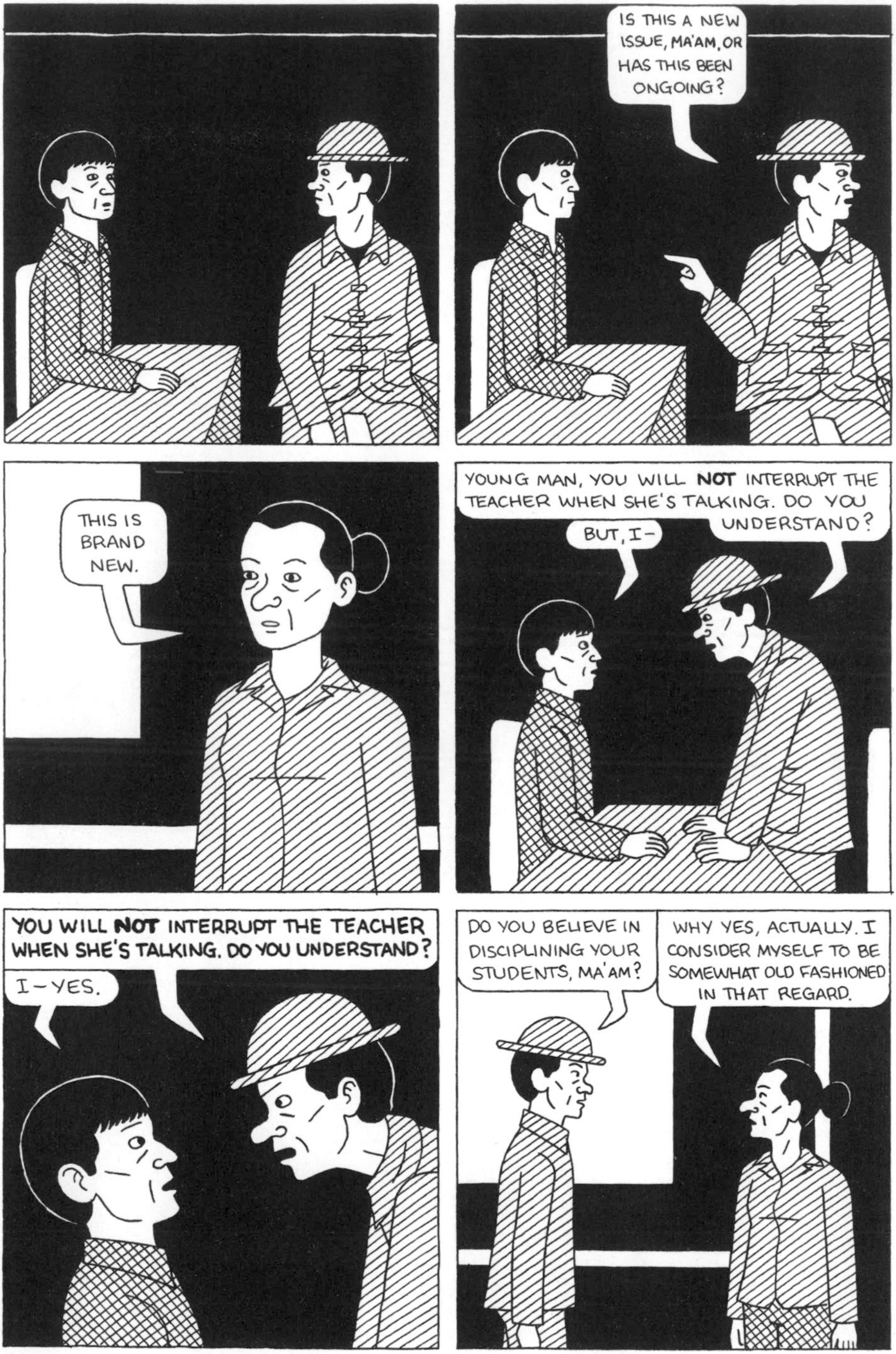

IS THIS A NEW ISSUE, MA'AM, OR HAS THIS BEEN ONGOING?
THIS IS BRAND NEW.
YOUNG MAN, YOU WILL **NOT** INTERRUPT THE TEACHER WHEN SHE'S TALKING. DO YOU UNDERSTAND?
BUT, I-
YOU WILL **NOT** INTERRUPT THE TEACHER WHEN SHE'S TALKING. DO YOU UNDERSTAND?
I-YES.
DO YOU BELIEVE IN DISCIPLINING YOUR STUDENTS, MA'AM?
WHY YES, ACTUALLY. I CONSIDER MYSELF TO BE SOMEWHAT OLD FASHIONED IN THAT REGARD.

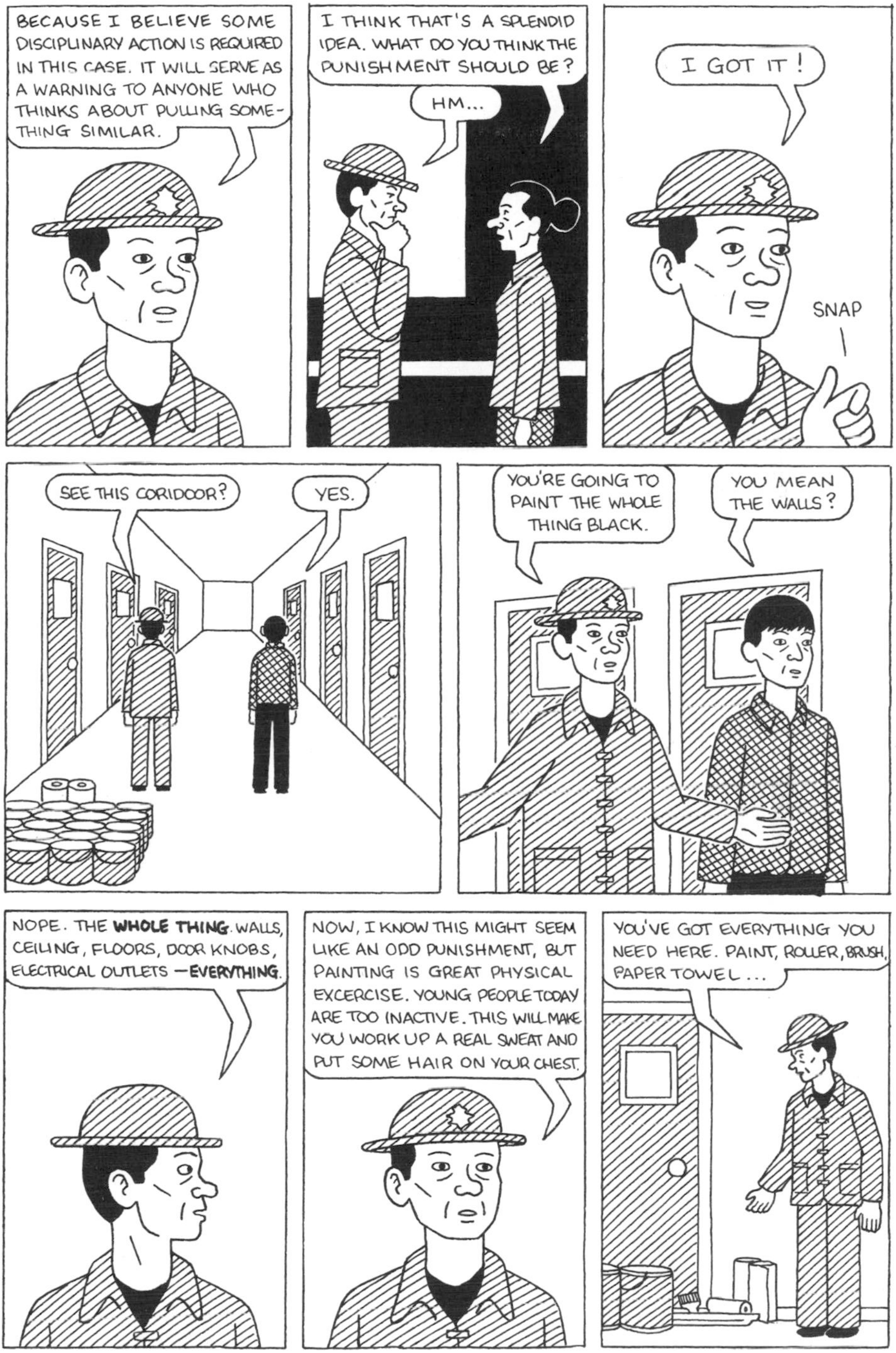

BECAUSE I BELIEVE SOME DISCIPLINARY ACTION IS REQUIRED IN THIS CASE. IT WILL SERVE AS A WARNING TO ANYONE WHO THINKS ABOUT PULLING SOMETHING SIMILAR.
I THINK THAT'S A SPLENDID IDEA. WHAT DO YOU THINK THE PUNISHMENT SHOULD BE?
HM...
I GOT IT!
SNAP
SEE THIS CORIDOOR?
YES.
YOU'RE GOING TO PAINT THE WHOLE THING BLACK.
YOU MEAN THE WALLS?
NOPE. THE **WHOLE THING**. WALLS, CEILING, FLOORS, DOOR KNOBS, ELECTRICAL OUTLETS —**EVERYTHING**.
NOW, I KNOW THIS MIGHT SEEM LIKE AN ODD PUNISHMENT, BUT PAINTING IS GREAT PHYSICAL EXCERCISE. YOUNG PEOPLE TODAY ARE TOO INACTIVE. THIS WILL MAKE YOU WORK UP A REAL SWEAT AND PUT SOME HAIR ON YOUR CHEST.
YOU'VE GOT EVERYTHING YOU NEED HERE. PAINT, ROLLER, BRUSH, PAPER TOWEL...

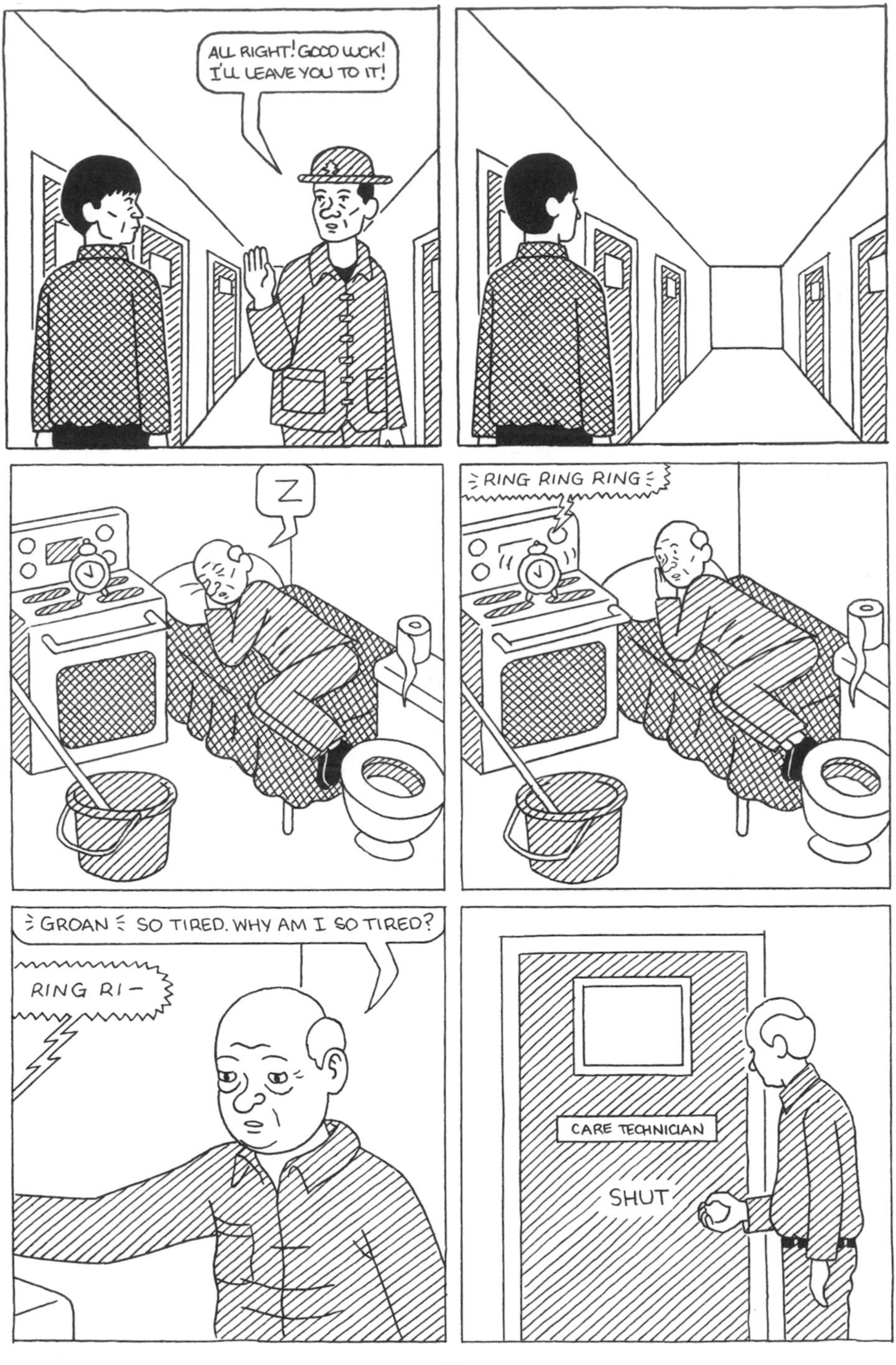
ALL RIGHT! GOOD LUCK! I'LL LEAVE YOU TO IT!
Z
RING RING RING
GROAN SO TIRED. WHY AM I SO TIRED?
RING RI—
CARE TECHNICIAN
SHUT

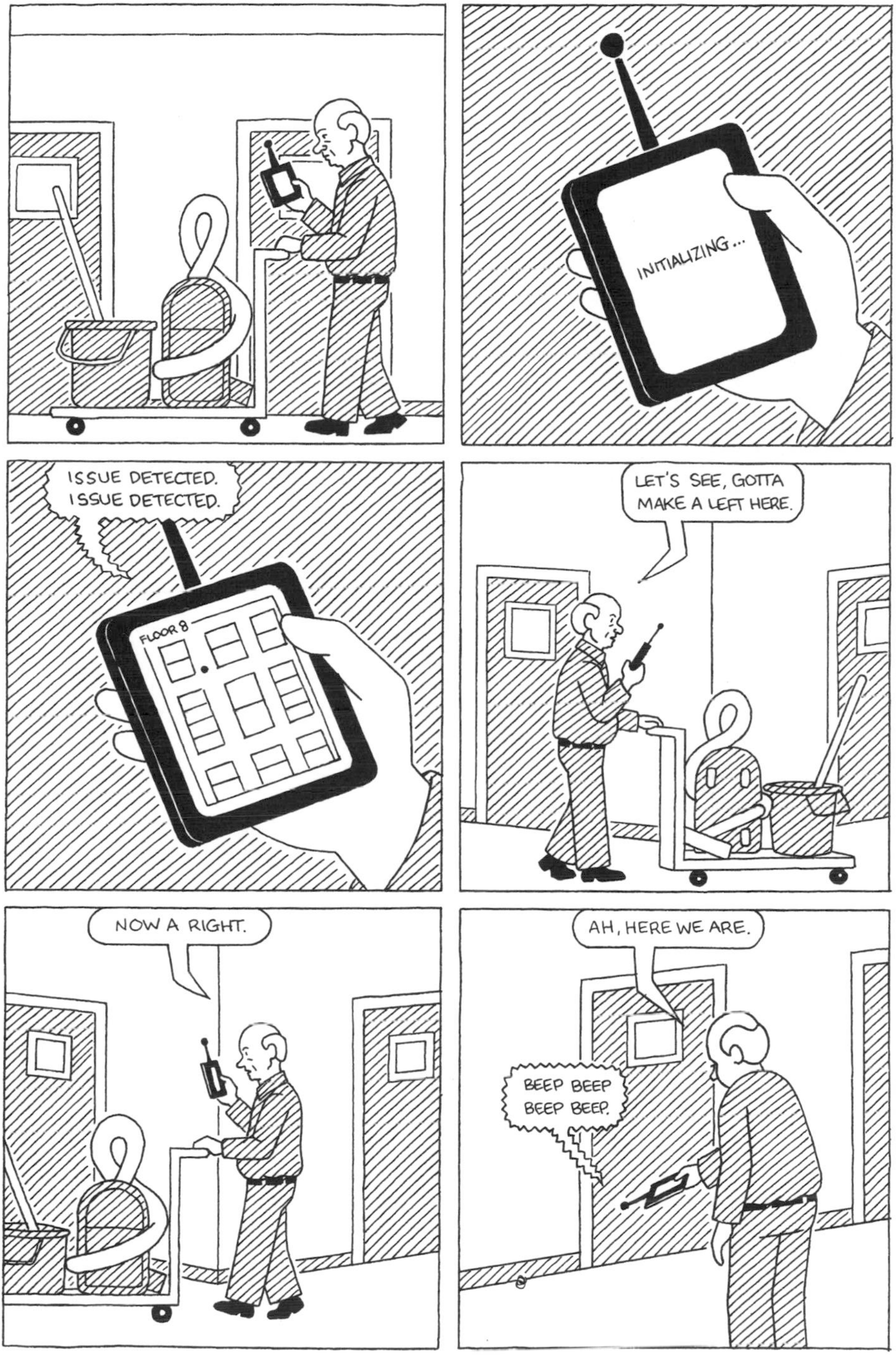
INITIALIZING...
ISSUE DETECTED. ISSUE DETECTED.
FLOOR 8
LET'S SEE, GOTTA MAKE A LEFT HERE.
NOW A RIGHT.
AH, HERE WE ARE.
BEEP BEEP BEEP BEEP.

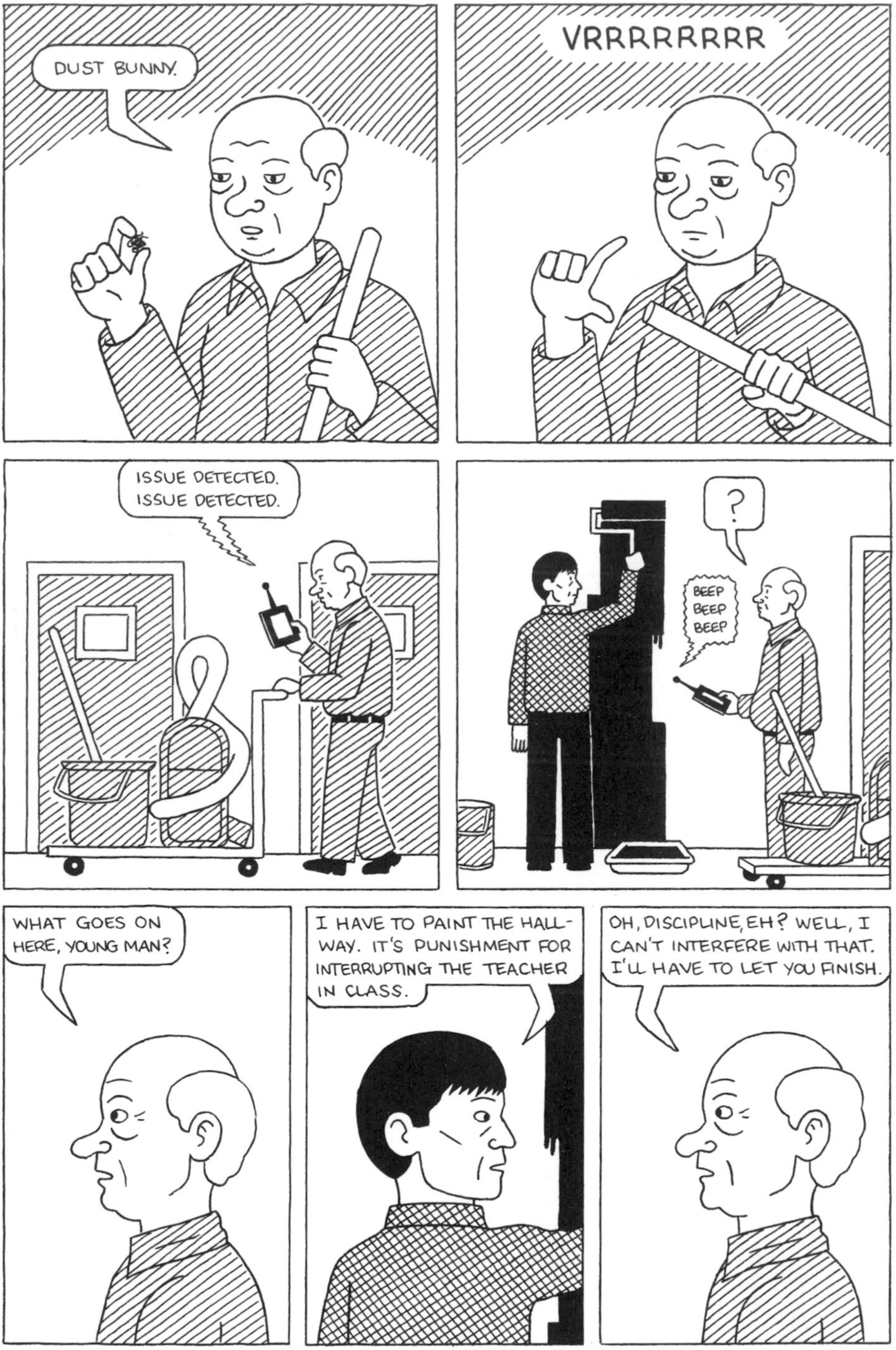
DUST BUNNY.
VRRRRRRRR
ISSUE DETECTED. ISSUE DETECTED.
?
BEEP BEEP BEEP
WHAT GOES ON HERE, YOUNG MAN?
I HAVE TO PAINT THE HALL-WAY. IT'S PUNISHMENT FOR INTERRUPTING THE TEACHER IN CLASS.
OH, DISCIPLINE, EH? WELL, I CAN'T INTERFERE WITH THAT. I'LL HAVE TO LET YOU FINISH.

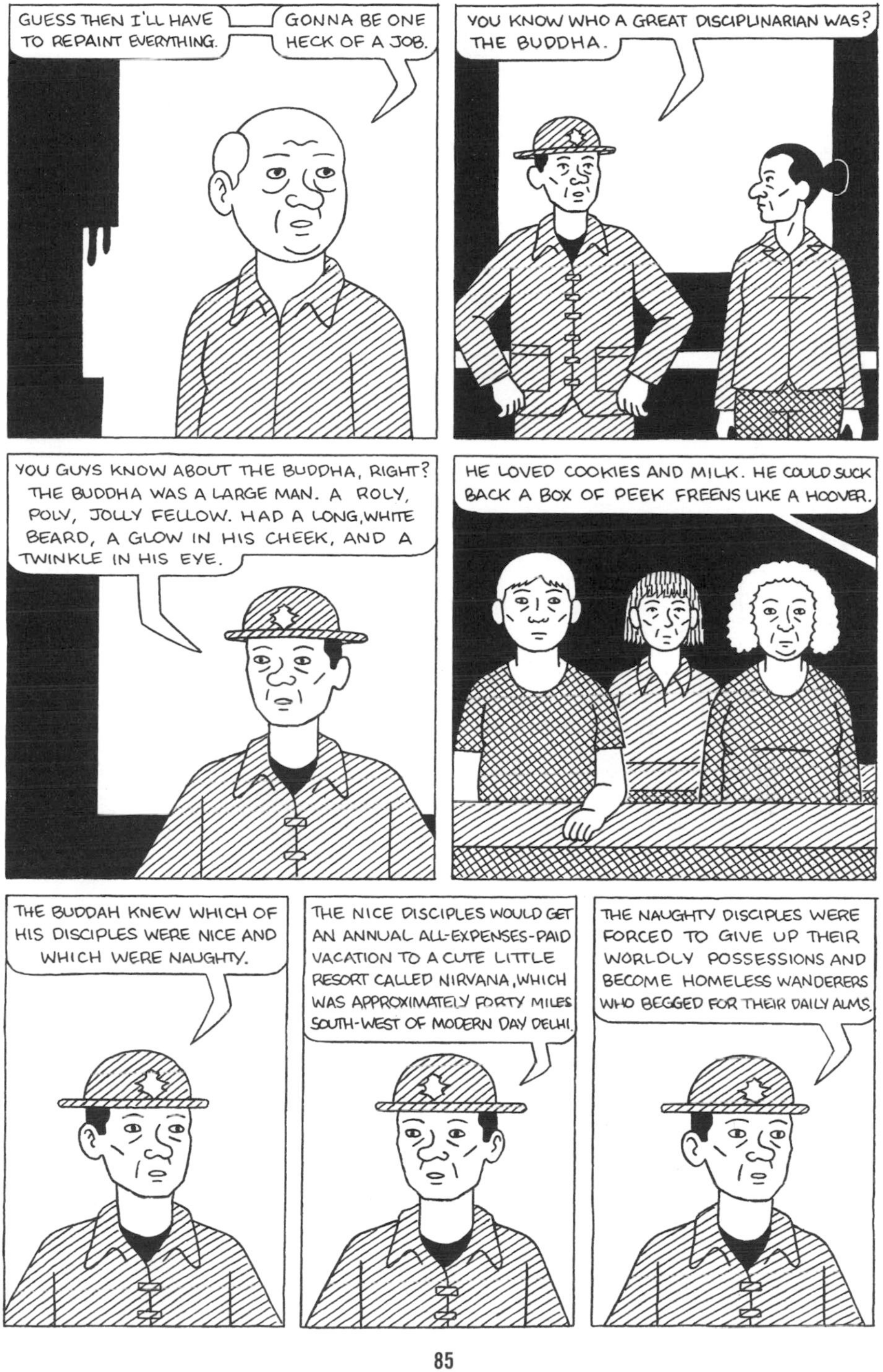
GUESS THEN I'LL HAVE TO REPAINT EVERYTHING.
GONNA BE ONE HECK OF A JOB.
YOU KNOW WHO A GREAT DISCIPLINARIAN WAS? THE BUDDHA.
YOU GUYS KNOW ABOUT THE BUDDHA, RIGHT? THE BUDDHA WAS A LARGE MAN. A ROLY, POLY, JOLLY FELLOW. HAD A LONG, WHITE BEARD, A GLOW IN HIS CHEEK, AND A TWINKLE IN HIS EYE.
HE LOVED COOKIES AND MILK. HE COULD SUCK BACK A BOX OF PEEK FREENS LIKE A HOOVER.
THE BUDDAH KNEW WHICH OF HIS DISCIPLES WERE NICE AND WHICH WERE NAUGHTY.
THE NICE DISCIPLES WOULD GET AN ANNUAL ALL-EXPENSES-PAID VACATION TO A CUTE LITTLE RESORT CALLED NIRVANA, WHICH WAS APPROXIMATELY FORTY MILES SOUTH-WEST OF MODERN DAY DELHI.
THE NAUGHTY DISCIPLES WERE FORCED TO GIVE UP THEIR WORLDLY POSSESSIONS AND BECOME HOMELESS WANDERERS WHO BEGGED FOR THEIR DAILY ALMS.

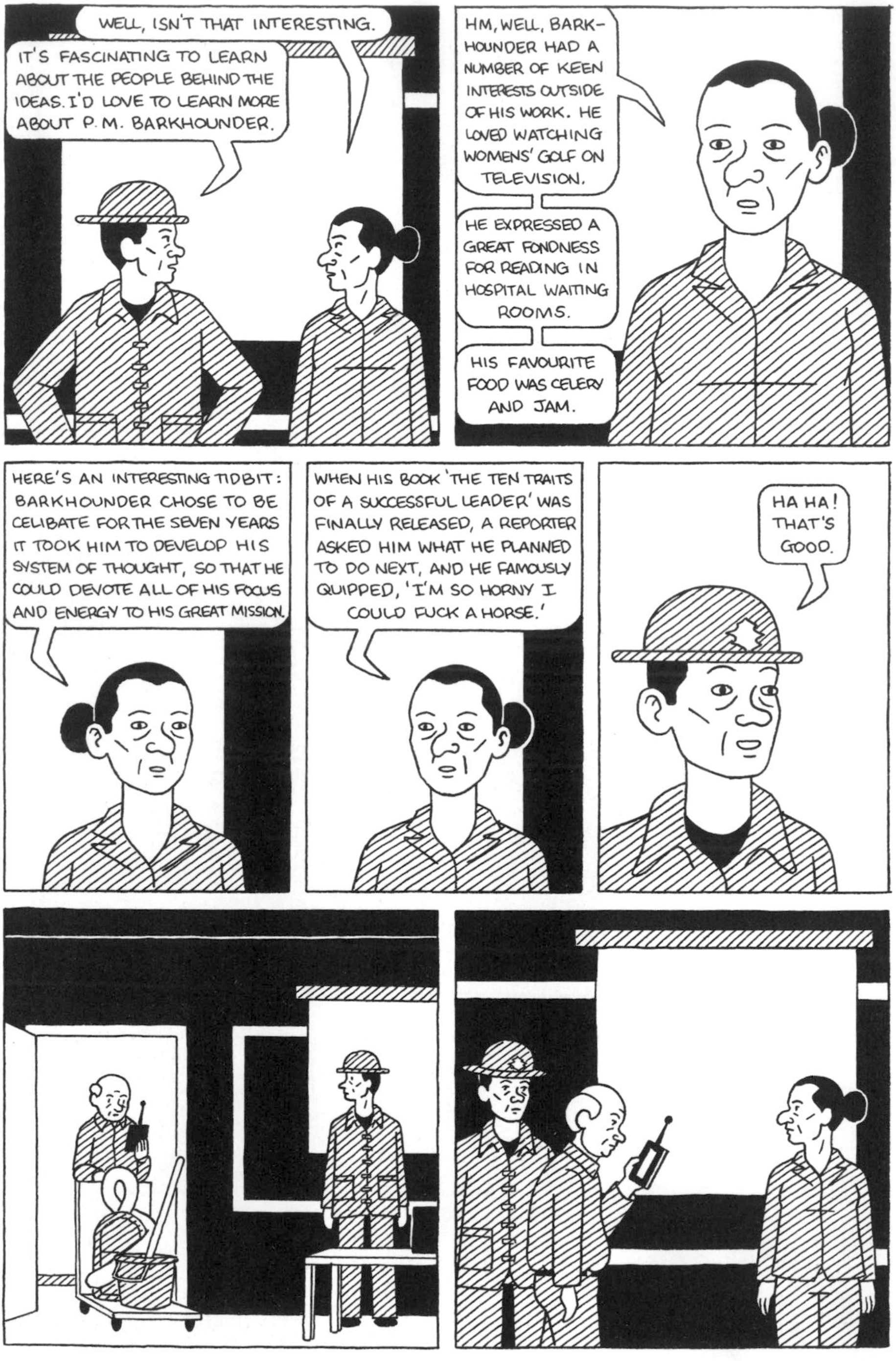
WELL, ISN'T THAT INTERESTING.
IT'S FASCINATING TO LEARN ABOUT THE PEOPLE BEHIND THE IDEAS. I'D LOVE TO LEARN MORE ABOUT P.M. BARKHOUNDER.
HM, WELL, BARKHOUNDER HAD A NUMBER OF KEEN INTERESTS OUTSIDE OF HIS WORK. HE LOVED WATCHING WOMENS' GOLF ON TELEVISION.
HE EXPRESSED A GREAT FONDNESS FOR READING IN HOSPITAL WAITING ROOMS.
HIS FAVOURITE FOOD WAS CELERY AND JAM.
HERE'S AN INTERESTING TIDBIT: BARKHOUNDER CHOSE TO BE CELIBATE FOR THE SEVEN YEARS IT TOOK HIM TO DEVELOP HIS SYSTEM OF THOUGHT, SO THAT HE COULD DEVOTE ALL OF HIS FOCUS AND ENERGY TO HIS GREAT MISSION.
WHEN HIS BOOK 'THE TEN TRAITS OF A SUCCESSFUL LEADER' WAS FINALLY RELEASED, A REPORTER ASKED HIM WHAT HE PLANNED TO DO NEXT, AND HE FAMOUSLY QUIPPED, 'I'M SO HORNY I COULD FUCK A HORSE.'
HA HA! THAT'S GOOD.

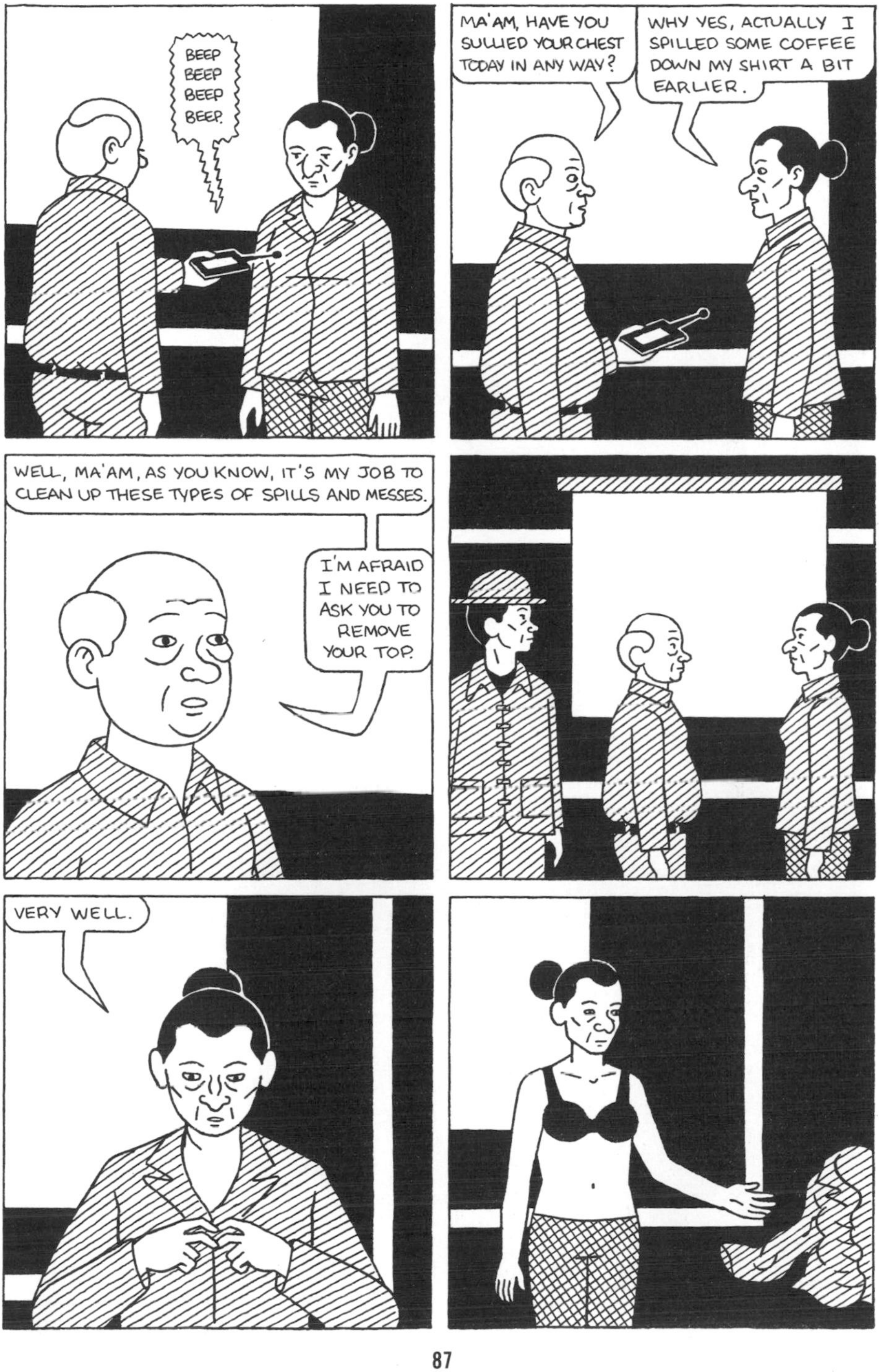
BEEP BEEP BEEP BEEP.
MA'AM, HAVE YOU SULLIED YOUR CHEST TODAY IN ANY WAY?
WHY YES, ACTUALLY I SPILLED SOME COFFEE DOWN MY SHIRT A BIT EARLIER.
WELL, MA'AM, AS YOU KNOW, IT'S MY JOB TO CLEAN UP THESE TYPES OF SPILLS AND MESSES.
I'M AFRAID I NEED TO ASK YOU TO REMOVE YOUR TOP.
VERY WELL.

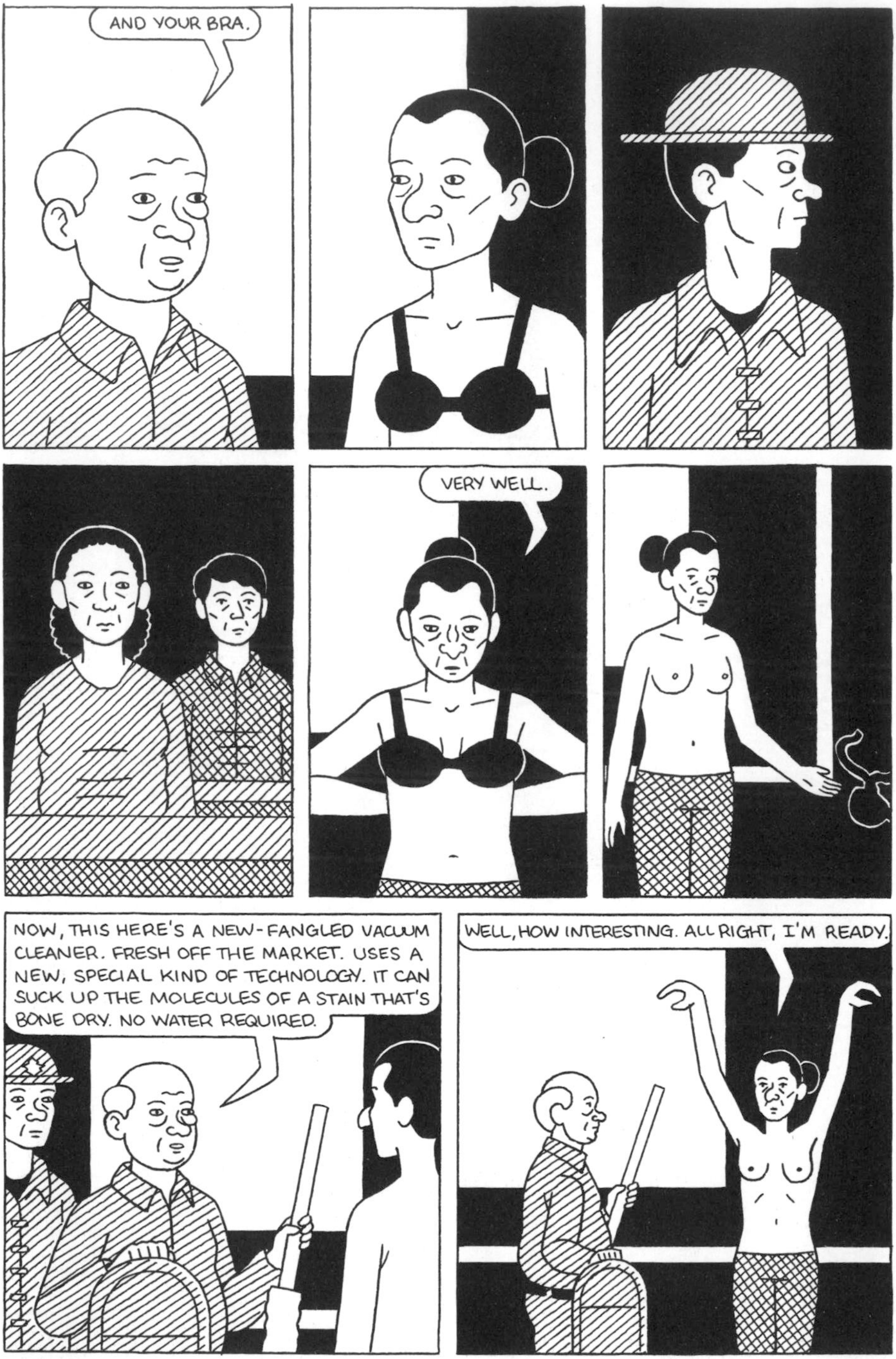
AND YOUR BRA.
VERY WELL.
NOW, THIS HERE'S A NEW-FANGLED VACUUM CLEANER. FRESH OFF THE MARKET. USES A NEW, SPECIAL KIND OF TECHNOLOGY. IT CAN SUCK UP THE MOLECULES OF A STAIN THAT'S BONE DRY. NO WATER REQUIRED.
WELL, HOW INTERESTING. ALL RIGHT, I'M READY.

VRRRRRRRRRRRRR
!
FOOMP!
TUG TUG!
FOP!
VRRRRRRRRRRRRR

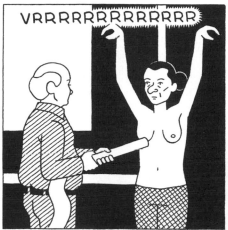

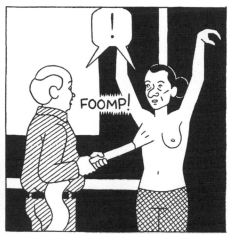

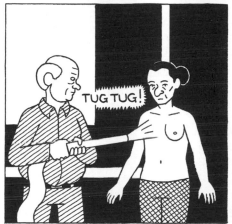

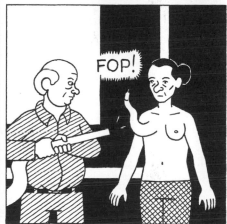

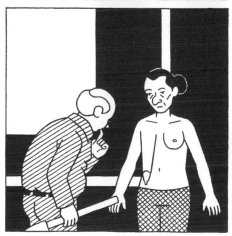

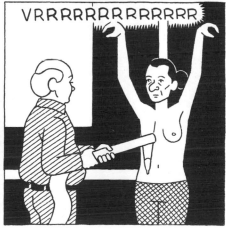

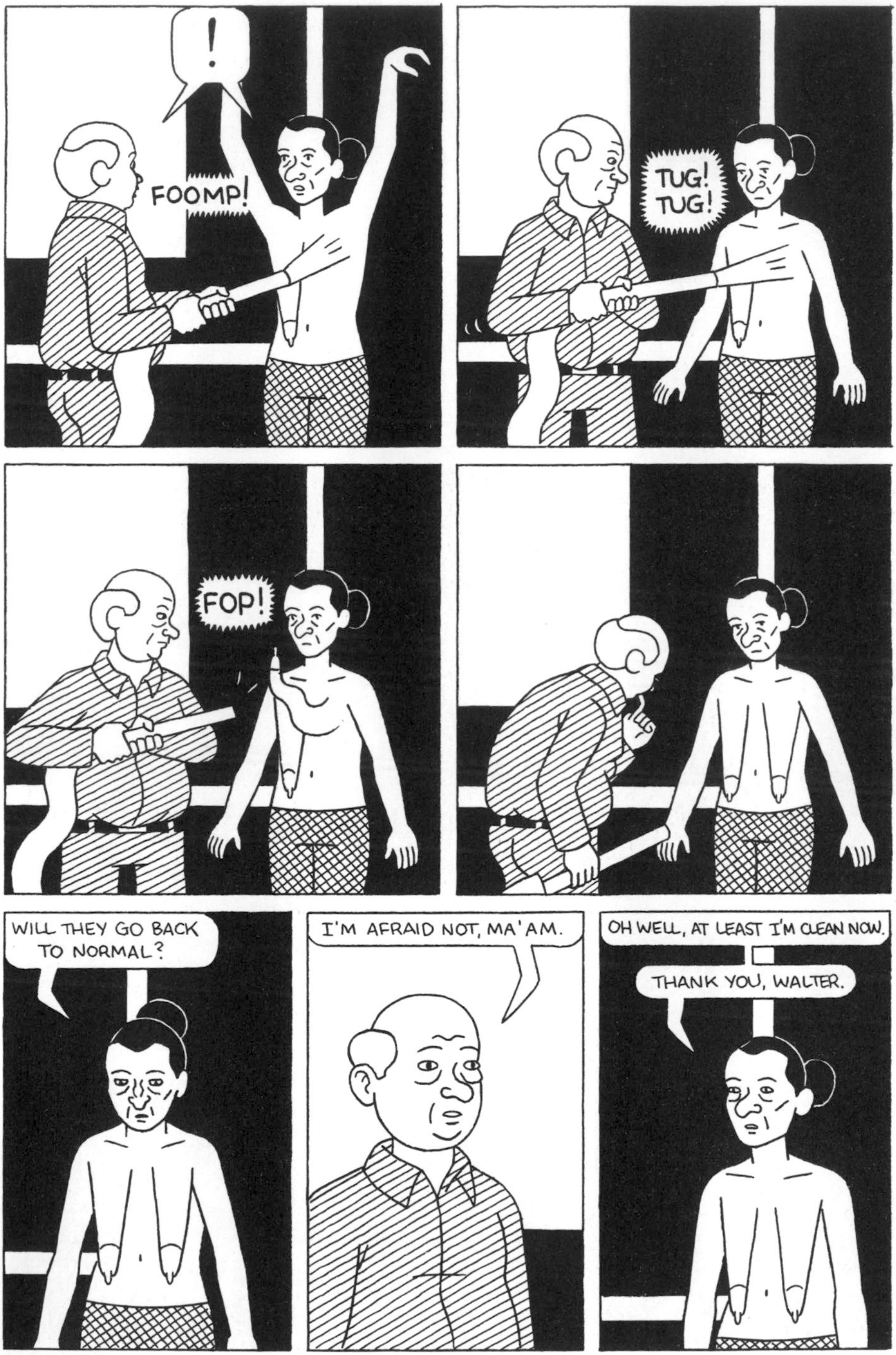
!
FOOMP!
TUG! TUG!
FOP!
WILL THEY GO BACK TO NORMAL?
I'M AFRAID NOT, MA'AM.
OH WELL, AT LEAST I'M CLEAN NOW.
THANK YOU, WALTER.

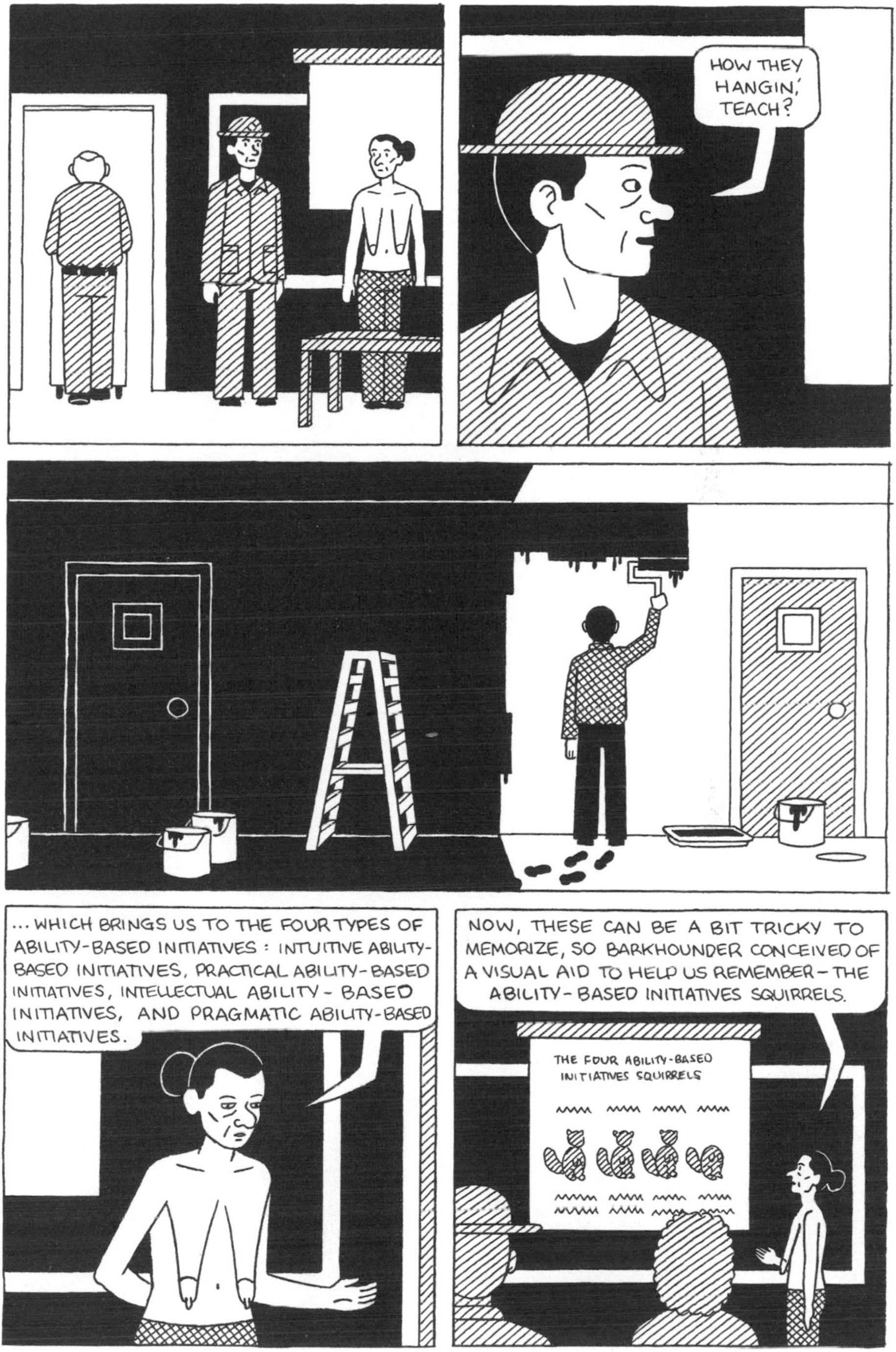

HOW THEY HANGIN,' TEACH?
...WHICH BRINGS US TO THE FOUR TYPES OF ABILITY-BASED INITIATIVES: INTUITIVE ABILITY-BASED INITIATIVES, PRACTICAL ABILITY-BASED INITIATIVES, INTELLECTUAL ABILITY-BASED INITIATIVES, AND PRAGMATIC ABILITY-BASED INITIATIVES.
NOW, THESE CAN BE A BIT TRICKY TO MEMORIZE, SO BARKHOUNDER CONCEIVED OF A VISUAL AID TO HELP US REMEMBER—THE ABILITY-BASED INITIATIVES SQUIRRELS.
THE FOUR ABILITY-BASED INITIATIVES SQUIRRELS

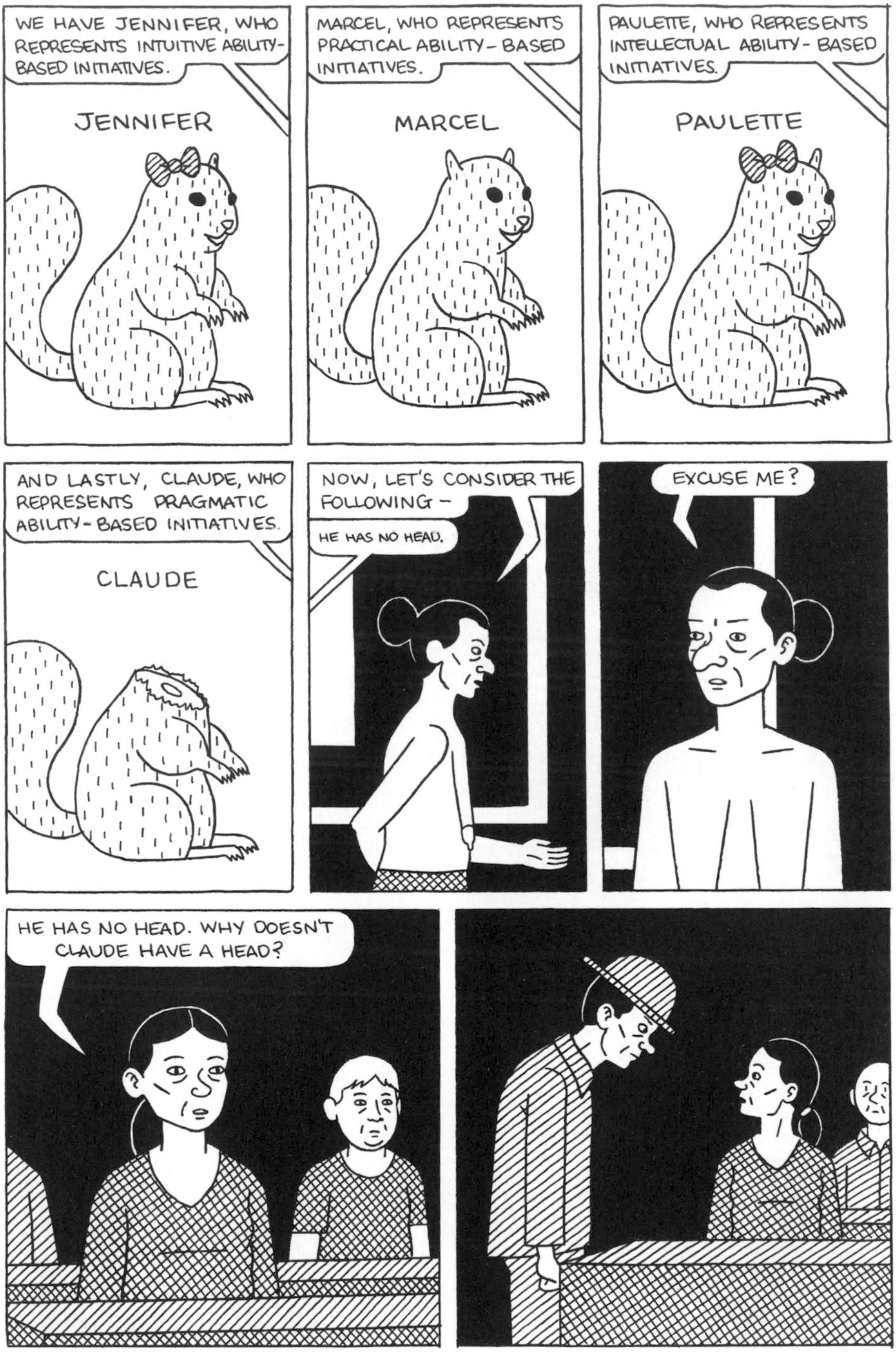
WE HAVE JENNIFER, WHO REPRESENTS INTUITIVE ABILITY-BASED INITIATIVES.
JENNIFER
MARCEL, WHO REPRESENTS PRACTICAL ABILITY-BASED INITIATIVES.
MARCEL
PAULETTE, WHO REPRESENTS INTELLECTUAL ABILITY-BASED INITIATIVES.
PAULETTE
AND LASTLY, CLAUDE, WHO REPRESENTS PRAGMATIC ABILITY-BASED INITIATIVES.
CLAUDE
NOW, LET'S CONSIDER THE FOLLOWING-
HE HAS NO HEAD.
EXCUSE ME?
HE HAS NO HEAD. WHY DOESN'T CLAUDE HAVE A HEAD?

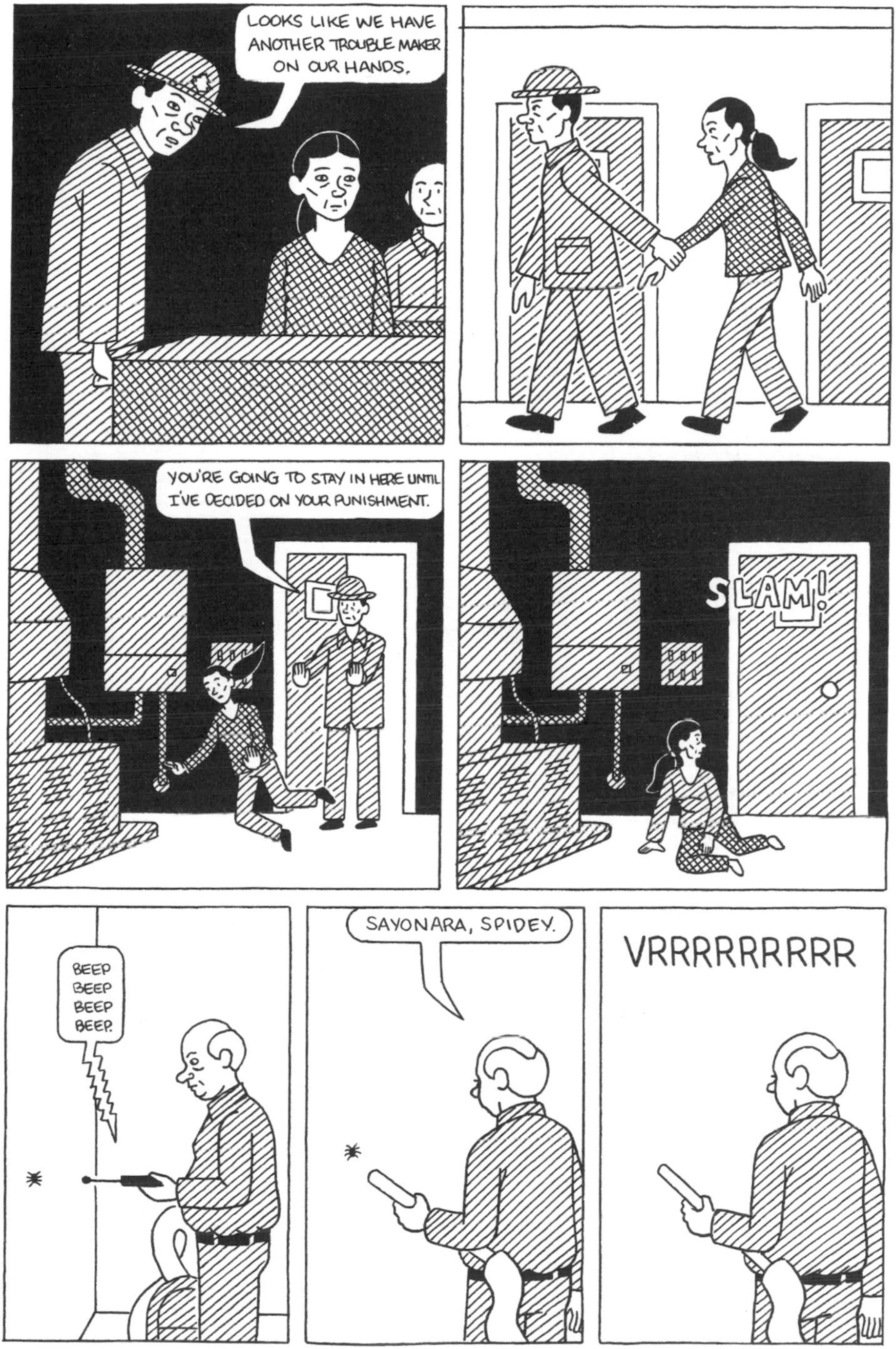
LOOKS LIKE WE HAVE ANOTHER TROUBLE MAKER ON OUR HANDS.
YOU'RE GOING TO STAY IN HERE UNTIL I'VE DECIDED ON YOUR PUNISHMENT.
SLAM!
BEEP BEEP BEEP BEEP.
SAYONARA, SPIDEY.
VRRRRRRRRR

WELL, JUST ABOUT QUITTING TIME.

I... I CAN'T REMEMBER WHERE MY CLOSET IS...

OH NO, IT'S ALL COMING BACK TO ME NOW...

I FORGET HOW TO GET BACK HOME **EVERY** DAY! **EVERY** DAY I FORGET AND END UP WANDERING THE HALLS FOR HOURS UNTIL I FINALLY STUMBLE ACROSS IT BY ACCIDENT!

AND THEN THERE'S ONLY TIME FOR ABOUT THREE OR FOUR HOURS OF SLEEP. AND WHEN I WAKE UP, I'VE FORGOTTEN THAT I FORGOT HOW TO GET HOME THE NIGHT BEFORE, AND THE WHOLE THING STARTS OVER AGAIN!

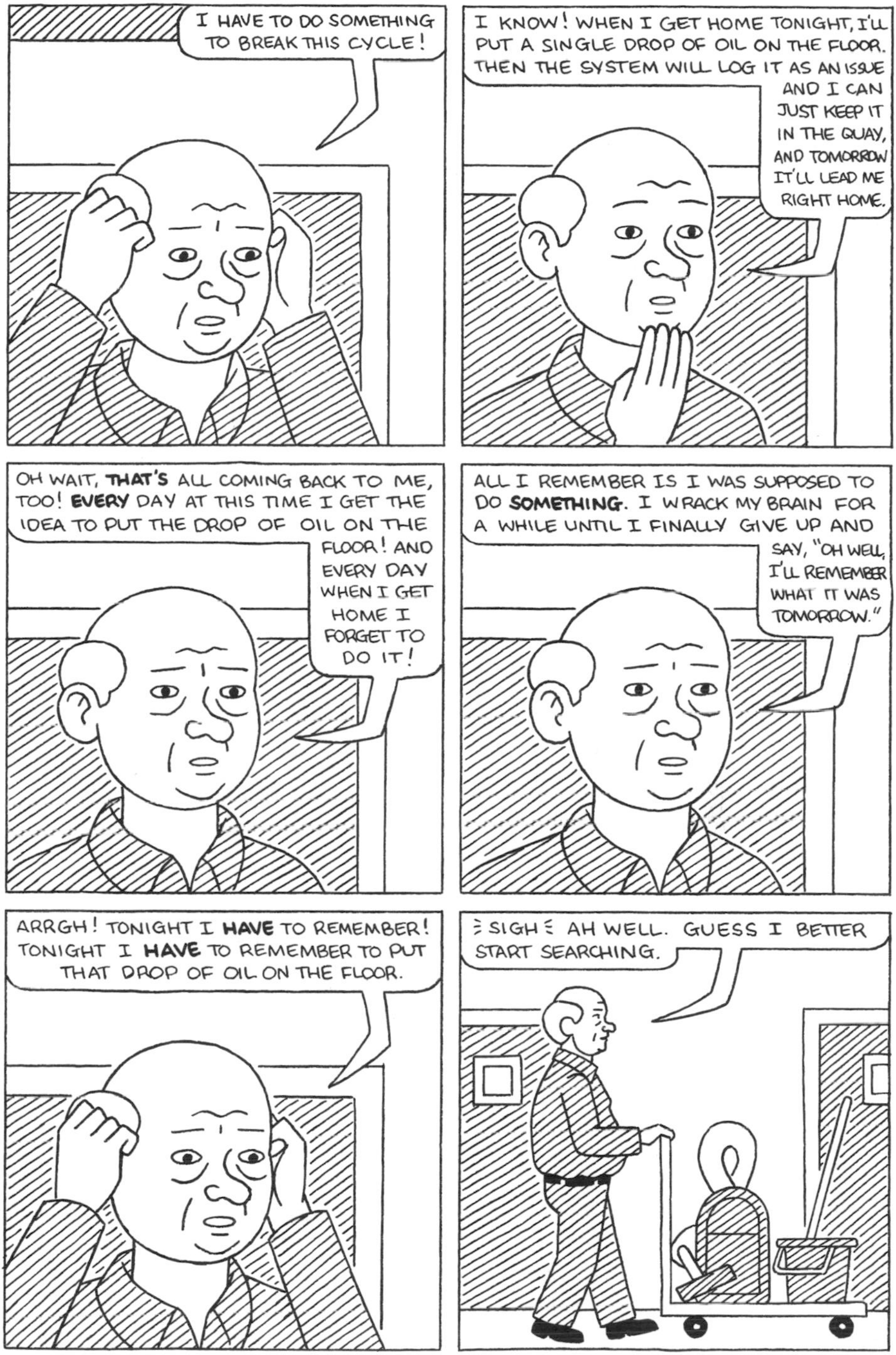
I HAVE TO DO SOMETHING TO BREAK THIS CYCLE!
I KNOW! WHEN I GET HOME TONIGHT, I'LL PUT A SINGLE DROP OF OIL ON THE FLOOR. THEN THE SYSTEM WILL LOG IT AS AN ISSUE AND I CAN JUST KEEP IT IN THE QUAY, AND TOMORROW IT'LL LEAD ME RIGHT HOME.
OH WAIT, **THAT'S** ALL COMING BACK TO ME, TOO! **EVERY** DAY AT THIS TIME I GET THE IDEA TO PUT THE DROP OF OIL ON THE FLOOR! AND EVERY DAY WHEN I GET HOME I FORGET TO DO IT!
ALL I REMEMBER IS I WAS SUPPOSED TO DO **SOMETHING**. I WRACK MY BRAIN FOR A WHILE UNTIL I FINALLY GIVE UP AND SAY, "OH WELL, I'LL REMEMBER WHAT IT WAS TOMORROW."
ARRGH! TONIGHT I **HAVE** TO REMEMBER! TONIGHT I **HAVE** TO REMEMBER TO PUT THAT DROP OF OIL ON THE FLOOR.
SIGH AH WELL. GUESS I BETTER START SEARCHING.

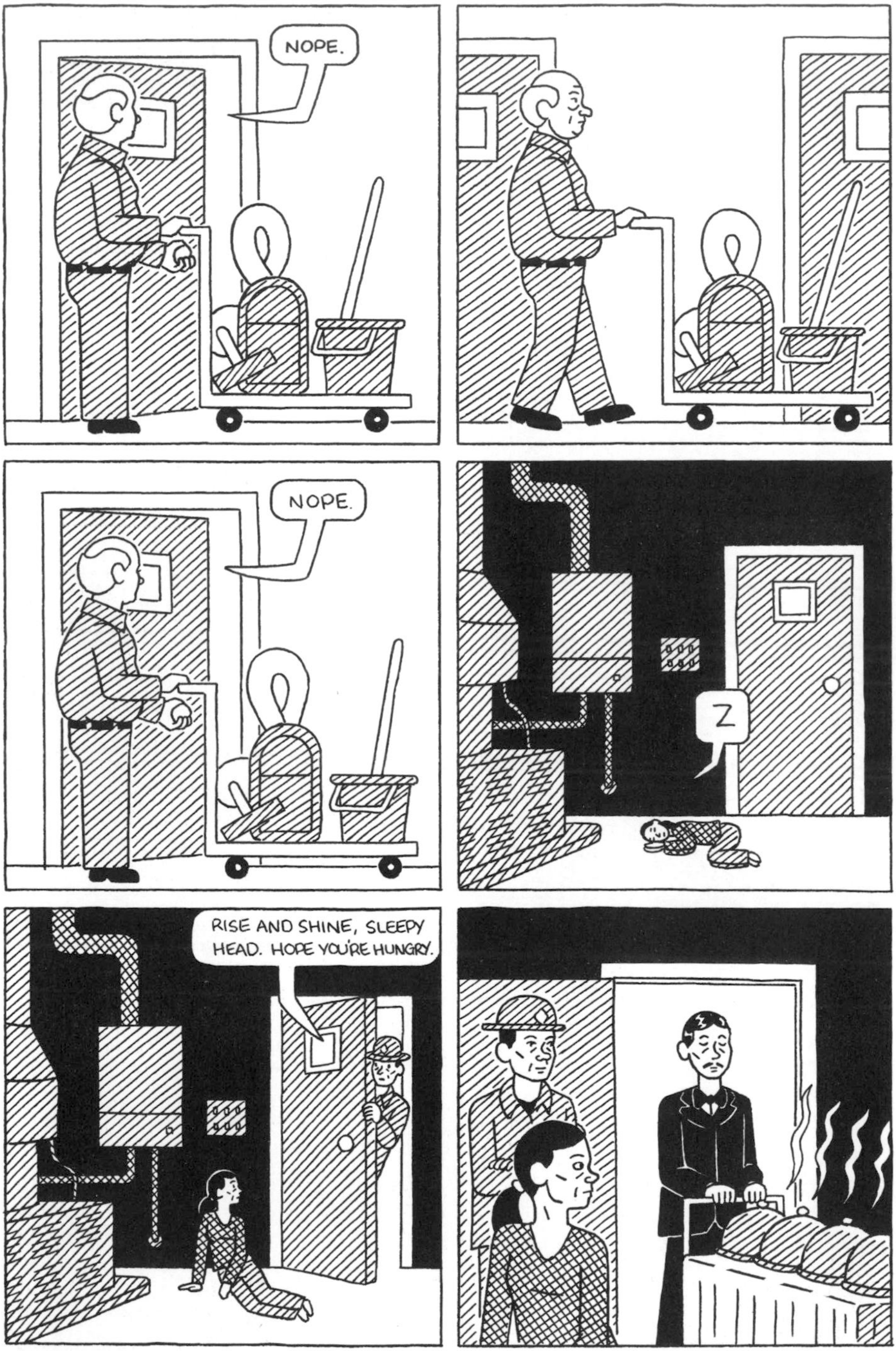
NOPE.
NOPE.
Z
RISE AND SHINE, SLEEPY HEAD. HOPE YOU'RE HUNGRY.

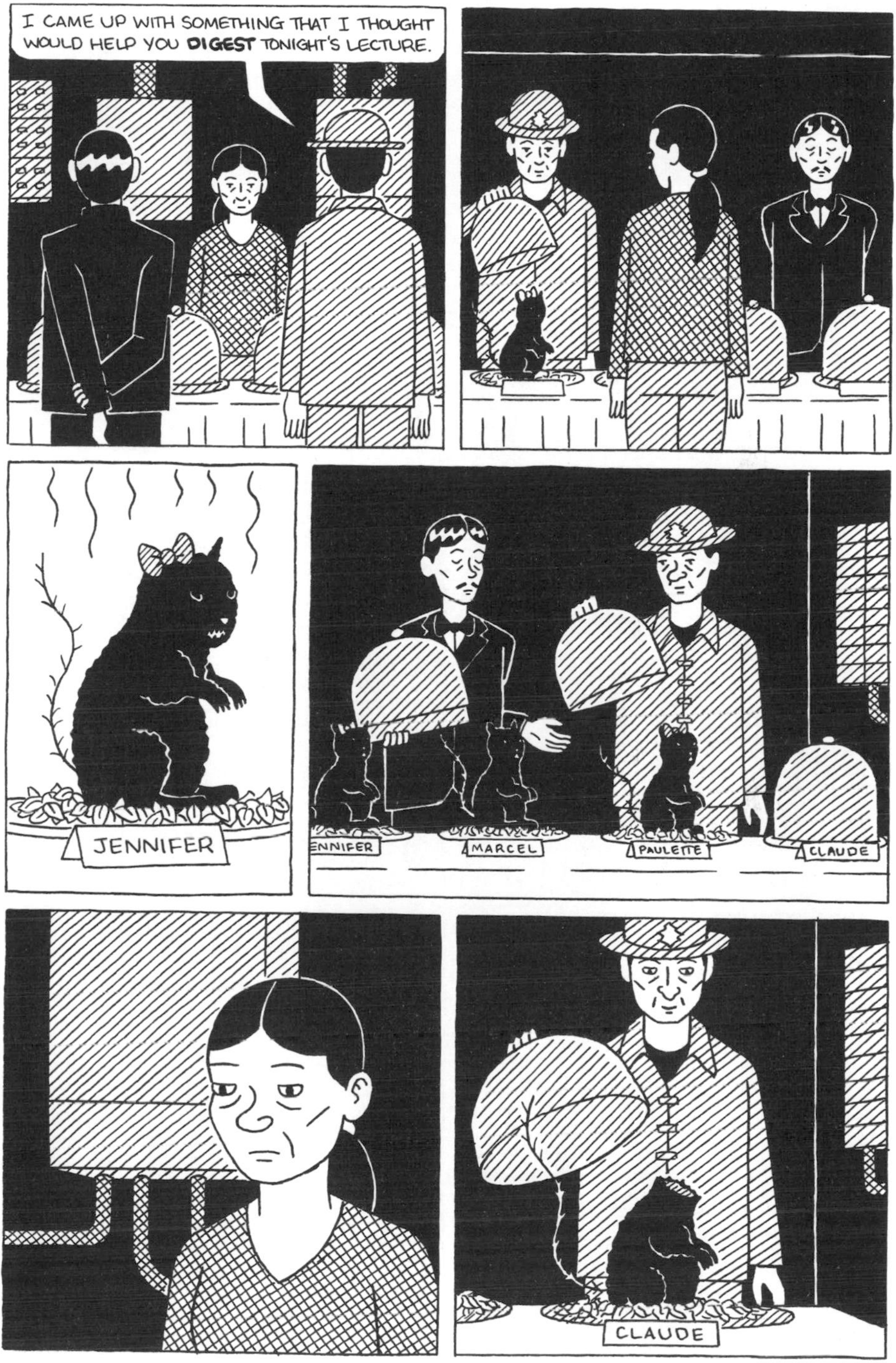
I CAME UP WITH SOMETHING THAT I THOUGHT WOULD HELP YOU **DIGEST** TONIGHT'S LECTURE.
JENNIFER
ENNIFER
MARCEL
PAULETTE
CLAUDE
CLAUDE

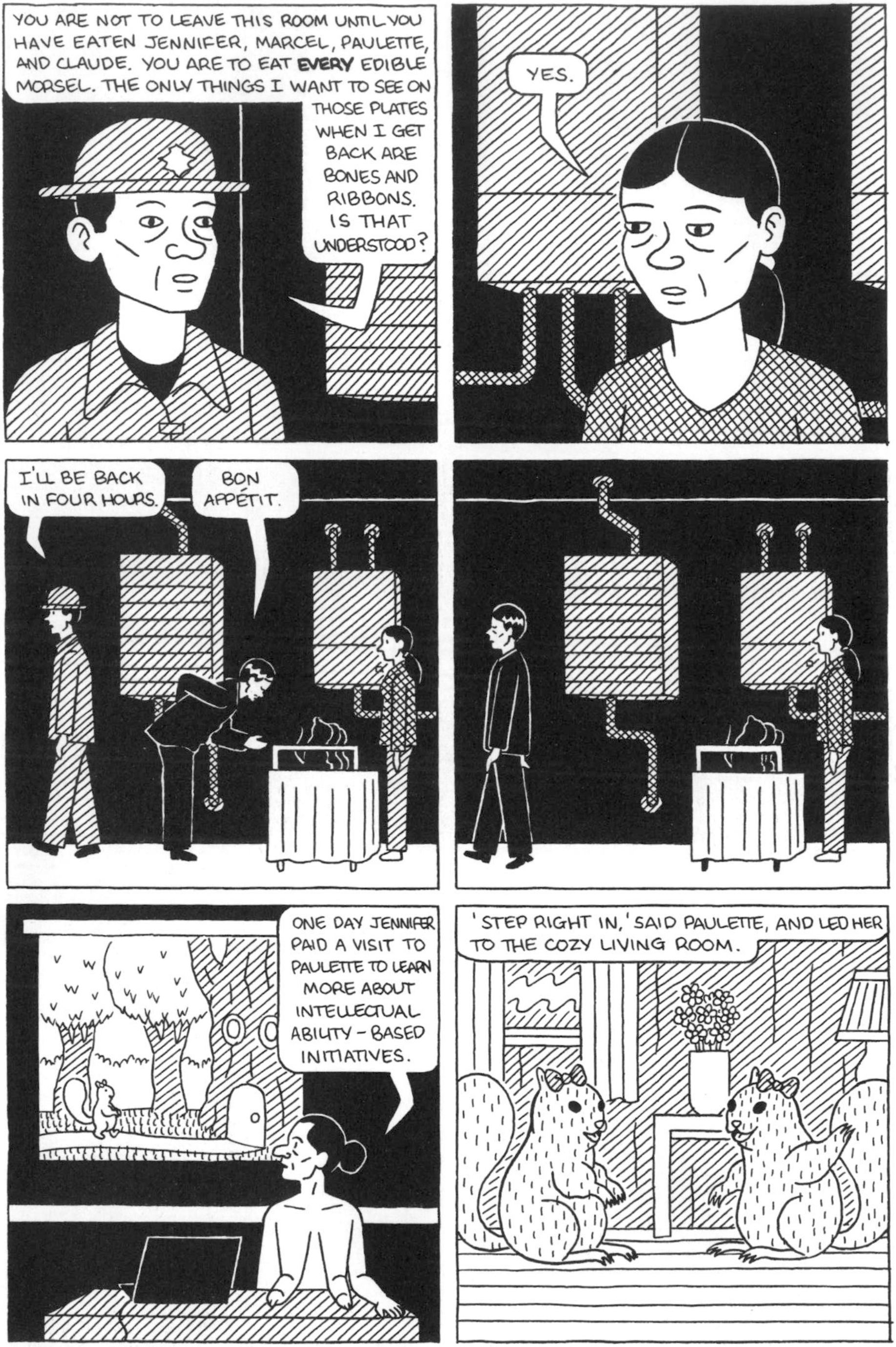

YOU ARE NOT TO LEAVE THIS ROOM UNTIL YOU HAVE EATEN JENNIFER, MARCEL, PAULETTE, AND CLAUDE. YOU ARE TO EAT **EVERY** EDIBLE MORSEL. THE ONLY THINGS I WANT TO SEE ON THOSE PLATES WHEN I GET BACK ARE BONES AND RIBBONS. IS THAT UNDERSTOOD?
YES.
I'LL BE BACK IN FOUR HOURS.
BON APPÉTIT.
ONE DAY JENNIFER PAID A VISIT TO PAULETTE TO LEARN MORE ABOUT INTELLECTUAL ABILITY-BASED INITIATIVES.
'STEP RIGHT IN,' SAID PAULETTE, AND LED HER TO THE COZY LIVING ROOM.

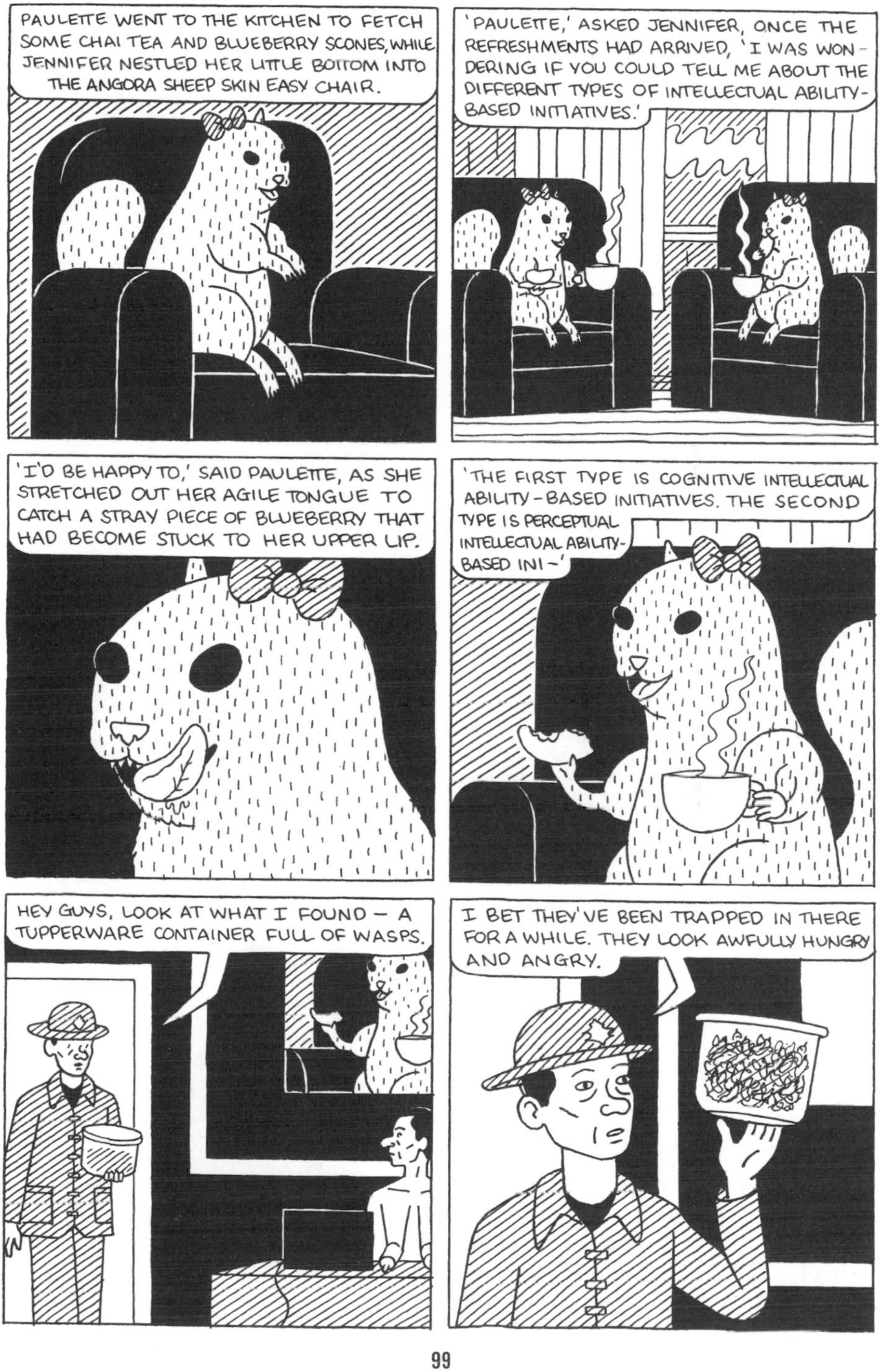
PAULETTE WENT TO THE KITCHEN TO FETCH SOME CHAI TEA AND BLUEBERRY SCONES, WHILE JENNIFER NESTLED HER LITTLE BOTTOM INTO THE ANGORA SHEEP SKIN EASY CHAIR.
'PAULETTE,' ASKED JENNIFER, ONCE THE REFRESHMENTS HAD ARRIVED, 'I WAS WONDERING IF YOU COULD TELL ME ABOUT THE DIFFERENT TYPES OF INTELLECTUAL ABILITY-BASED INITIATIVES.'
'I'D BE HAPPY TO,' SAID PAULETTE, AS SHE STRETCHED OUT HER AGILE TONGUE TO CATCH A STRAY PIECE OF BLUEBERRY THAT HAD BECOME STUCK TO HER UPPER LIP.
'THE FIRST TYPE IS COGNITIVE INTELLECTUAL ABILITY-BASED INITIATIVES. THE SECOND TYPE IS PERCEPTUAL INTELLECTUAL ABILITY-BASED INI~'
HEY GUYS, LOOK AT WHAT I FOUND — A TUPPERWARE CONTAINER FULL OF WASPS.
I BET THEY'VE BEEN TRAPPED IN THERE FOR A WHILE. THEY LOOK AWFULLY HUNGRY AND ANGRY.

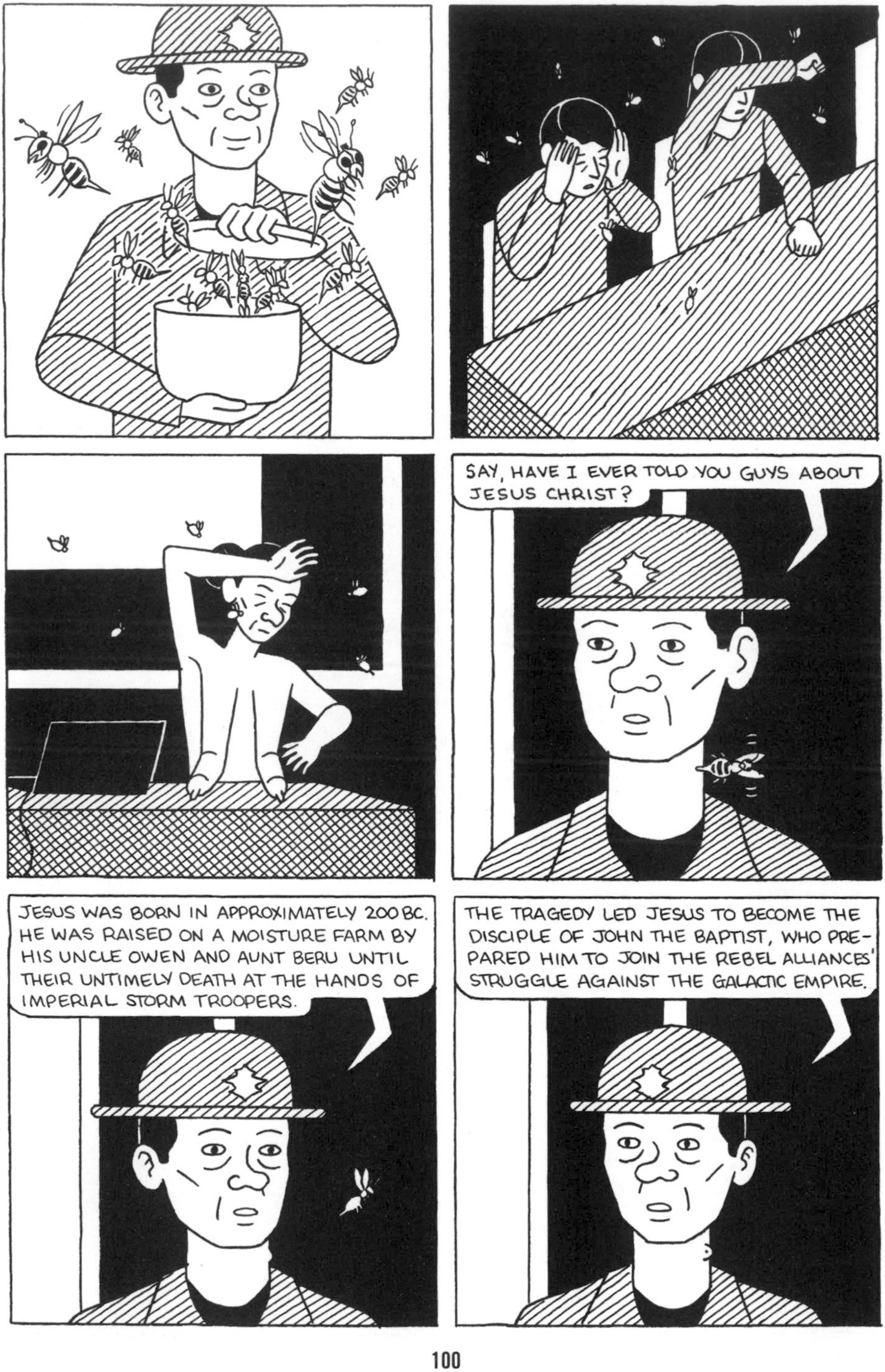
SAY, HAVE I EVER TOLD YOU GUYS ABOUT JESUS CHRIST?
JESUS WAS BORN IN APPROXIMATELY 200 BC. HE WAS RAISED ON A MOISTURE FARM BY HIS UNCLE OWEN AND AUNT BERU UNTIL THEIR UNTIMELY DEATH AT THE HANDS OF IMPERIAL STORM TROOPERS.
THE TRAGEDY LED JESUS TO BECOME THE DISCIPLE OF JOHN THE BAPTIST, WHO PREPARED HIM TO JOIN THE REBEL ALLIANCES' STRUGGLE AGAINST THE GALACTIC EMPIRE.

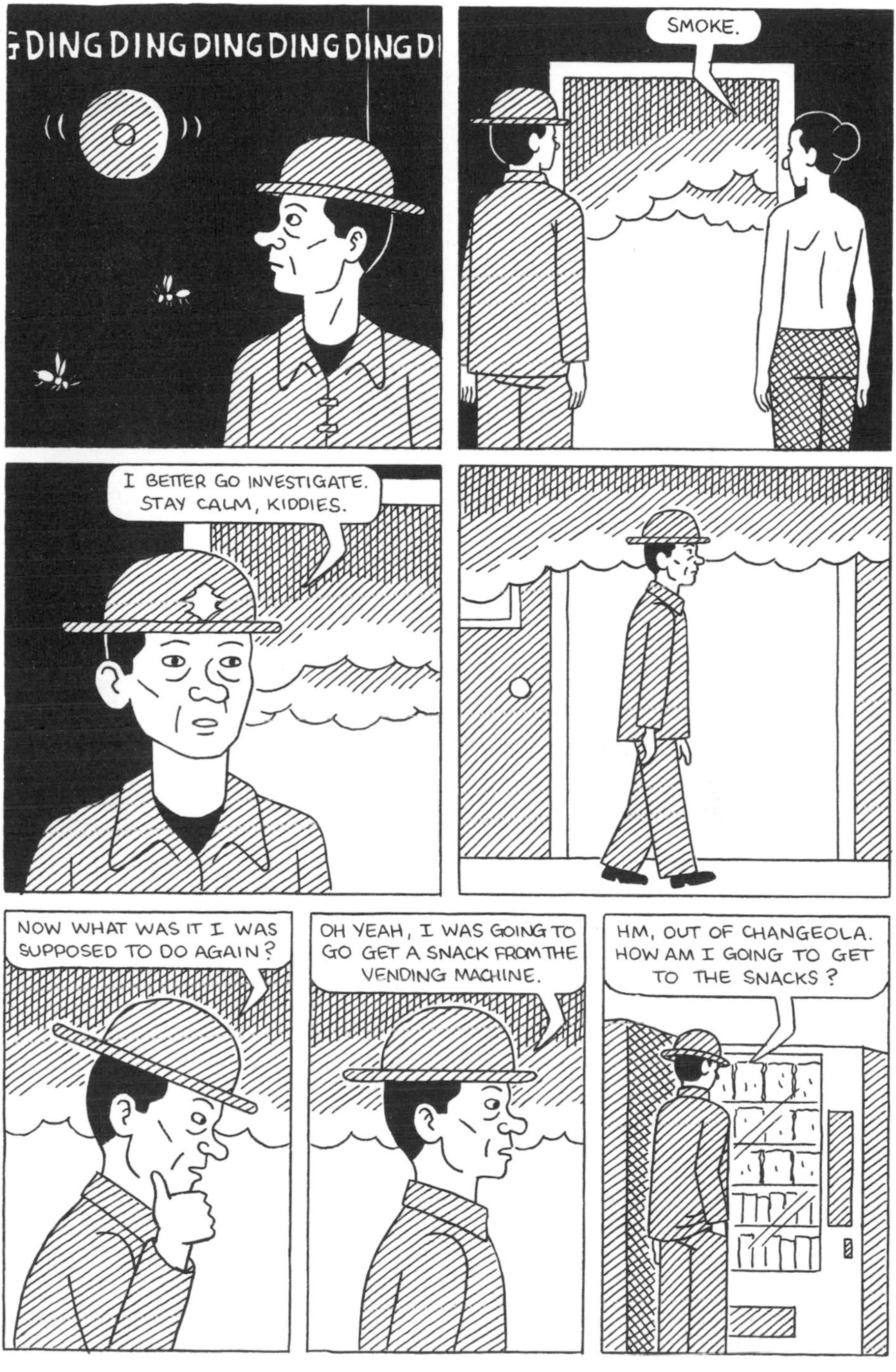
DING DING DING DING DING DI
SMOKE.
I BETTER GO INVESTIGATE. STAY CALM, KIDDIES.
NOW WHAT WAS IT I WAS SUPPOSED TO DO AGAIN?
OH YEAH, I WAS GOING TO GO GET A SNACK FROM THE VENDING MACHINE.
HM, OUT OF CHANGEOLA. HOW AM I GOING TO GET TO THE SNACKS?

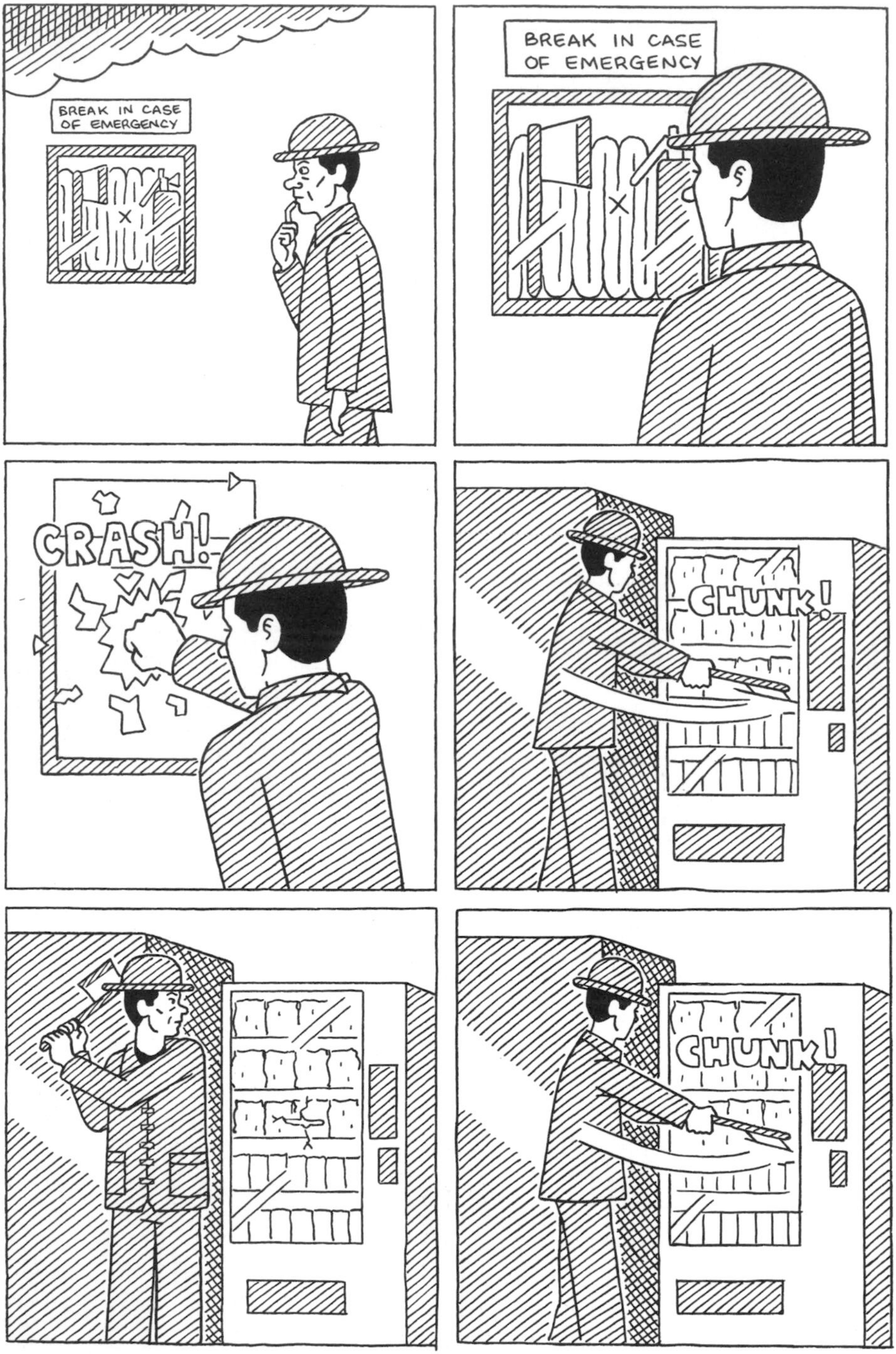
BREAK IN CASE OF EMERGENCY
BREAK IN CASE OF EMERGENCY
CRASH!
CHUNK!
CHUNK!

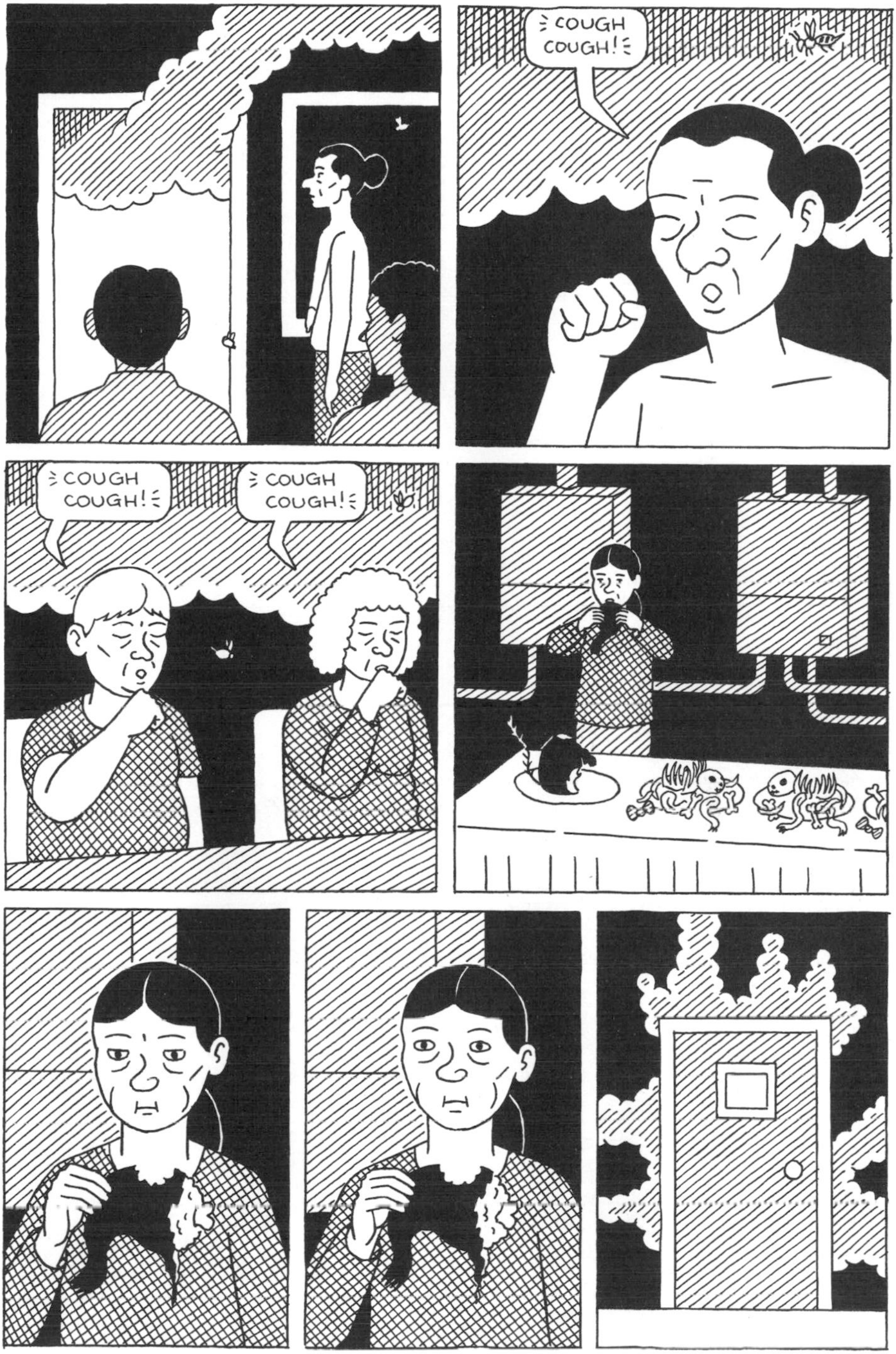
COUGH COUGH!
COUGH COUGH!
COUGH COUGH!

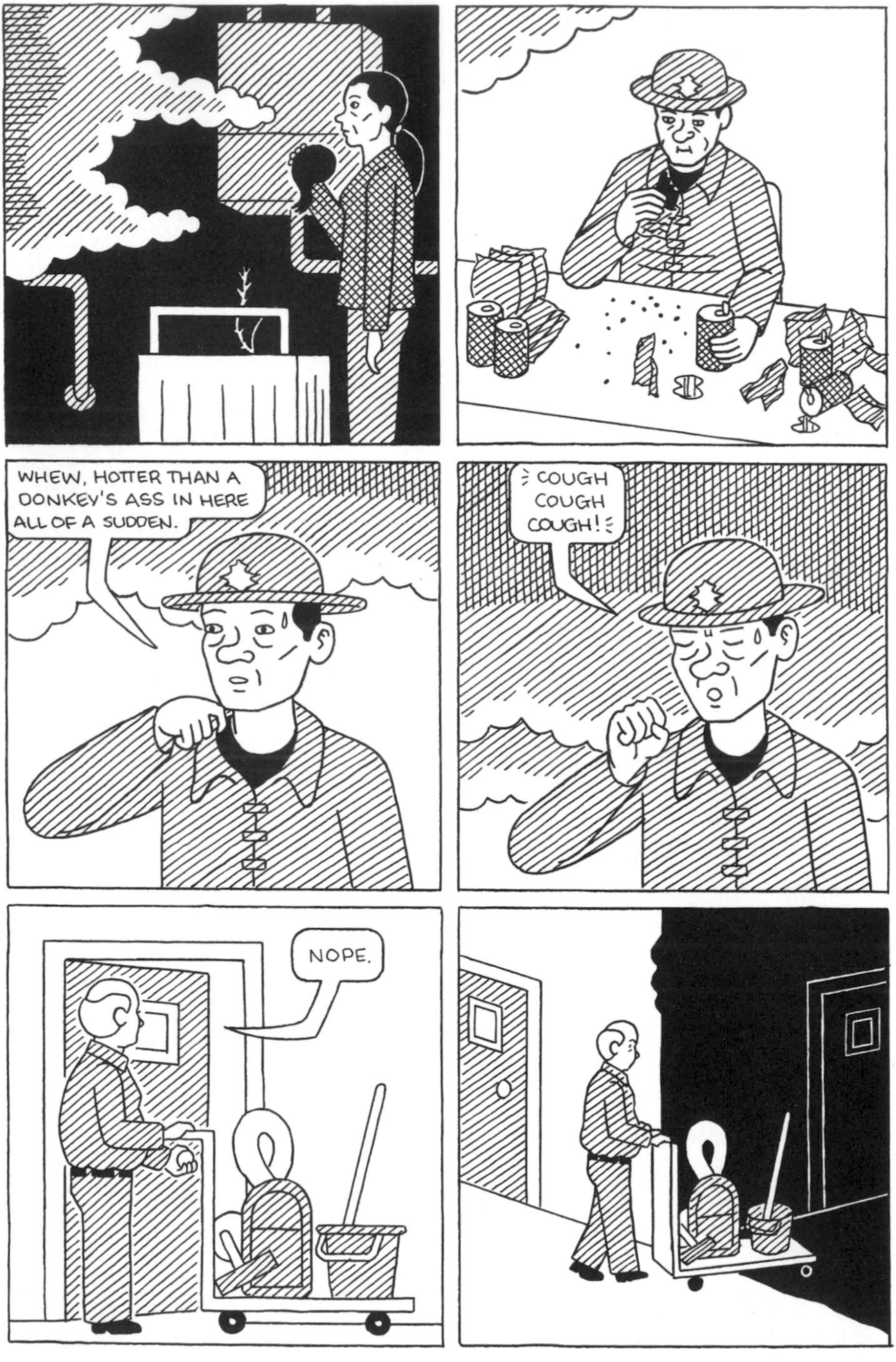
WHEW, HOTTER THAN A DONKEY'S ASS IN HERE ALL OF A SUDDEN.
COUGH COUGH COUGH!
NOPE.

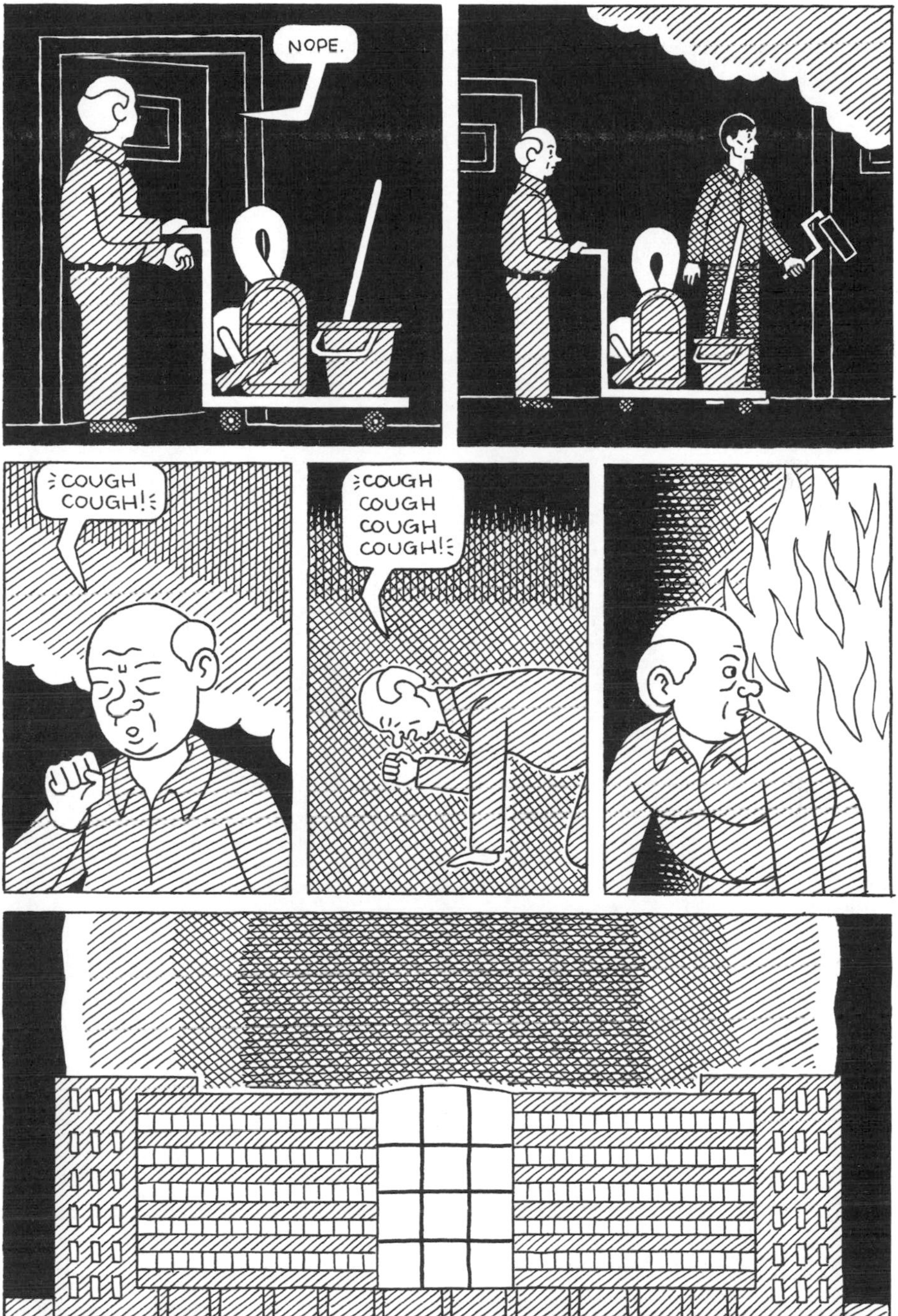
NOPE.
COUGH COUGH!
COUGH COUGH COUGH COUGH!

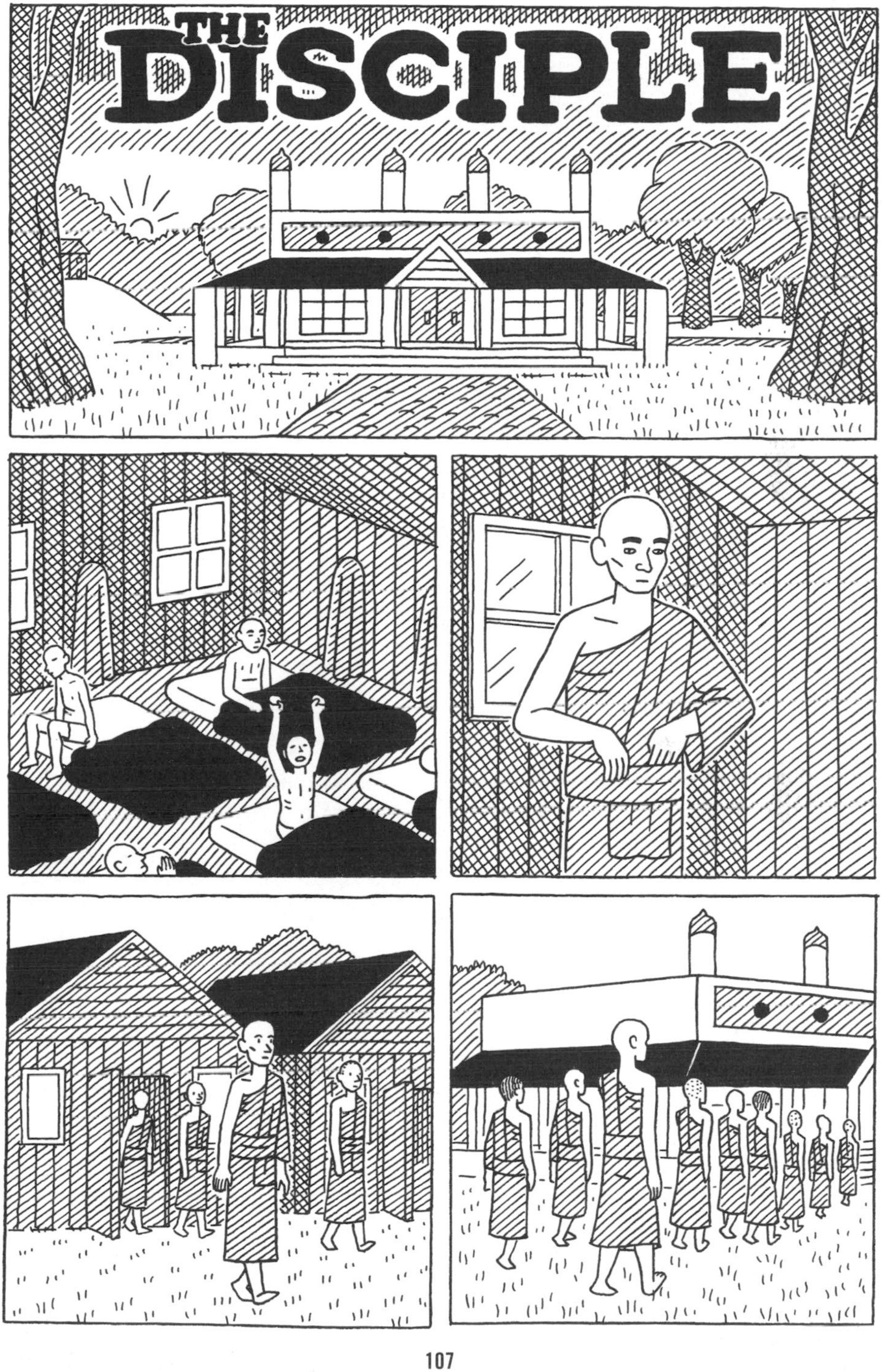
THE DISCIPLE

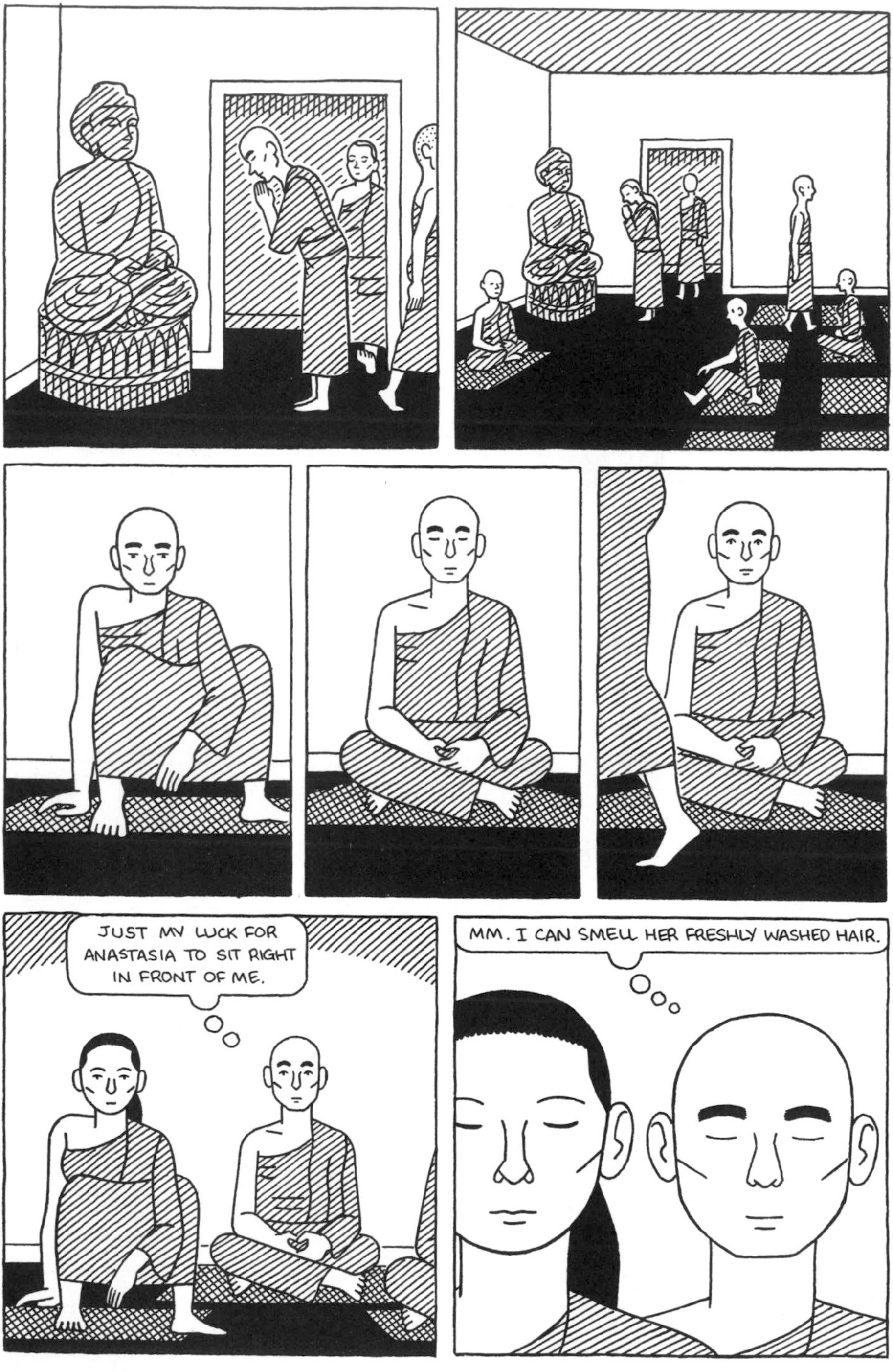
JUST MY LUCK FOR ANASTASIA TO SIT RIGHT IN FRONT OF ME.
MM. I CAN SMELL HER FRESHLY WASHED HAIR.

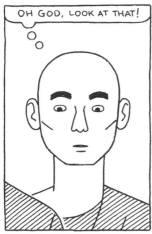

OH GOD, LOOK AT THAT!

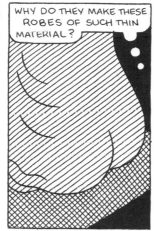

WHY DO THEY MAKE THESE ROBES OF SUCH THIN MATERIAL?

≥SIGH≤ THIS MAY PROVE TO BE A DISTRACTING SESSION.

GOOD MORNING, EVERYONE. LET US BEGIN OUR MORNING MEDITATION.

TIIIIIIIIIIIIIIIING

OKAY, TIME TO CONCENTRATE. DEEP BREATHS. RELAX THE BODY. FOCUS THE MIND.

FOCUSING ON INHALATION, EXHALATION, THE RISE AND FALL OF THE ABDOMEN.

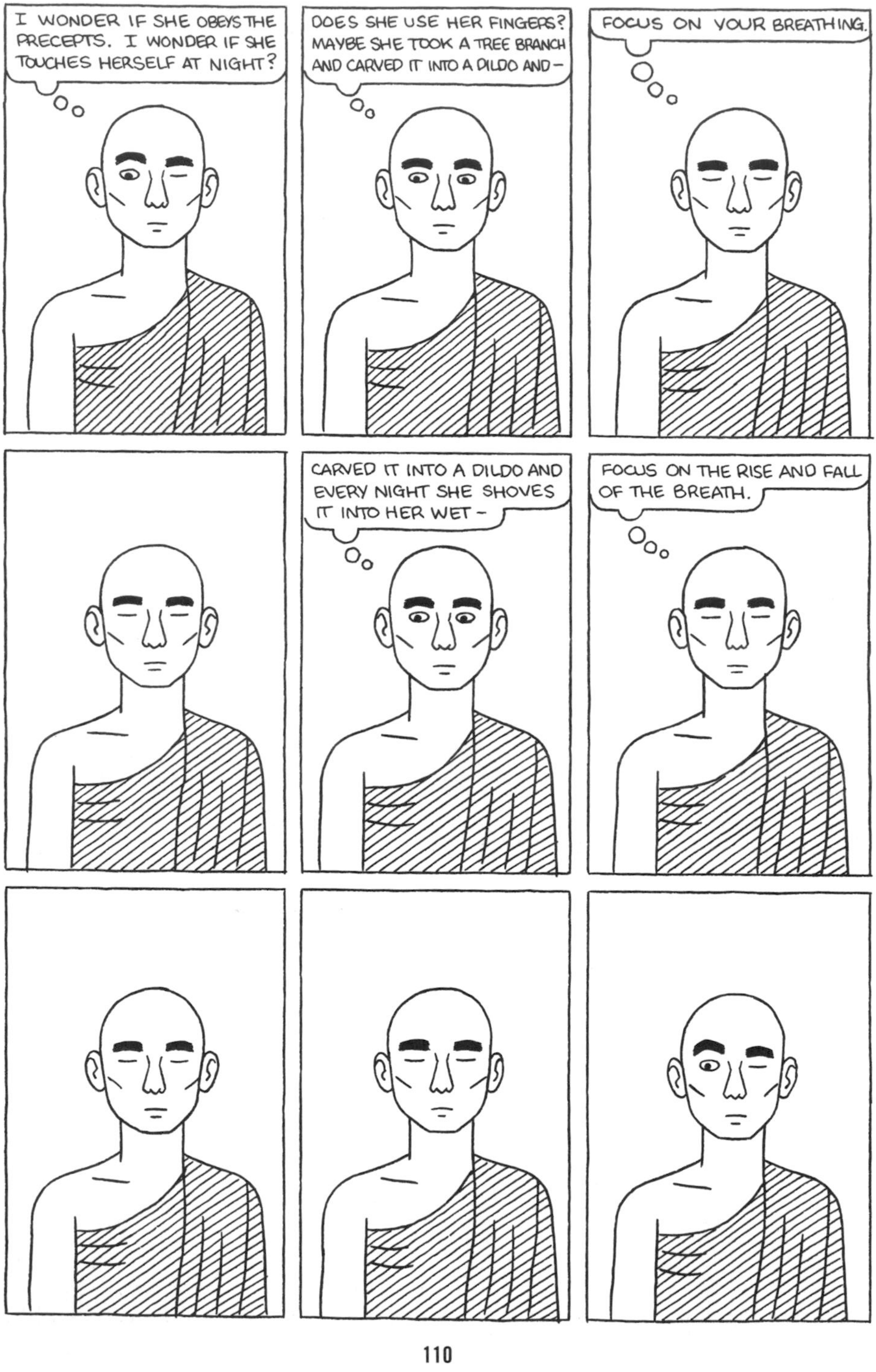
I WONDER IF SHE OBEYS THE PRECEPTS. I WONDER IF SHE TOUCHES HERSELF AT NIGHT?
DOES SHE USE HER FINGERS? MAYBE SHE TOOK A TREE BRANCH AND CARVED IT INTO A DILDO AND—
FOCUS ON YOUR BREATHING.
CARVED IT INTO A DILDO AND EVERY NIGHT SHE SHOVES IT INTO HER WET—
FOCUS ON THE RISE AND FALL OF THE BREATH.

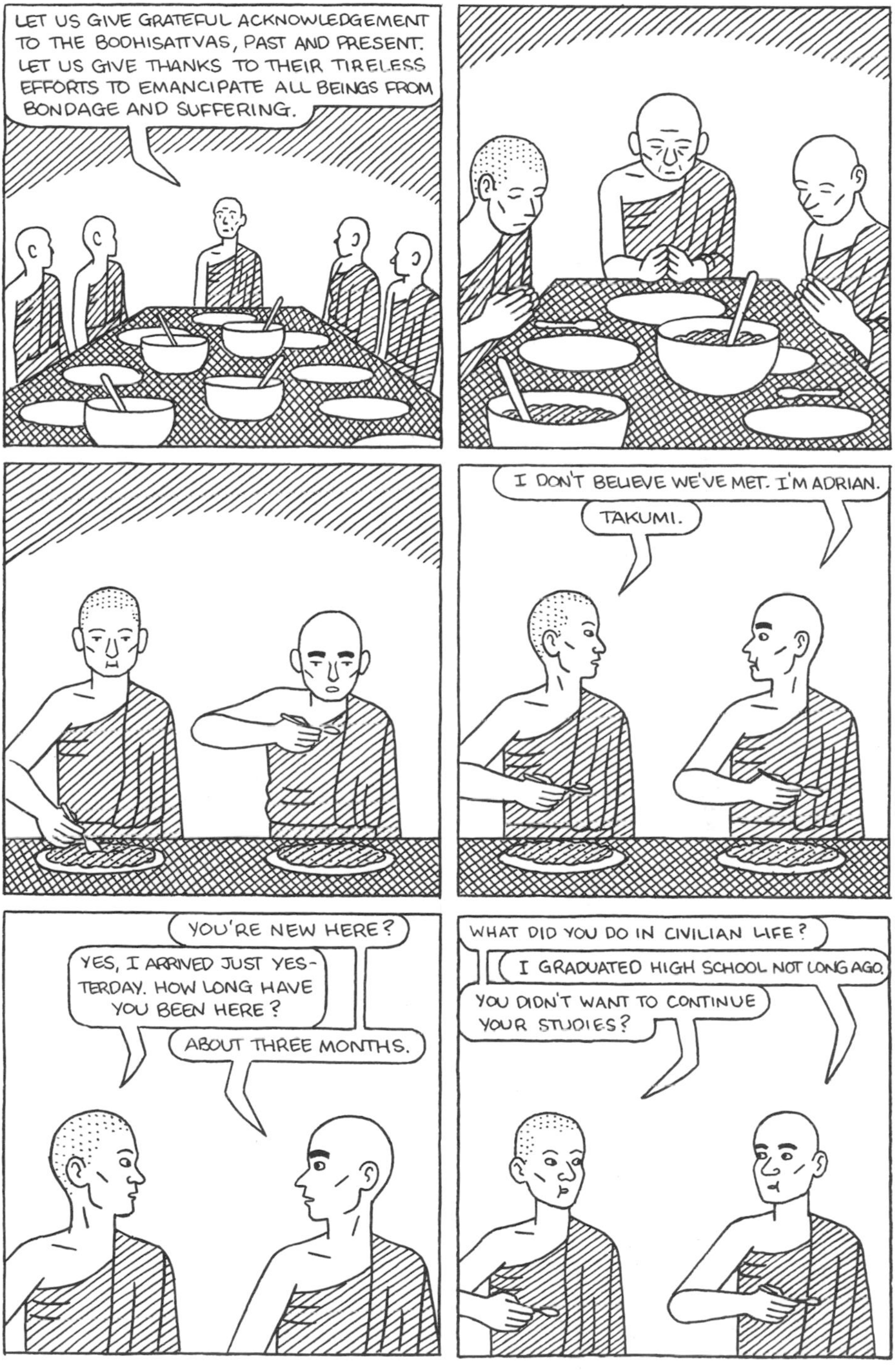
LET US GIVE GRATEFUL ACKNOWLEDGEMENT TO THE BODHISATTVAS, PAST AND PRESENT. LET US GIVE THANKS TO THEIR TIRELESS EFFORTS TO EMANCIPATE ALL BEINGS FROM BONDAGE AND SUFFERING.
I DON'T BELIEVE WE'VE MET. I'M ADRIAN.
TAKUMI.
YOU'RE NEW HERE?
YES, I ARRIVED JUST YESTERDAY. HOW LONG HAVE YOU BEEN HERE?
ABOUT THREE MONTHS.
WHAT DID YOU DO IN CIVILIAN LIFE?
I GRADUATED HIGH SCHOOL NOT LONG AGO.
YOU DIDN'T WANT TO CONTINUE YOUR STUDIES?

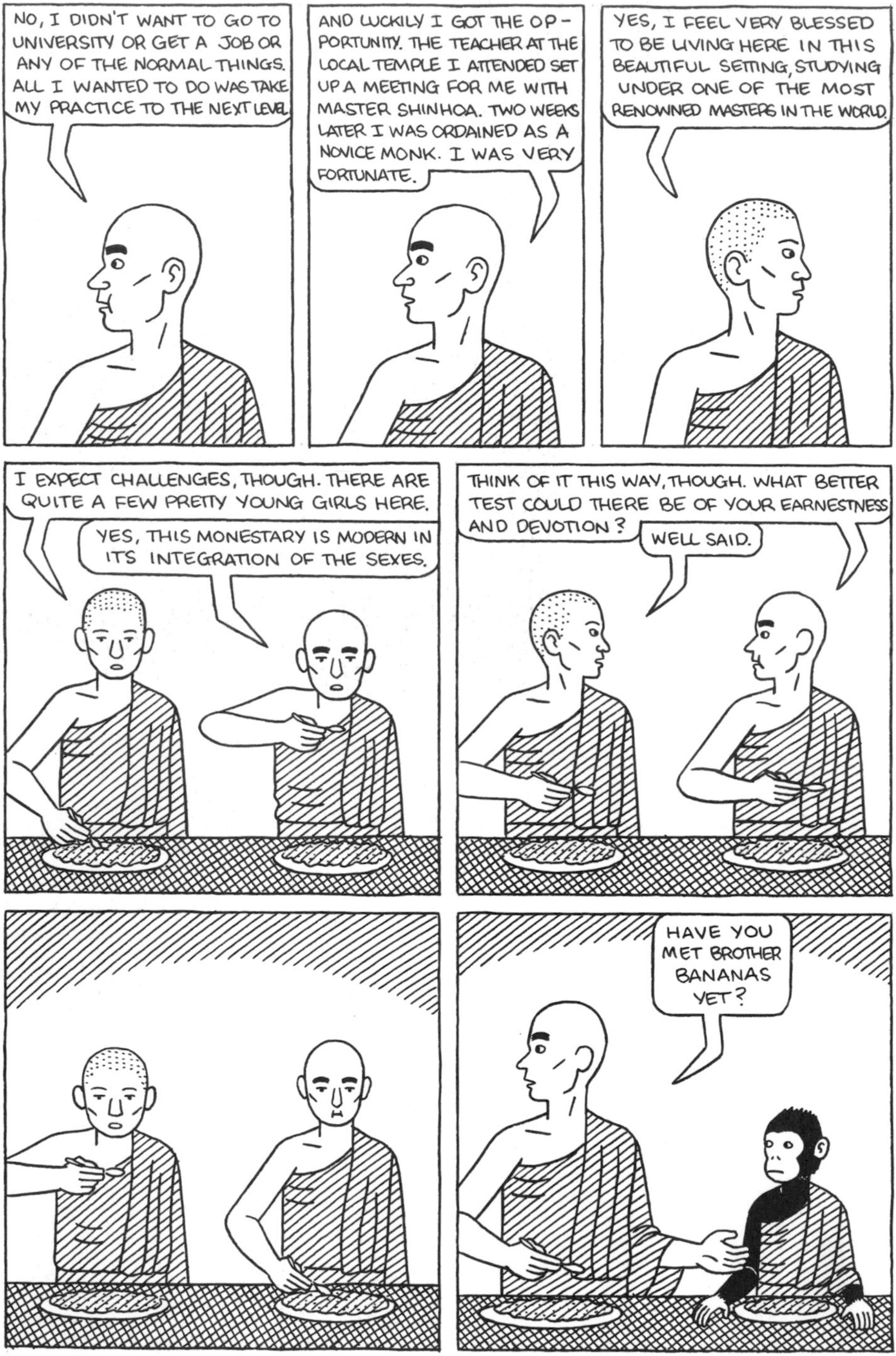
NO, I DIDN'T WANT TO GO TO UNIVERSITY OR GET A JOB OR ANY OF THE NORMAL THINGS. ALL I WANTED TO DO WAS TAKE MY PRACTICE TO THE NEXT LEVEL.
AND LUCKILY I GOT THE OP-PORTUNITY. THE TEACHER AT THE LOCAL TEMPLE I ATTENDED SET UP A MEETING FOR ME WITH MASTER SHINHOA. TWO WEEKS LATER I WAS ORDAINED AS A NOVICE MONK. I WAS VERY FORTUNATE.
YES, I FEEL VERY BLESSED TO BE LIVING HERE IN THIS BEAUTIFUL SETTING, STUDYING UNDER ONE OF THE MOST RENOWNED MASTERS IN THE WORLD.
I EXPECT CHALLENGES, THOUGH. THERE ARE QUITE A FEW PRETTY YOUNG GIRLS HERE.
YES, THIS MONESTARY IS MODERN IN ITS INTEGRATION OF THE SEXES.
THINK OF IT THIS WAY, THOUGH. WHAT BETTER TEST COULD THERE BE OF YOUR EARNESTNESS AND DEVOTION?
WELL SAID.
HAVE YOU MET BROTHER BANANAS YET?

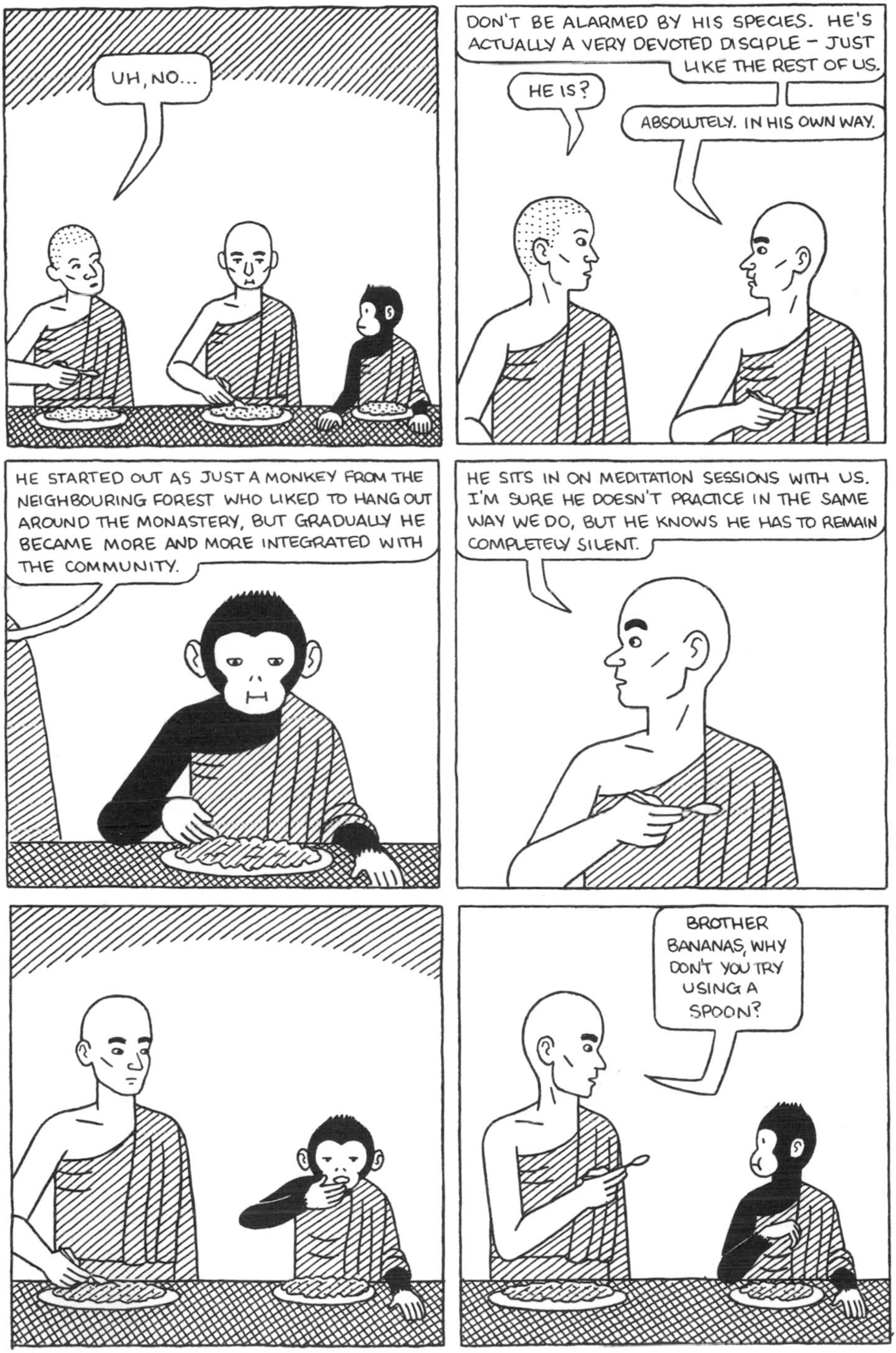
UH, NO...
DON'T BE ALARMED BY HIS SPECIES. HE'S ACTUALLY A VERY DEVOTED DISCIPLE – JUST LIKE THE REST OF US.
HE IS?
ABSOLUTELY. IN HIS OWN WAY.
HE STARTED OUT AS JUST A MONKEY FROM THE NEIGHBOURING FOREST WHO LIKED TO HANG OUT AROUND THE MONASTERY, BUT GRADUALLY HE BECAME MORE AND MORE INTEGRATED WITH THE COMMUNITY.
HE SITS IN ON MEDITATION SESSIONS WITH US. I'M SURE HE DOESN'T PRACTICE IN THE SAME WAY WE DO, BUT HE KNOWS HE HAS TO REMAIN COMPLETELY SILENT.
BROTHER BANANAS, WHY DON'T YOU TRY USING A SPOON?

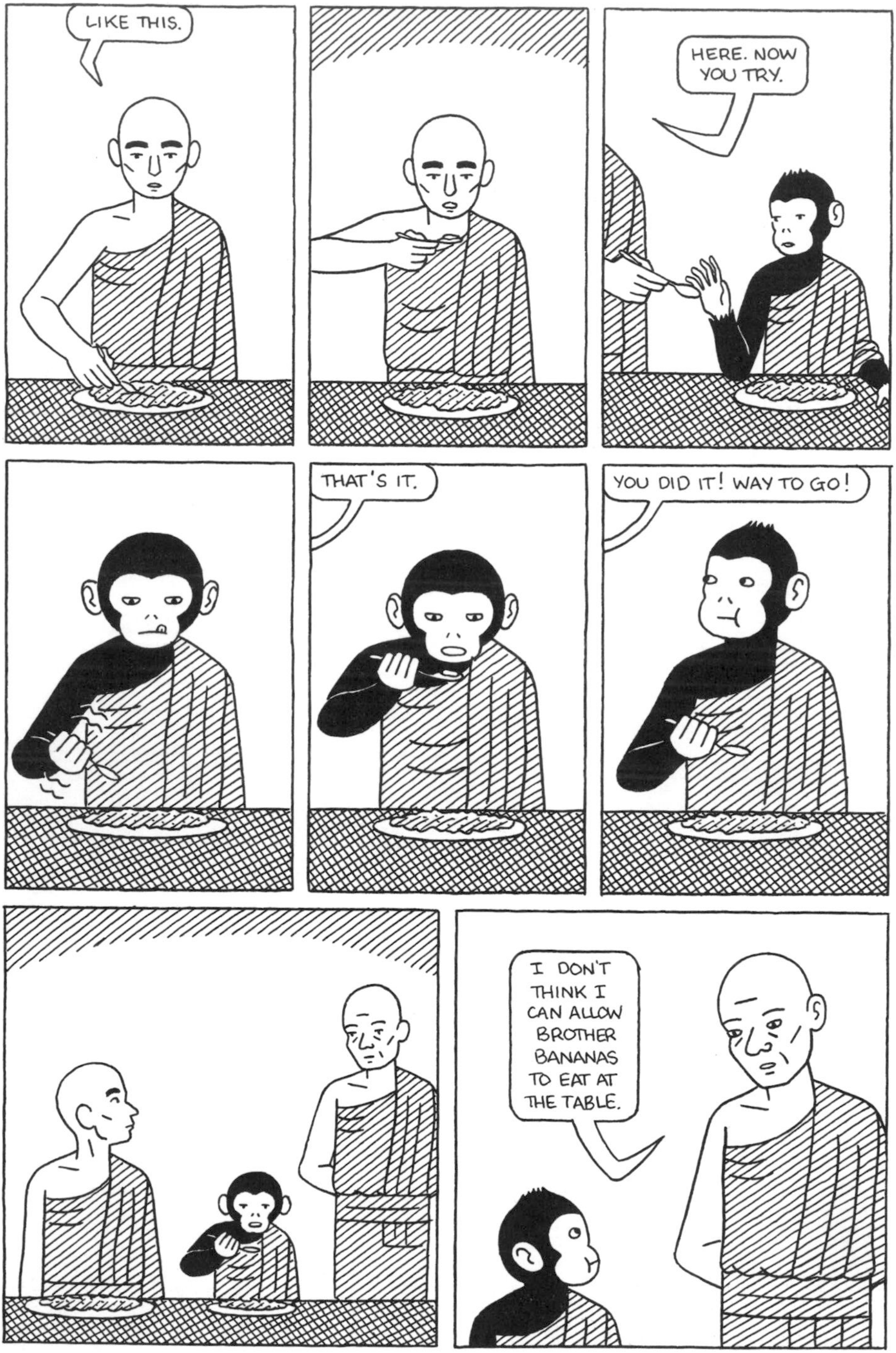
LIKE THIS.
HERE. NOW YOU TRY.
THAT'S IT.
YOU DID IT! WAY TO GO!
I DON'T THINK I CAN ALLOW BROTHER BANANAS TO EAT AT THE TABLE.

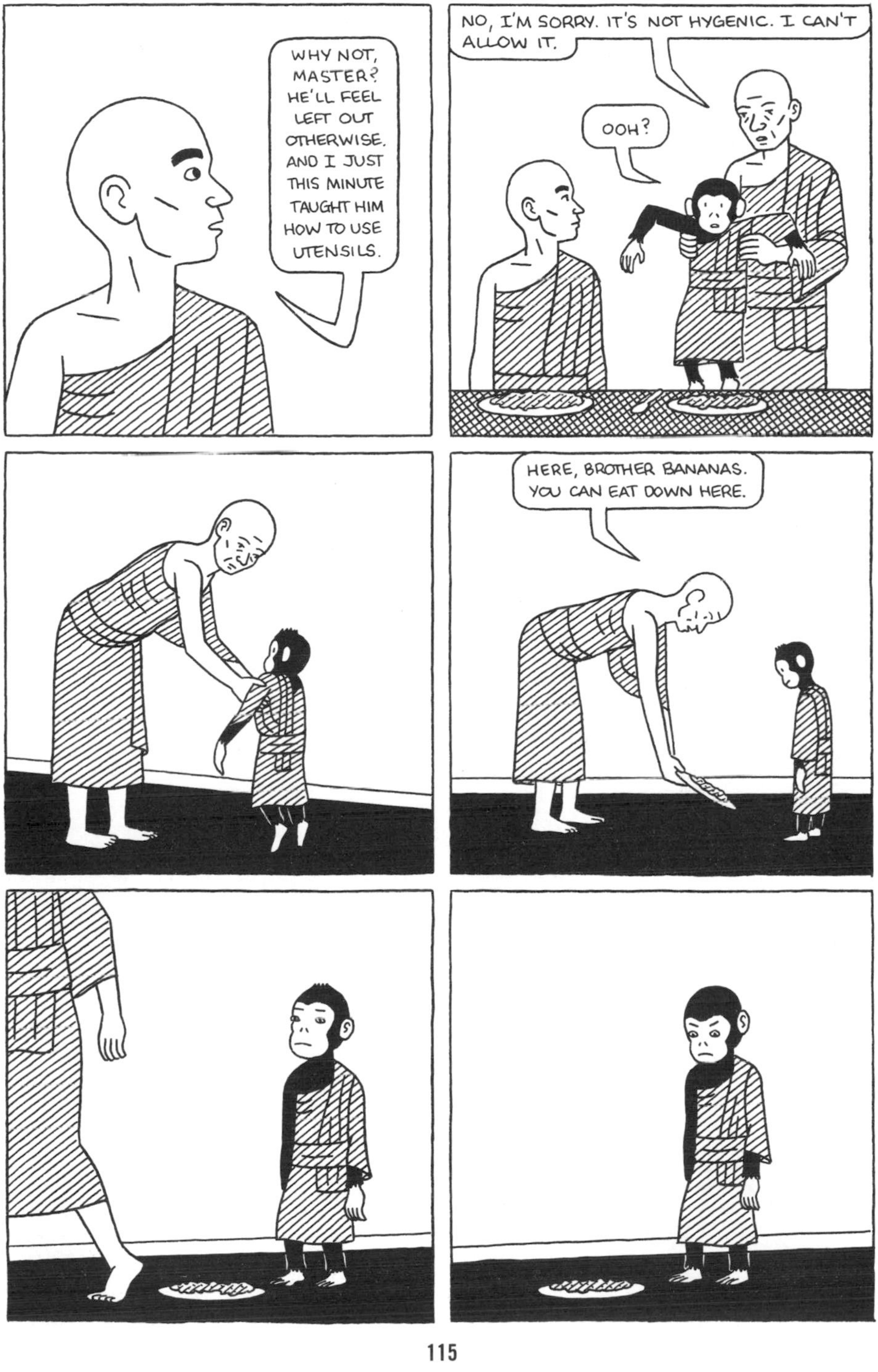
WHY NOT, MASTER? HE'LL FEEL LEFT OUT OTHERWISE. AND I JUST THIS MINUTE TAUGHT HIM HOW TO USE UTENSILS.
NO, I'M SORRY. IT'S NOT HYGENIC. I CAN'T ALLOW IT.
OOH?
HERE, BROTHER BANANAS. YOU CAN EAT DOWN HERE.

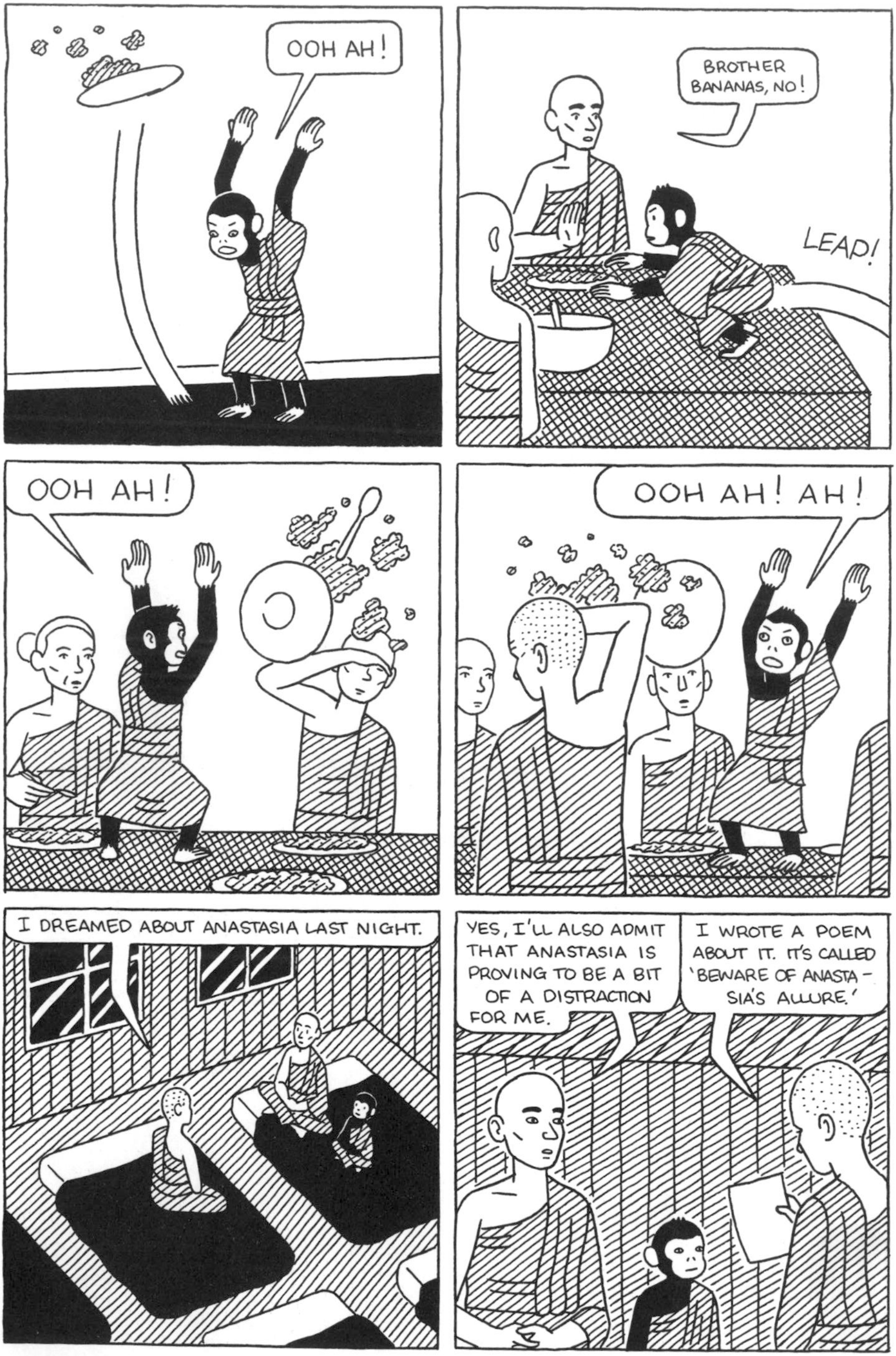
OOH AH!
BROTHER BANANAS, NO!
LEAP!
OOH AH!
OOH AH! AH!
I DREAMED ABOUT ANASTASIA LAST NIGHT.
YES, I'LL ALSO ADMIT THAT ANASTASIA IS PROVING TO BE A BIT OF A DISTRACTION FOR ME.
I WROTE A POEM ABOUT IT. IT'S CALLED 'BEWARE OF ANASTA-SIA'S ALLURE.'

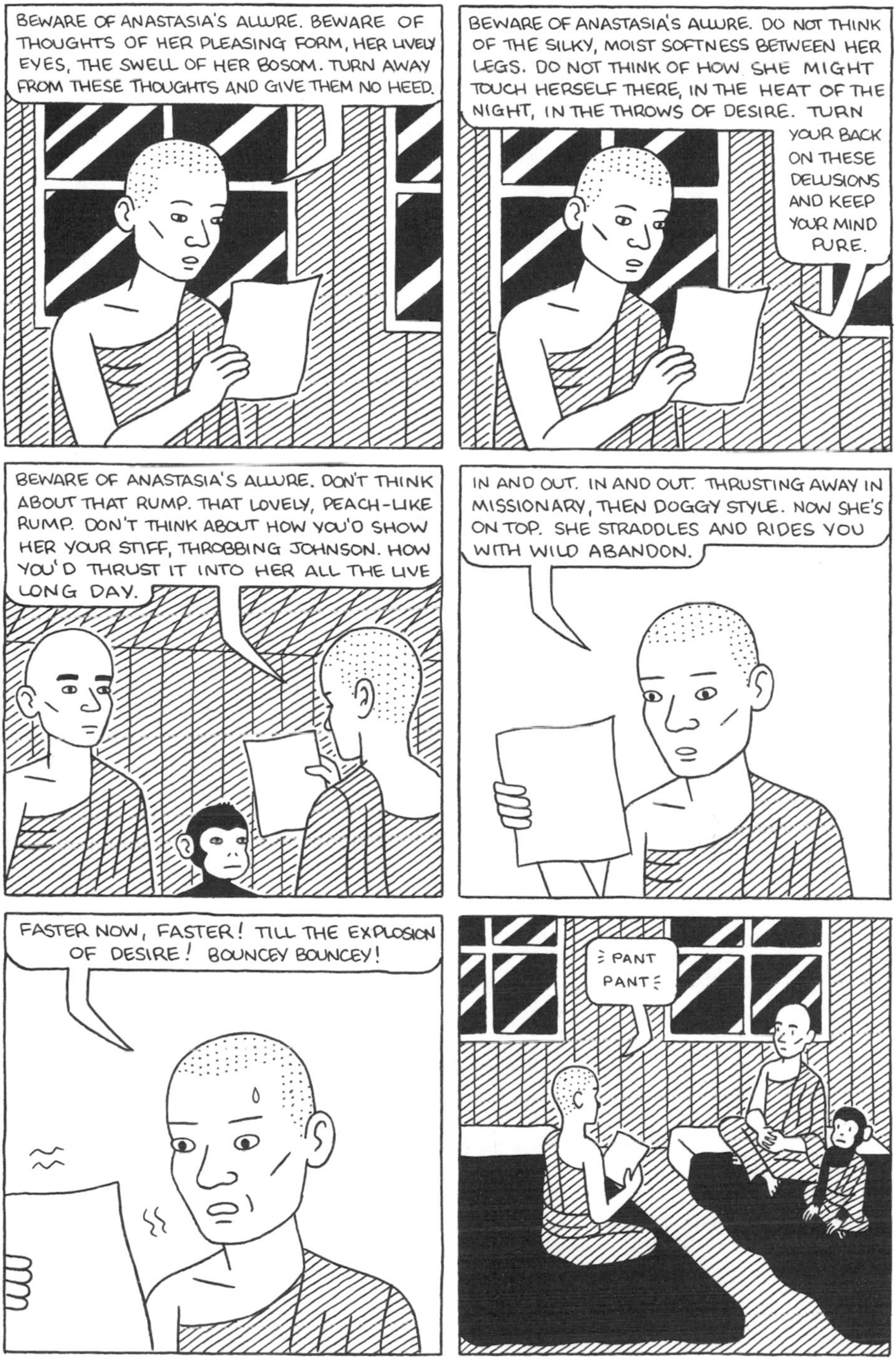
BEWARE OF ANASTASIA'S ALLURE. BEWARE OF THOUGHTS OF HER PLEASING FORM, HER LIVELY EYES, THE SWELL OF HER BOSOM. TURN AWAY FROM THESE THOUGHTS AND GIVE THEM NO HEED.
BEWARE OF ANASTASIA'S ALLURE. DO NOT THINK OF THE SILKY, MOIST SOFTNESS BETWEEN HER LEGS. DO NOT THINK OF HOW SHE MIGHT TOUCH HERSELF THERE, IN THE HEAT OF THE NIGHT, IN THE THROWS OF DESIRE. TURN YOUR BACK ON THESE DELUSIONS AND KEEP YOUR MIND PURE.
BEWARE OF ANASTASIA'S ALLURE. DON'T THINK ABOUT THAT RUMP. THAT LOVELY, PEACH-LIKE RUMP. DON'T THINK ABOUT HOW YOU'D SHOW HER YOUR STIFF, THROBBING JOHNSON. HOW YOU'D THRUST IT INTO HER ALL THE LIVE LONG DAY.
IN AND OUT. IN AND OUT. THRUSTING AWAY IN MISSIONARY, THEN DOGGY STYLE. NOW SHE'S ON TOP. SHE STRADDLES AND RIDES YOU WITH WILD ABANDON.
FASTER NOW, FASTER! TILL THE EXPLOSION OF DESIRE! BOUNCEY BOUNCEY!
PANT PANT

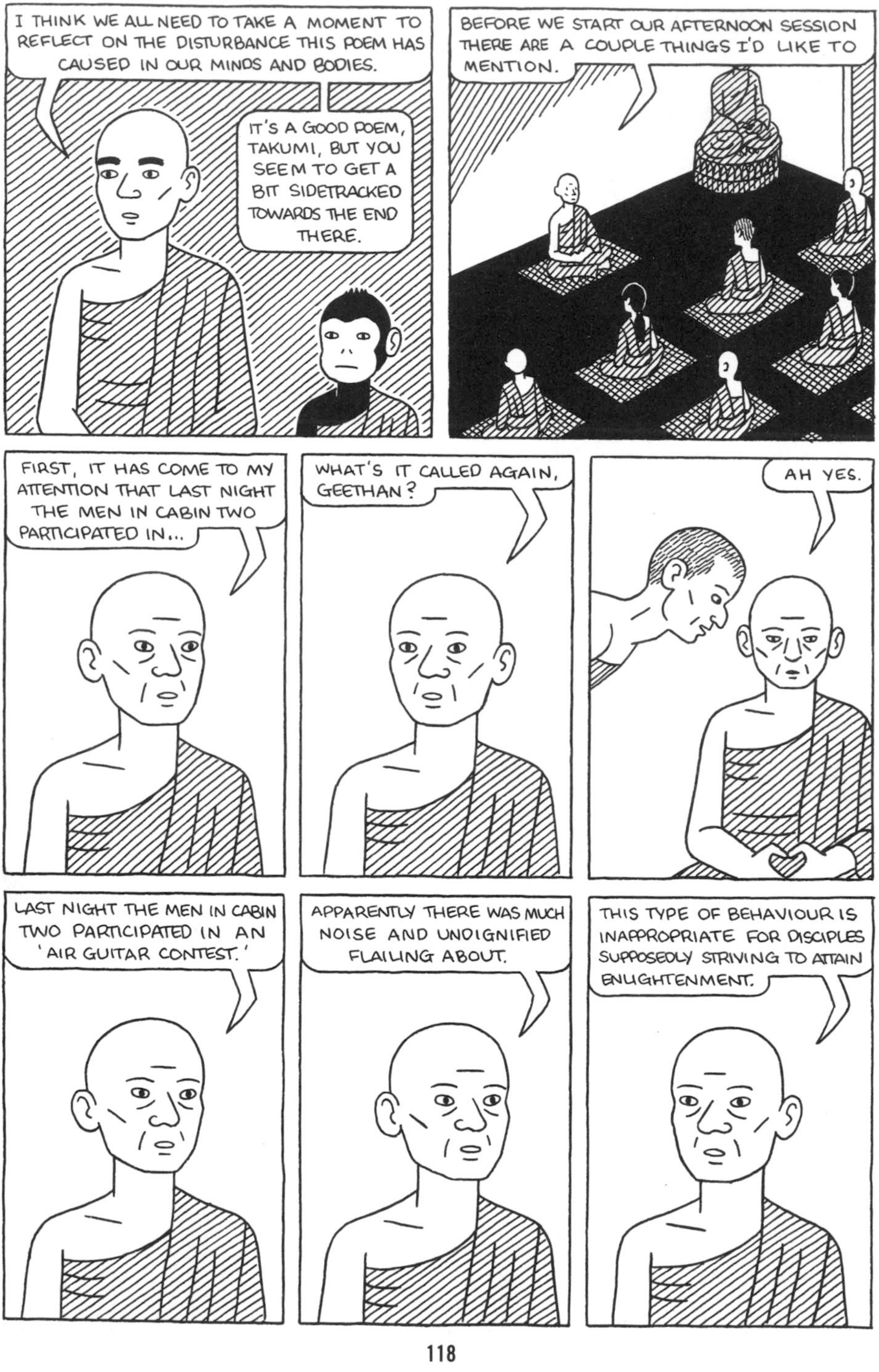

I THINK WE ALL NEED TO TAKE A MOMENT TO REFLECT ON THE DISTURBANCE THIS POEM HAS CAUSED IN OUR MINDS AND BODIES.
IT'S A GOOD POEM, TAKUMI, BUT YOU SEEM TO GET A BIT SIDETRACKED TOWARDS THE END THERE.
BEFORE WE START OUR AFTERNOON SESSION THERE ARE A COUPLE THINGS I'D LIKE TO MENTION.
FIRST, IT HAS COME TO MY ATTENTION THAT LAST NIGHT THE MEN IN CABIN TWO PARTICIPATED IN...
WHAT'S IT CALLED AGAIN, GEETHAN?
AH YES.
LAST NIGHT THE MEN IN CABIN TWO PARTICIPATED IN AN 'AIR GUITAR CONTEST.'
APPARENTLY THERE WAS MUCH NOISE AND UNDIGNIFIED FLAILING ABOUT.
THIS TYPE OF BEHAVIOUR IS INAPPROPRIATE FOR DISCIPLES SUPPOSEDLY STRIVING TO ATTAIN ENLIGHTENMENT.

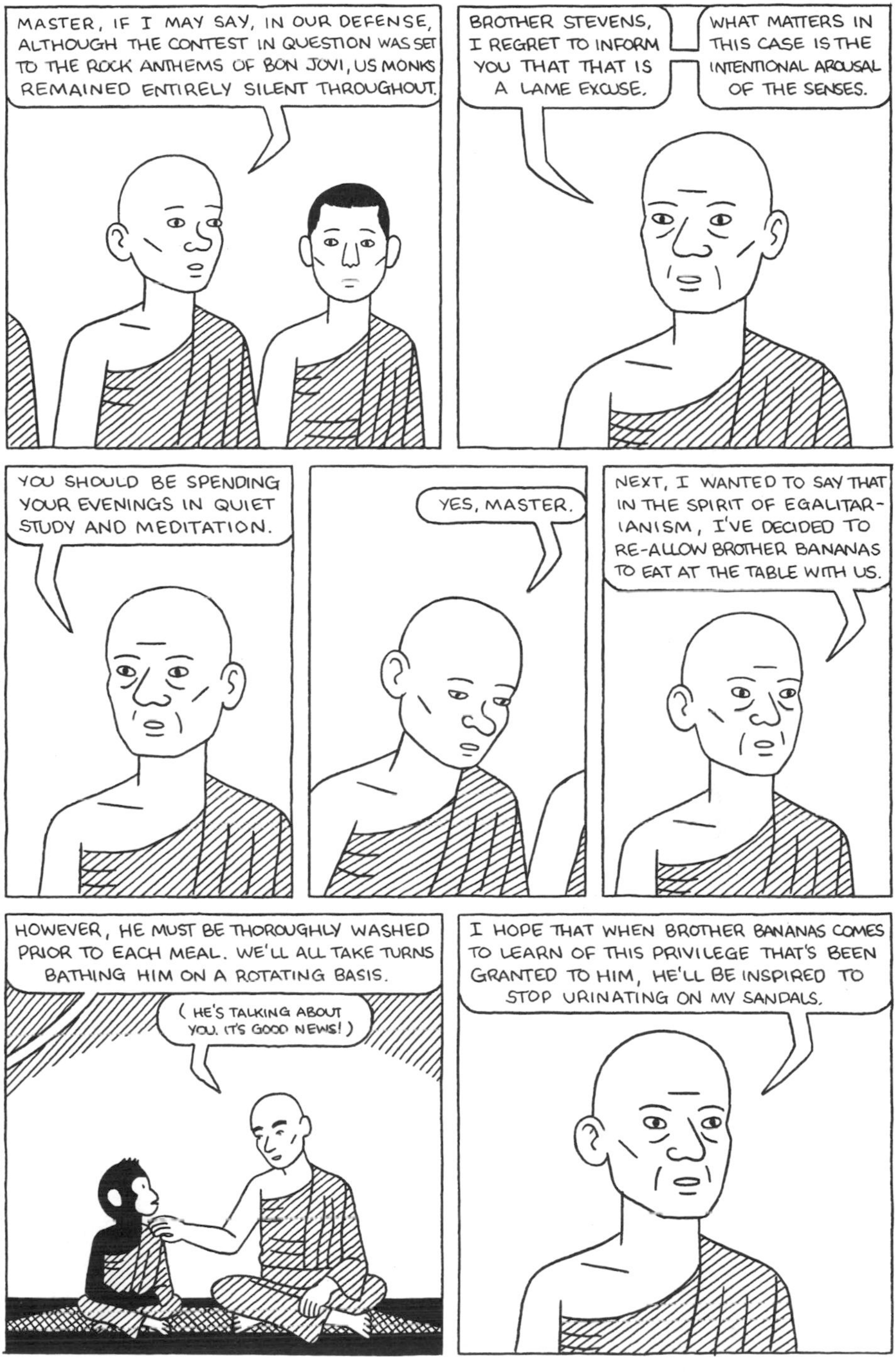
MASTER, IF I MAY SAY, IN OUR DEFENSE, ALTHOUGH THE CONTEST IN QUESTION WAS SET TO THE ROCK ANTHEMS OF BON JOVI, US MONKS REMAINED ENTIRELY SILENT THROUGHOUT.
BROTHER STEVENS, I REGRET TO INFORM YOU THAT THAT IS A LAME EXCUSE.
WHAT MATTERS IN THIS CASE IS THE INTENTIONAL AROUSAL OF THE SENSES.
YOU SHOULD BE SPENDING YOUR EVENINGS IN QUIET STUDY AND MEDITATION.
YES, MASTER.
NEXT, I WANTED TO SAY THAT IN THE SPIRIT OF EGALITARIANISM, I'VE DECIDED TO RE-ALLOW BROTHER BANANAS TO EAT AT THE TABLE WITH US.
HOWEVER, HE MUST BE THOROUGHLY WASHED PRIOR TO EACH MEAL. WE'LL ALL TAKE TURNS BATHING HIM ON A ROTATING BASIS.
(HE'S TALKING ABOUT YOU. IT'S GOOD NEWS!)
I HOPE THAT WHEN BROTHER BANANAS COMES TO LEARN OF THIS PRIVILEGE THAT'S BEEN GRANTED TO HIM, HE'LL BE INSPIRED TO STOP URINATING ON MY SANDALS.

MASTER, ONE OF THE WOMENS' SHOWER HEADS ISN'T WORKING.

WHICH ONE?

THE FAR ONE TO THE SOUTH.

BROTHER O'CONNOR WILL BE JOINING US FOR A RETREAT ON MONDAY. HE KNOWS A LOT ABOUT PLUMBING. I'LL ASK HIM ABOUT IT.

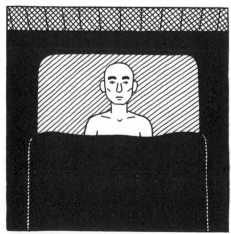

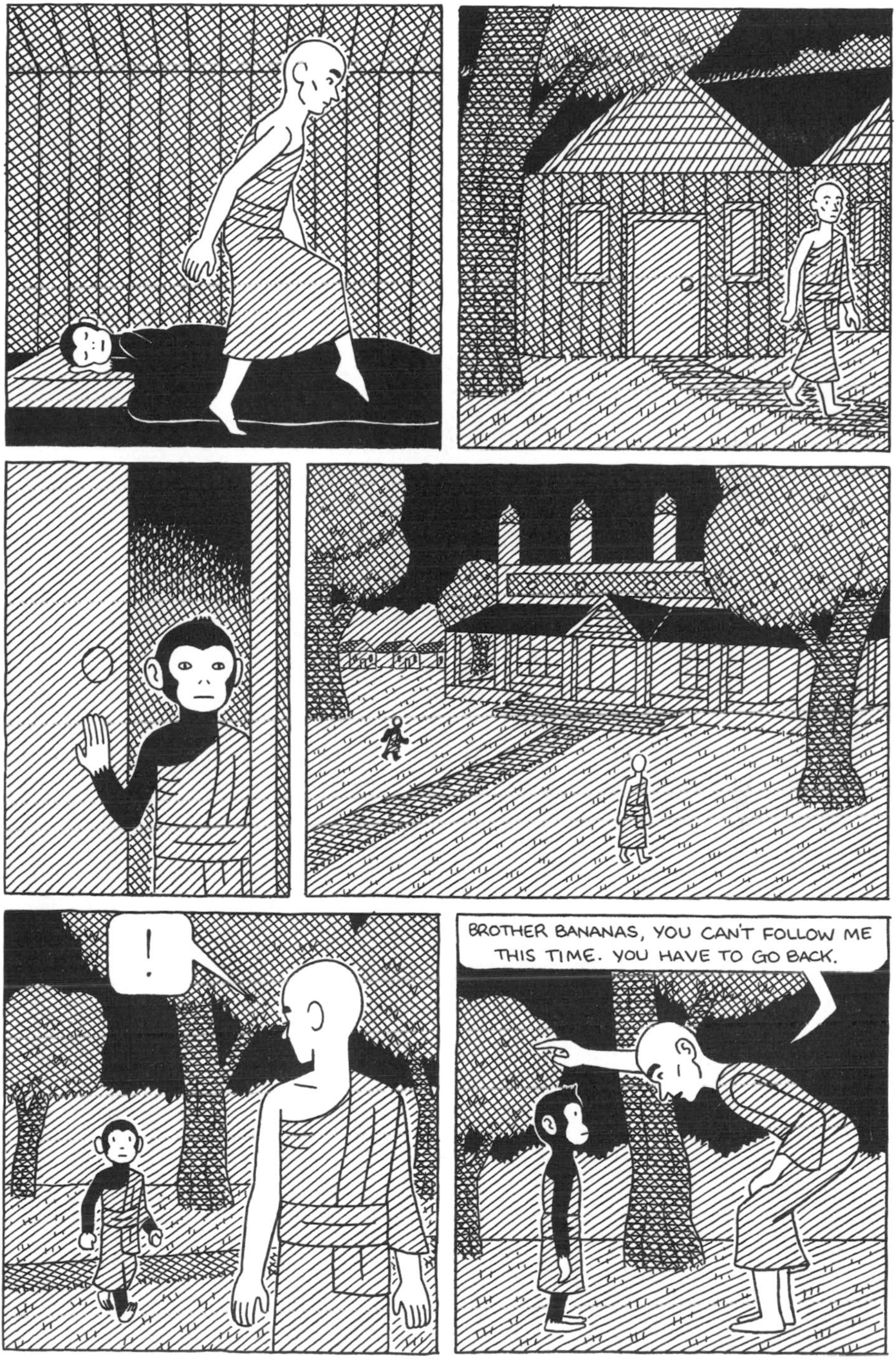
!
BROTHER BANANAS, YOU CAN'T FOLLOW ME THIS TIME. YOU HAVE TO GO BACK.

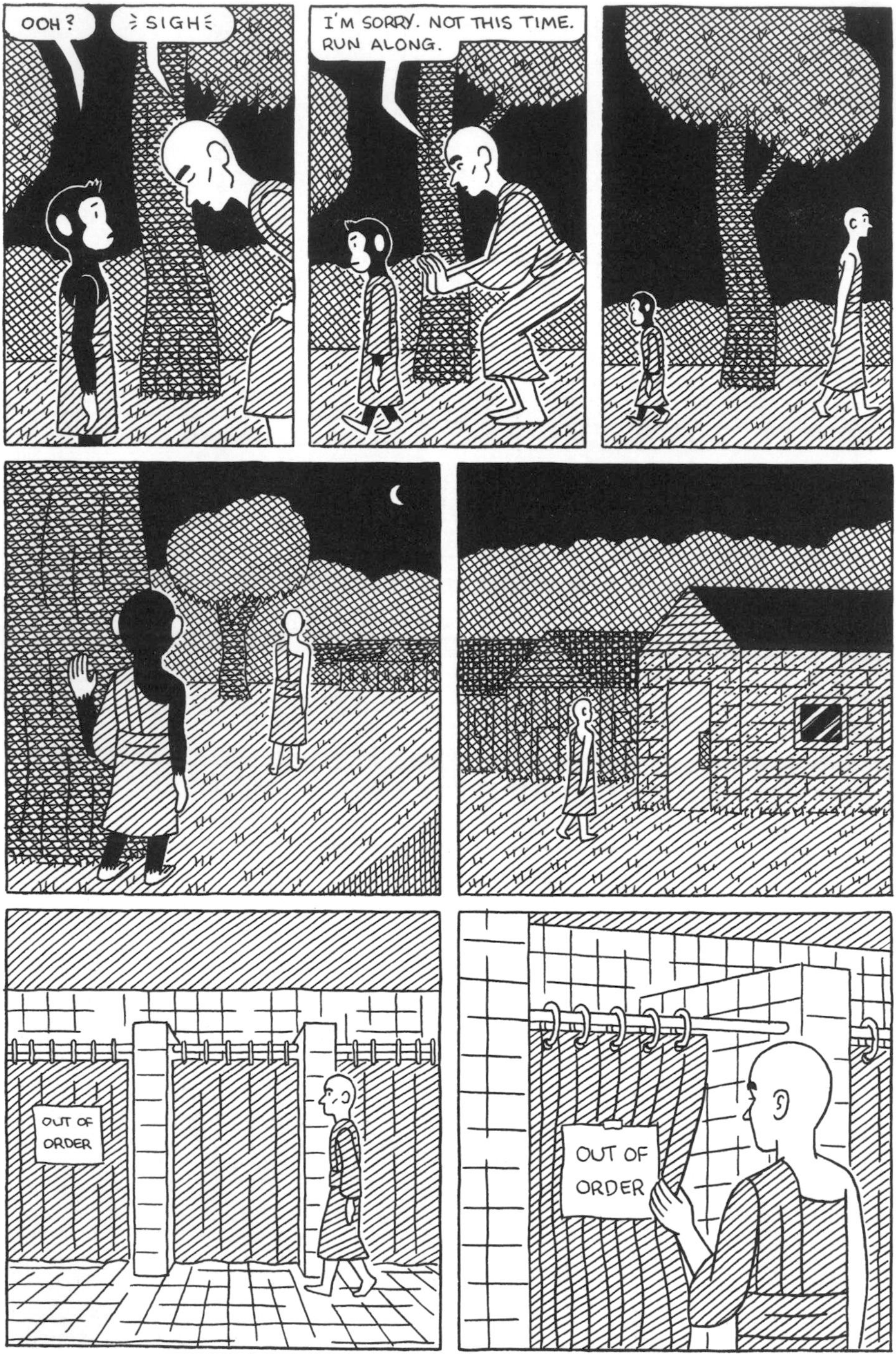
OOH?
SIGH
I'M SORRY. NOT THIS TIME. RUN ALONG.
OUT OF ORDER
OUT OF ORDER

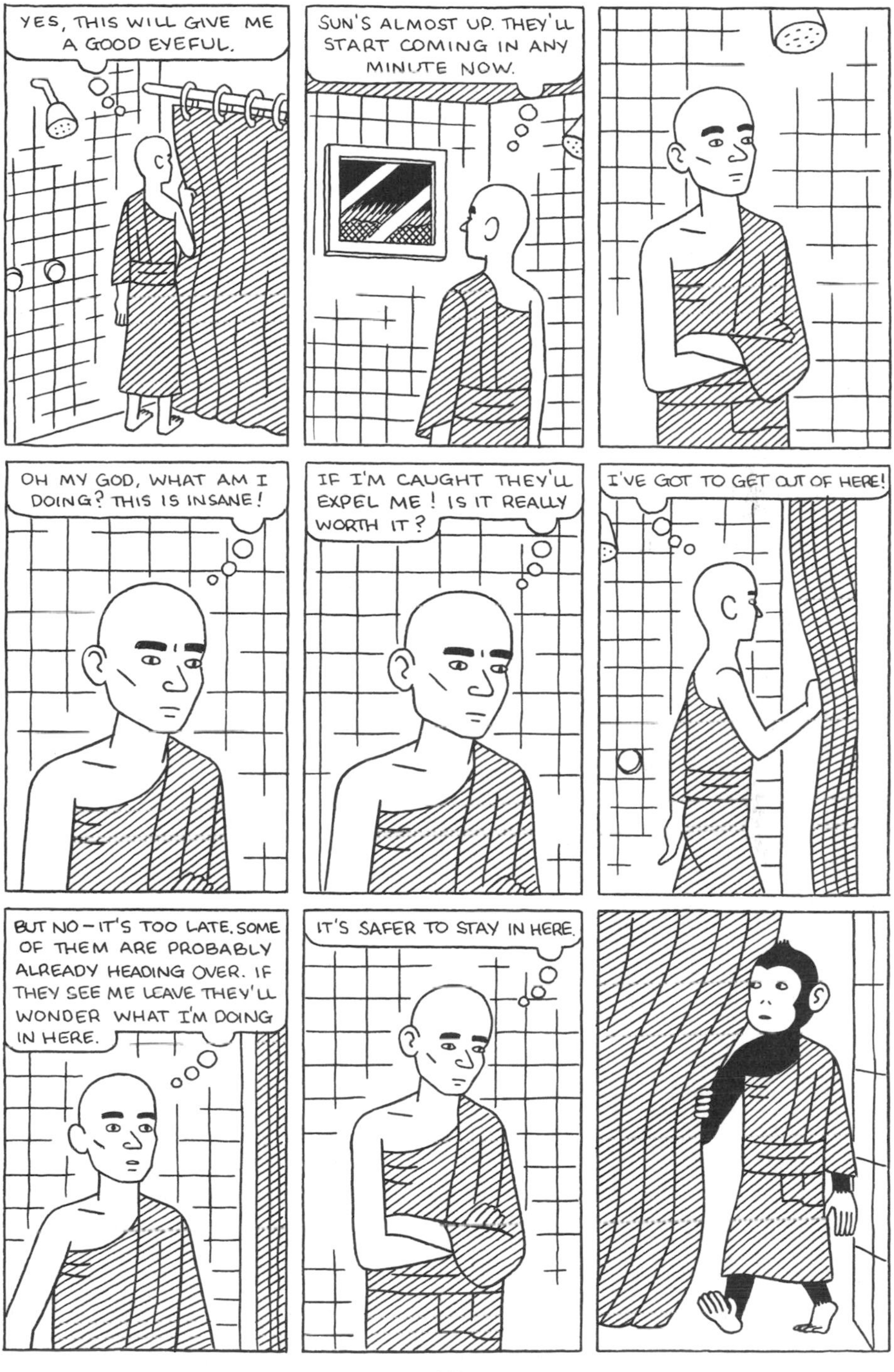
YES, THIS WILL GIVE ME A GOOD EYEFUL.
SUN'S ALMOST UP. THEY'LL START COMING IN ANY MINUTE NOW.
OH MY GOD, WHAT AM I DOING? THIS IS INSANE!
IF I'M CAUGHT THEY'LL EXPEL ME! IS IT REALLY WORTH IT?
I'VE GOT TO GET OUT OF HERE!
BUT NO – IT'S TOO LATE. SOME OF THEM ARE PROBABLY ALREADY HEADING OVER. IF THEY SEE ME LEAVE THEY'LL WONDER WHAT I'M DOING IN HERE.
IT'S SAFER TO STAY IN HERE.

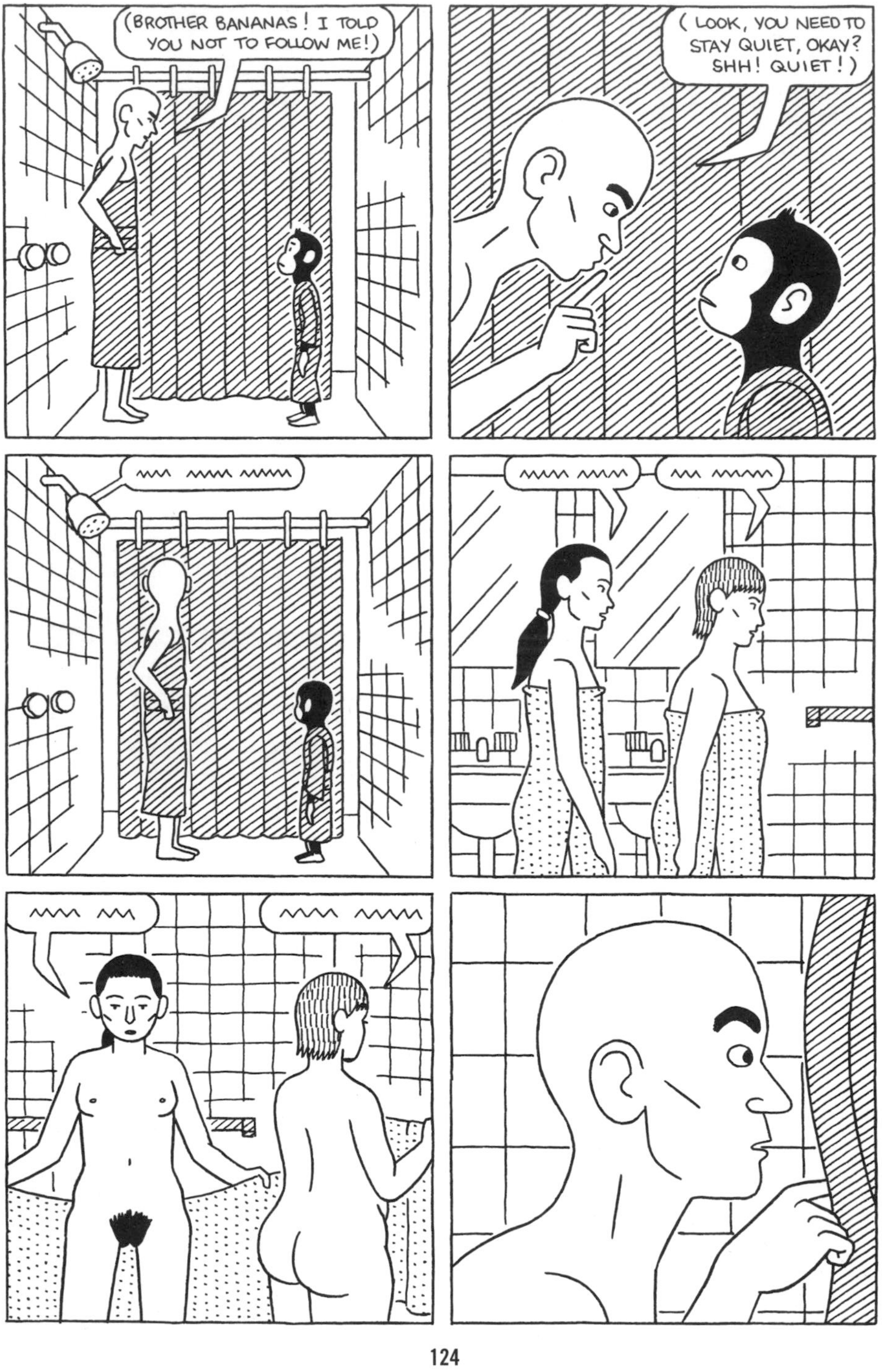
(BROTHER BANANAS! I TOLD YOU NOT TO FOLLOW ME!)
(LOOK, YOU NEED TO STAY QUIET, OKAY? SHH! QUIET!)

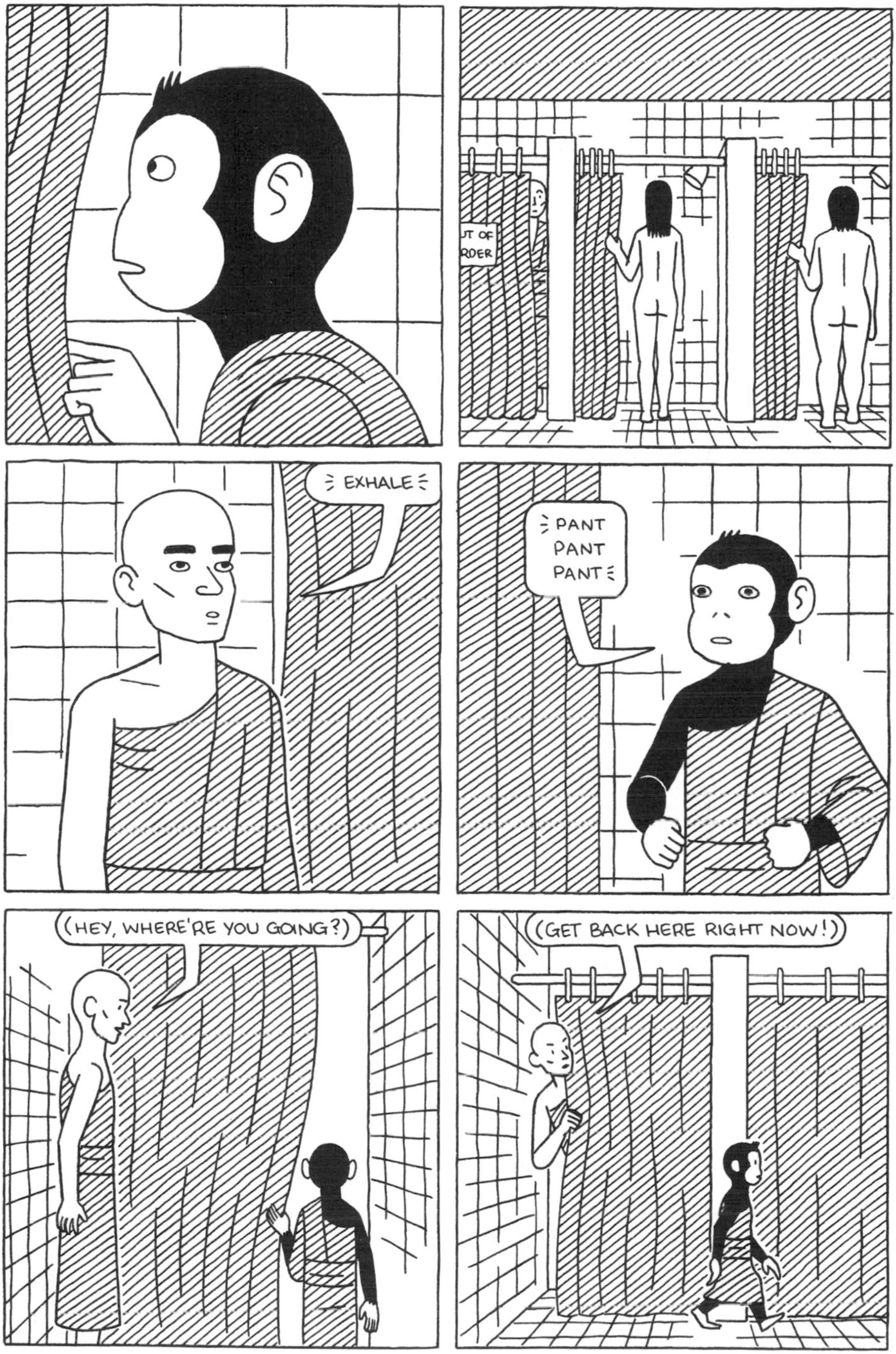
UT OF
RDER
EXHALE
PANT
PANT
PANT
(HEY, WHERE'RE YOU GOING?)
(GET BACK HERE RIGHT NOW!)

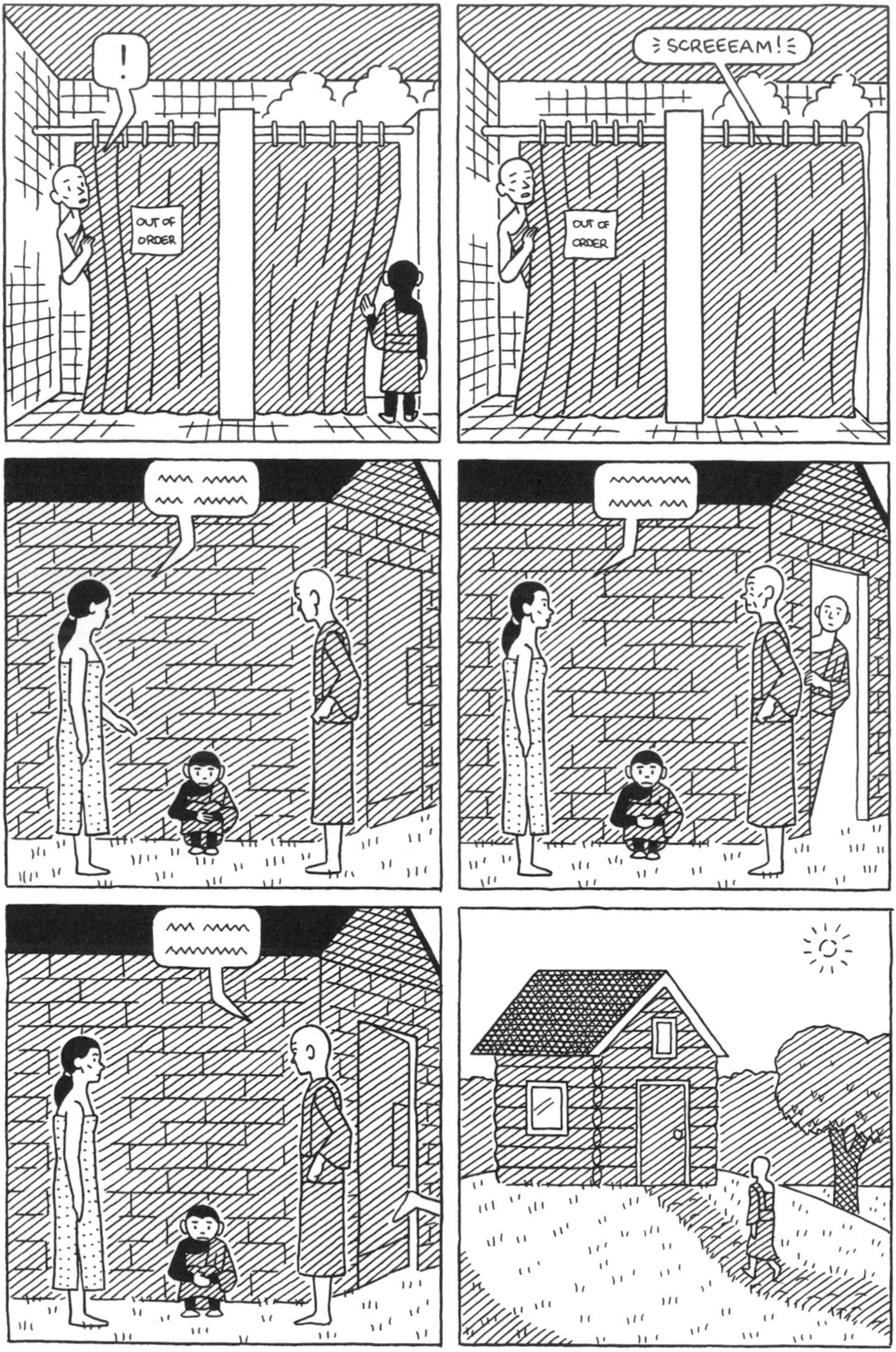

!
OUT OF ORDER
SCREEEAM!
OUT OF ORDER

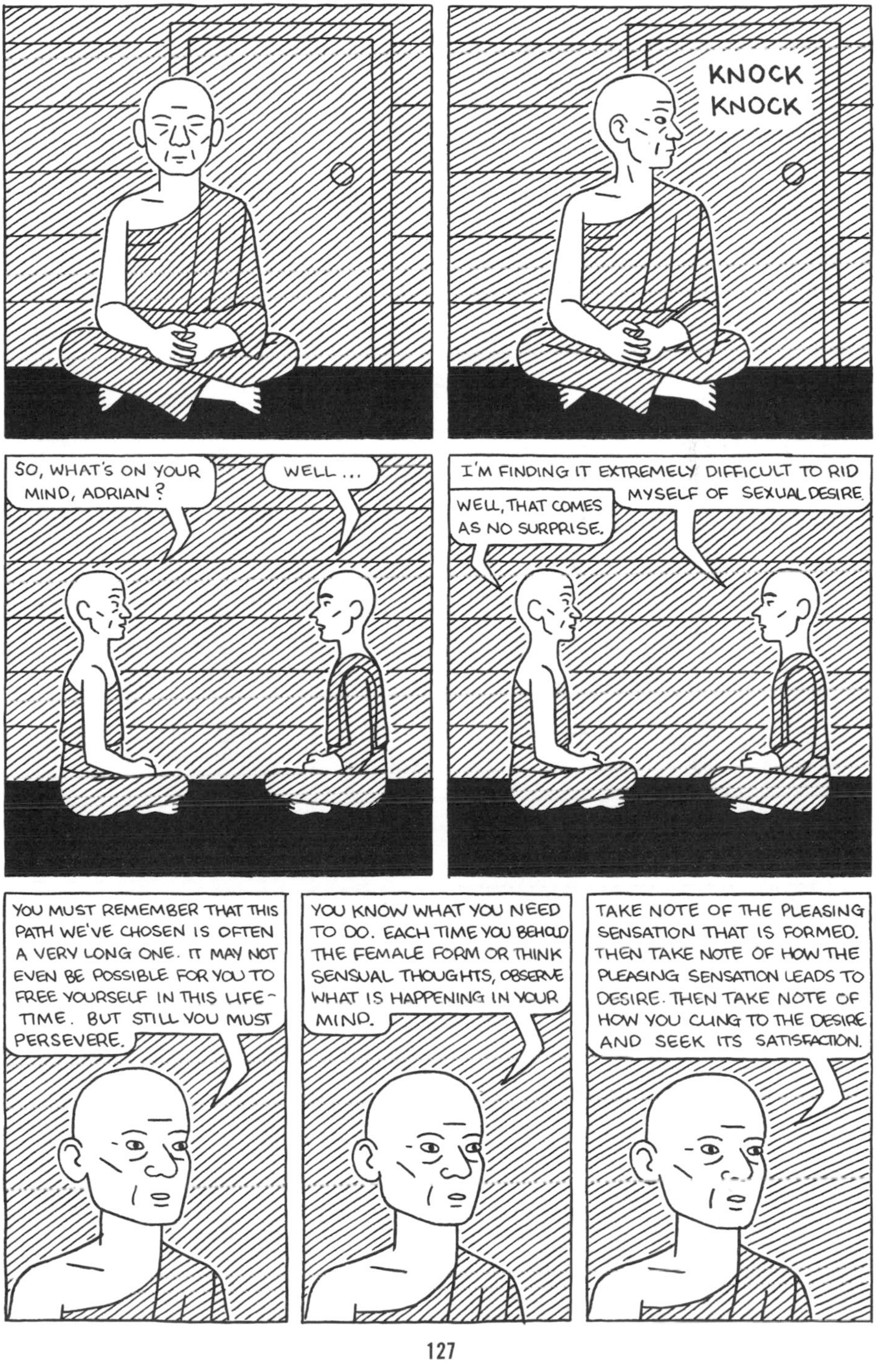
KNOCK KNOCK
SO, WHAT'S ON YOUR MIND, ADRIAN?
WELL...
I'M FINDING IT EXTREMELY DIFFICULT TO RID MYSELF OF SEXUAL DESIRE.
WELL, THAT COMES AS NO SURPRISE.
YOU MUST REMEMBER THAT THIS PATH WE'VE CHOSEN IS OFTEN A VERY LONG ONE. IT MAY NOT EVEN BE POSSIBLE FOR YOU TO FREE YOURSELF IN THIS LIFE-TIME. BUT STILL YOU MUST PERSEVERE.
YOU KNOW WHAT YOU NEED TO DO. EACH TIME YOU BEHOLD THE FEMALE FORM OR THINK SENSUAL THOUGHTS, OBSERVE WHAT IS HAPPENING IN YOUR MIND.
TAKE NOTE OF THE PLEASING SENSATION THAT IS FORMED. THEN TAKE NOTE OF HOW THE PLEASING SENSATION LEADS TO DESIRE. THEN TAKE NOTE OF HOW YOU CLING TO THE DESIRE AND SEEK ITS SATISFACTION.

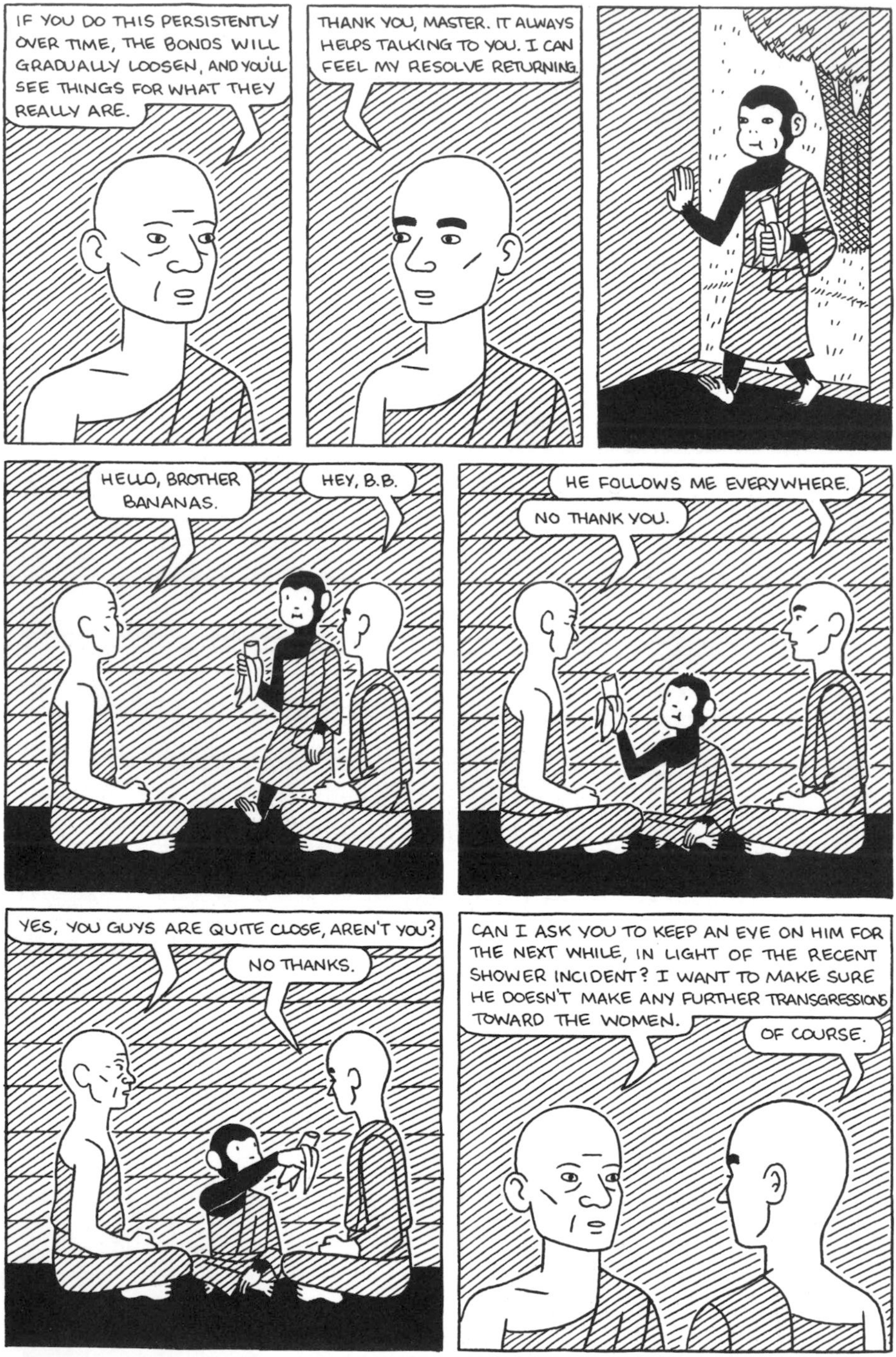
IF YOU DO THIS PERSISTENTLY OVER TIME, THE BONDS WILL GRADUALLY LOOSEN, AND YOU'LL SEE THINGS FOR WHAT THEY REALLY ARE.
THANK YOU, MASTER. IT ALWAYS HELPS TALKING TO YOU. I CAN FEEL MY RESOLVE RETURNING.
HELLO, BROTHER BANANAS.
HEY, B.B.
HE FOLLOWS ME EVERYWHERE.
NO THANK YOU.
YES, YOU GUYS ARE QUITE CLOSE, AREN'T YOU?
NO THANKS.
CAN I ASK YOU TO KEEP AN EYE ON HIM FOR THE NEXT WHILE, IN LIGHT OF THE RECENT SHOWER INCIDENT? I WANT TO MAKE SURE HE DOESN'T MAKE ANY FURTHER TRANSGRESSIONS TOWARD THE WOMEN.
OF COURSE.

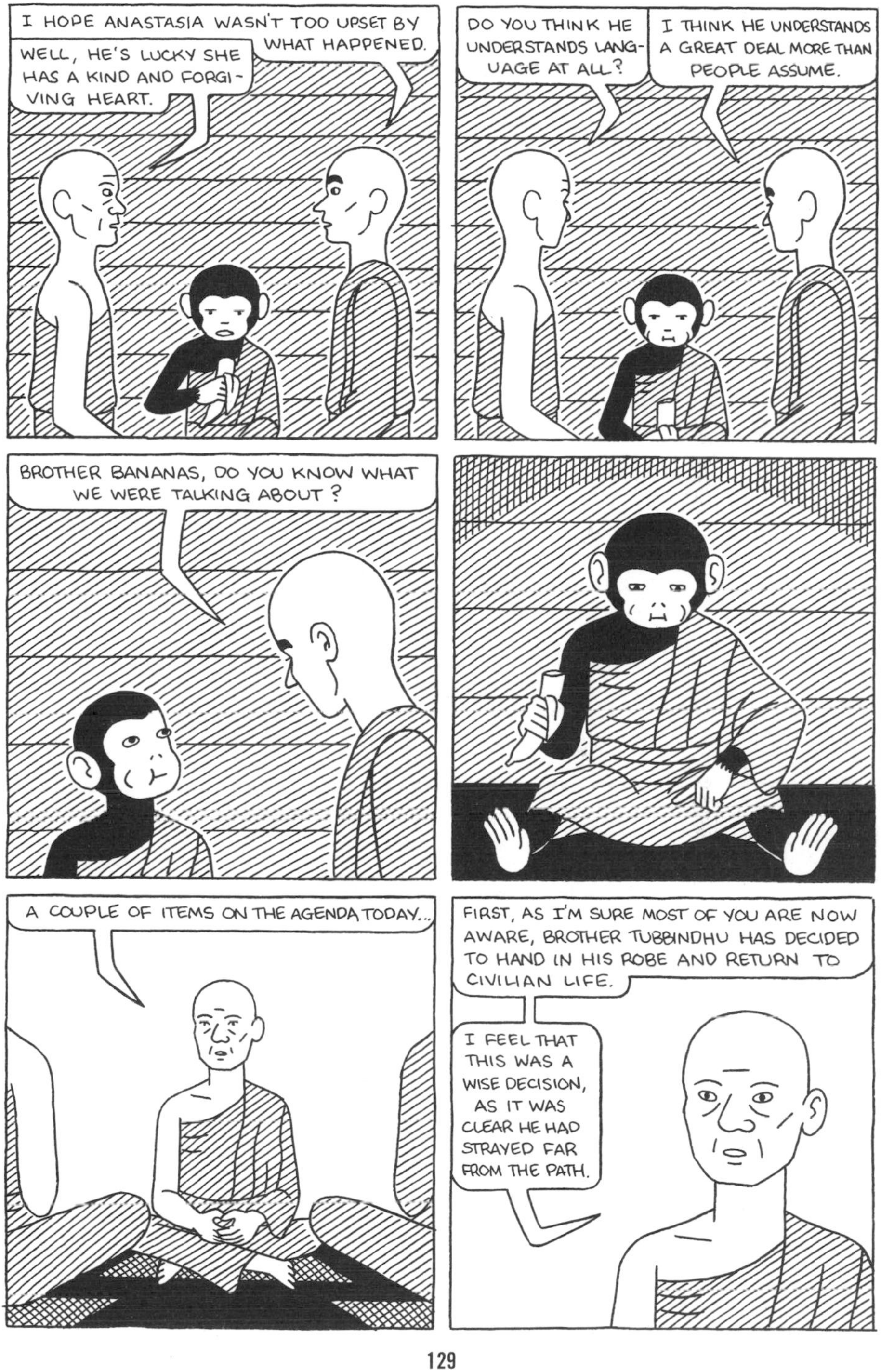
I HOPE ANASTASIA WASN'T TOO UPSET BY WHAT HAPPENED.
WELL, HE'S LUCKY SHE HAS A KIND AND FORGI-VING HEART.
DO YOU THINK HE UNDERSTANDS LANG-UAGE AT ALL?
I THINK HE UNDERSTANDS A GREAT DEAL MORE THAN PEOPLE ASSUME.
BROTHER BANANAS, DO YOU KNOW WHAT WE WERE TALKING ABOUT?
A COUPLE OF ITEMS ON THE AGENDA TODAY...
FIRST, AS I'M SURE MOST OF YOU ARE NOW AWARE, BROTHER TUBBINDHU HAS DECIDED TO HAND IN HIS ROBE AND RETURN TO CIVILIAN LIFE.
I FEEL THAT THIS WAS A WISE DECISION, AS IT WAS CLEAR HE HAD STRAYED FAR FROM THE PATH.

HE HAD, OF COURSE, A PRO-CLIVITY TO CONSUME EXCESSIVE AMOUNTS OF FOOD. WE ALL SUSPECTED HIM OF SNEAKING INTO THE KITCHEN IN THE MIDDLE OF THE NIGHT, AS THERE WAS NO OTHER WAY TO ACCOUNT FOR HIS SUBSTANTIAL GIRTH.

UNSATISFIED WITH HIS RATIONS AT MEAL TIMES, HE WOULD OFTEN REQUEST SECOND PORTIONS WITH THE WEAKEST OF EXCUSES.

I RECALL ONE OCCASION WHERE HE ARGUED THAT AS THE SELF TRANSFORMS FROM INSTANT TO INSTANT, HE HAD YET TO HAVE HIS FIRST PORTION.

AND, SAD TO SAY, IN ADDITION TO GLUTTONY, BROTHER TUBBINDHU ALSO EXEMPLIFIED SLOTH. IN FACT, I WOULD SAY HE WAS THE ULTI-MATE PROCRASTINATOR.

THERE WAS ONE POINT WHERE I ASKED HIM IF HE WOULD BE ABLE TO BUILD US A TOOL SHED, AS I KNEW HE HAD BEEN A CONTRAC-TOR IN CIVILIAN LIFE.

MONTHS WENT BY, AND HE HAD NOT YET BEGUN TO LAY THE FOUNDATION. WHEN I ASKED HIM WHY HE HADN'T STARTED THE PROJECT, HE SAID I'D INDICATED NO DEAD-LINE, AND THAT HE'D LIKELY GET AROUND TO IT IN HIS NEXT LIFE.

SO, I THINK THAT BROTHER TUBBINDHU WAS NOT QUITE READY FOR MONASTIC LIFE. BUT LET US SEND OUR HEARTS OUT TO HIM, AND HOPE THAT SOMEDAY HE FINDS HIS WAY BACK TO THE NOBLE PATH.

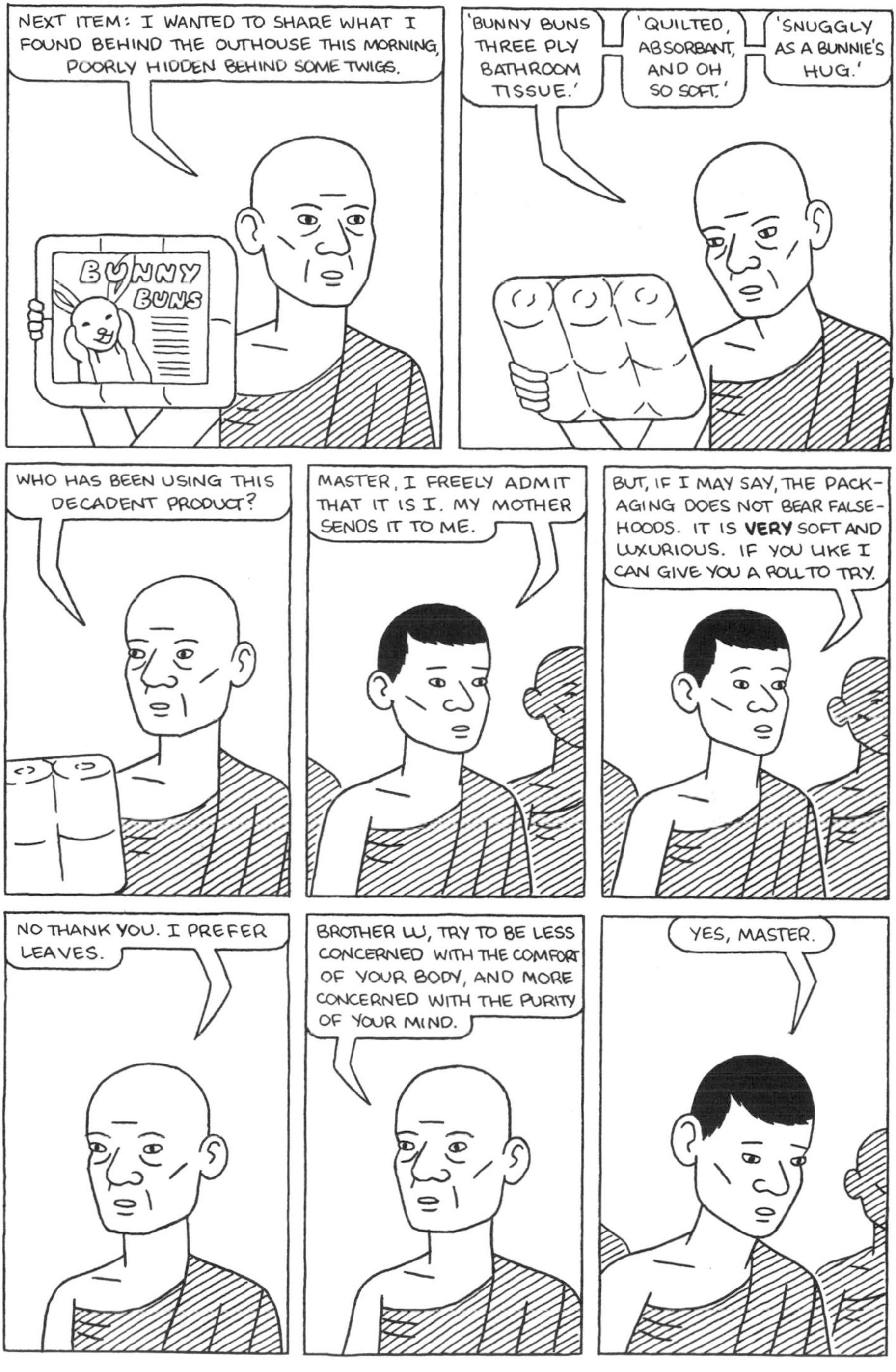
NEXT ITEM: I WANTED TO SHARE WHAT I FOUND BEHIND THE OUTHOUSE THIS MORNING, POORLY HIDDEN BEHIND SOME TWIGS.
BUNNY BUNS
'BUNNY BUNS THREE PLY BATHROOM TISSUE.'
'QUILTED, ABSORBANT, AND OH SO SOFT.'
'SNUGGLY AS A BUNNIE'S HUG.'
WHO HAS BEEN USING THIS DECADENT PRODUCT?
MASTER, I FREELY ADMIT THAT IT IS I. MY MOTHER SENDS IT TO ME.
BUT, IF I MAY SAY, THE PACKAGING DOES NOT BEAR FALSEHOODS. IT IS **VERY** SOFT AND LUXURIOUS. IF YOU LIKE I CAN GIVE YOU A ROLL TO TRY.
NO THANK YOU. I PREFER LEAVES.
BROTHER LU, TRY TO BE LESS CONCERNED WITH THE COMFORT OF YOUR BODY, AND MORE CONCERNED WITH THE PURITY OF YOUR MIND.
YES, MASTER.

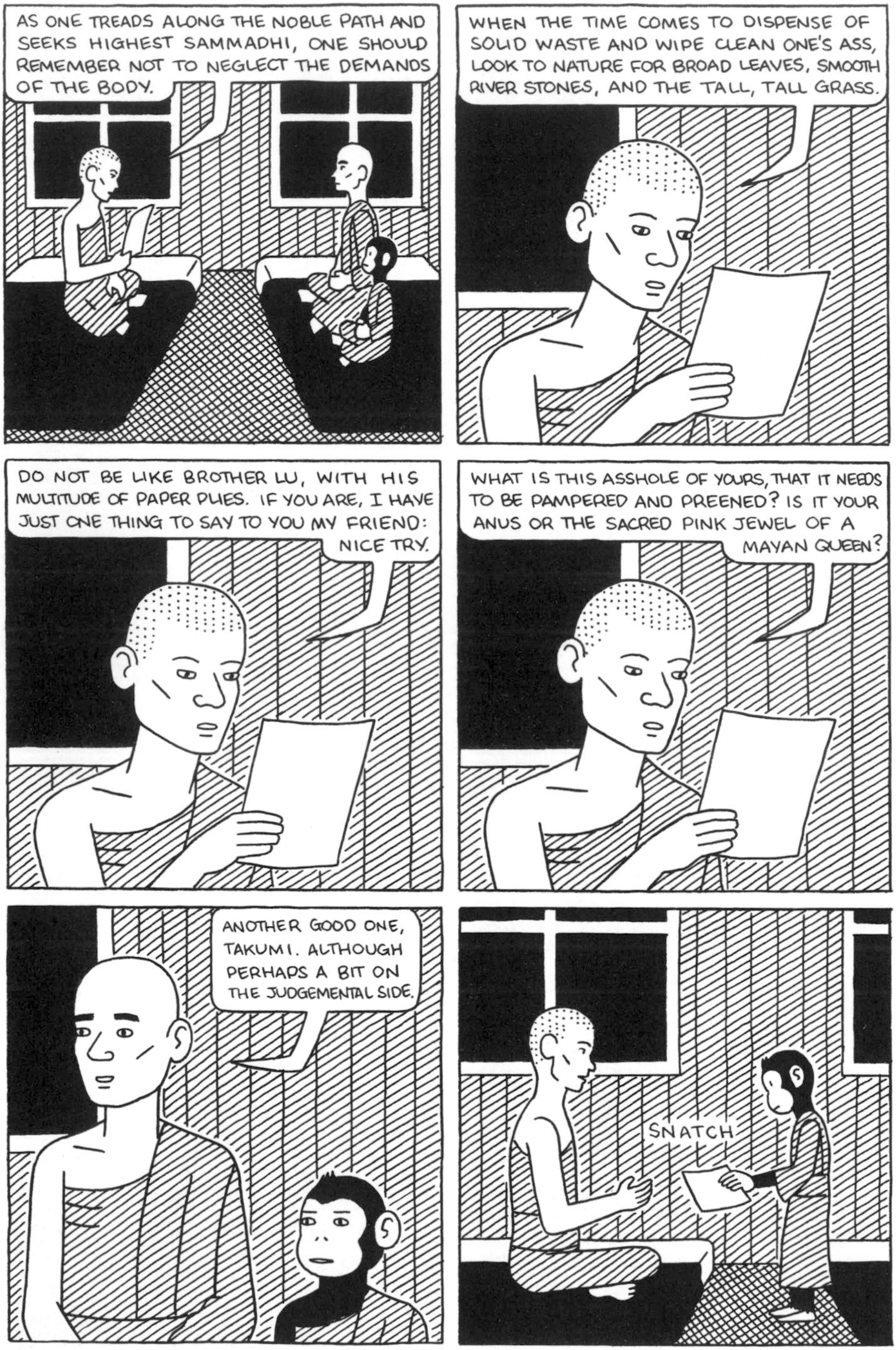
AS ONE TREADS ALONG THE NOBLE PATH AND SEEKS HIGHEST SAMMADHI, ONE SHOULD REMEMBER NOT TO NEGLECT THE DEMANDS OF THE BODY.
WHEN THE TIME COMES TO DISPENSE OF SOLID WASTE AND WIPE CLEAN ONE'S ASS, LOOK TO NATURE FOR BROAD LEAVES, SMOOTH RIVER STONES, AND THE TALL, TALL GRASS.
DO NOT BE LIKE BROTHER LU, WITH HIS MULTITUDE OF PAPER PLIES. IF YOU ARE, I HAVE JUST ONE THING TO SAY TO YOU MY FRIEND: NICE TRY.
WHAT IS THIS ASSHOLE OF YOURS, THAT IT NEEDS TO BE PAMPERED AND PREENED? IS IT YOUR ANUS OR THE SACRED PINK JEWEL OF A MAYAN QUEEN?
ANOTHER GOOD ONE, TAKUMI. ALTHOUGH PERHAPS A BIT ON THE JUDGEMENTAL SIDE.
SNATCH

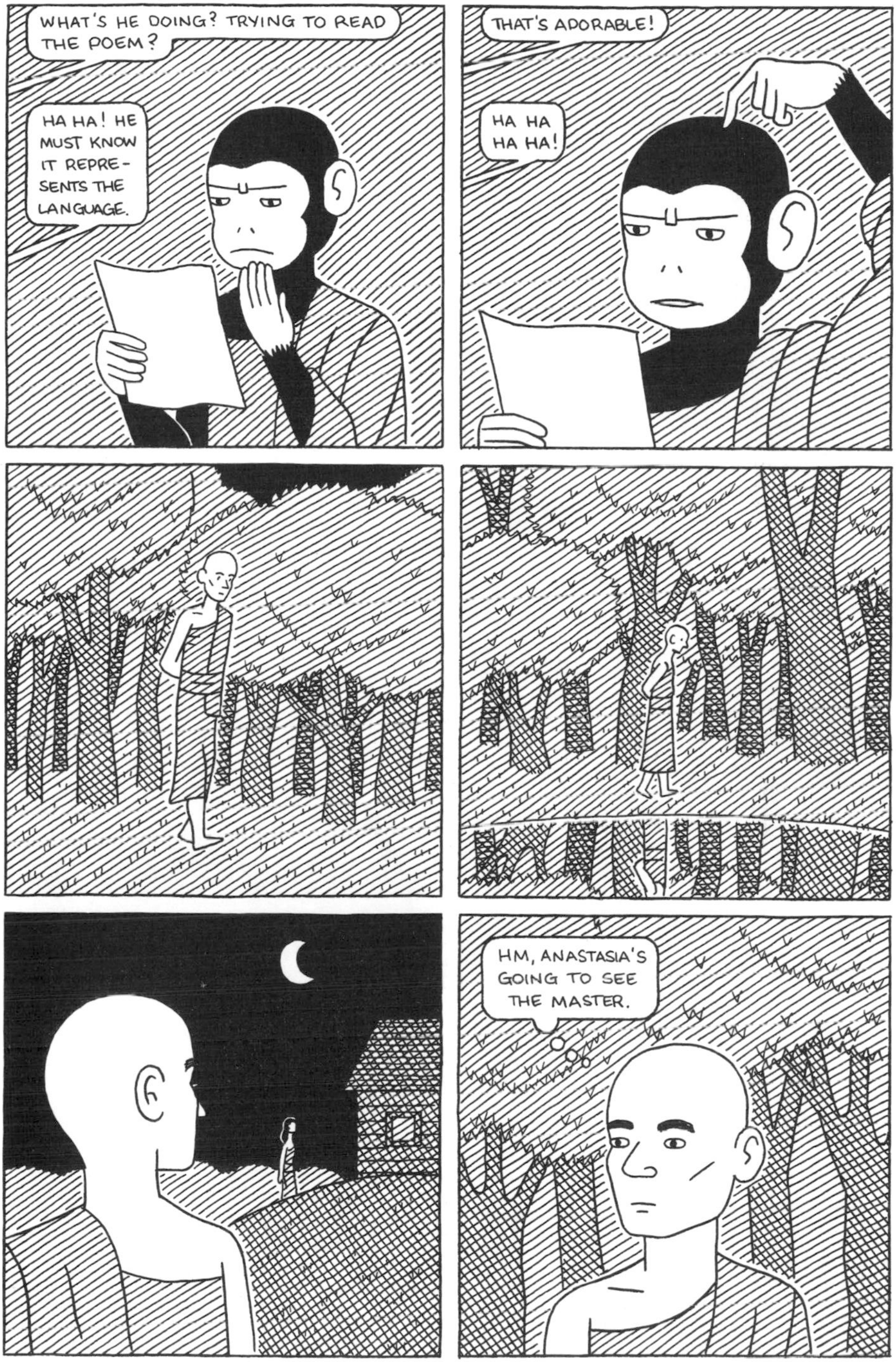
WHAT'S HE DOING? TRYING TO READ THE POEM?
HA HA! HE MUST KNOW IT REPRESENTS THE LANGUAGE.
THAT'S ADORABLE!
HA HA HA HA!
HM, ANASTASIA'S GOING TO SEE THE MASTER.

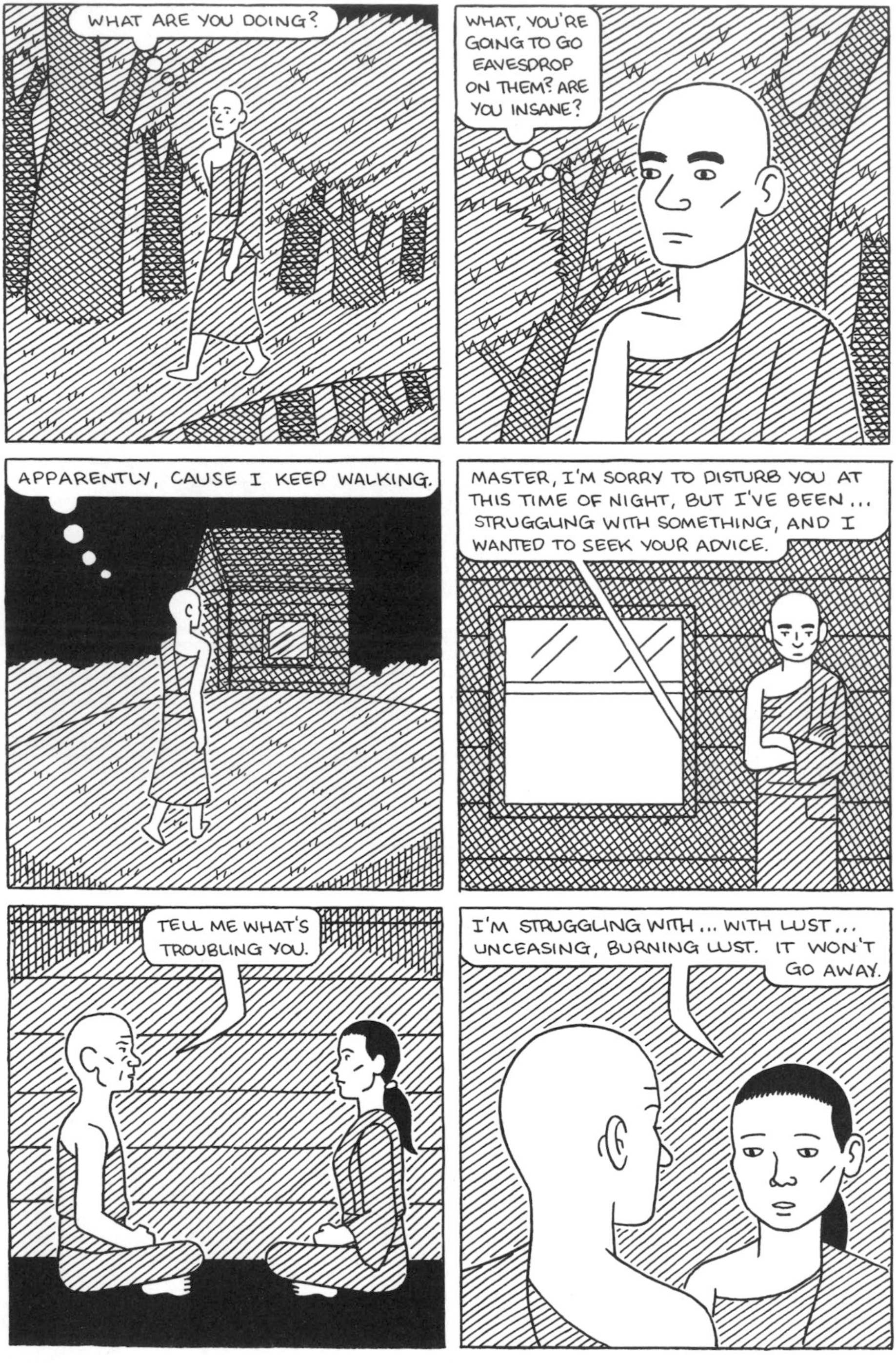
WHAT ARE YOU DOING?
WHAT, YOU'RE GOING TO GO EAVESDROP ON THEM? ARE YOU INSANE?
APPARENTLY, CAUSE I KEEP WALKING.
MASTER, I'M SORRY TO DISTURB YOU AT THIS TIME OF NIGHT, BUT I'VE BEEN... STRUGGLING WITH SOMETHING, AND I WANTED TO SEEK YOUR ADVICE.
TELL ME WHAT'S TROUBLING YOU.
I'M STRUGGLING WITH... WITH LUST... UNCEASING, BURNING LUST. IT WON'T GO AWAY.

I HAVE A CONFESSION: I BROKE ONE OF THE PRECEPTS LAST NIGHT. I ENGAGED IN SEXUAL ACTIVITY. I USED MY HAIRBRUSH... ON MYSELF.

AND I KNOW THAT I ALONE AM TO BLAME FOR THIS, BUT I HAVE TO SAY, IT DOESN'T HELP THAT AT THIS MONASTERY I'M SURROUNDED BY FELLOW BUDDHISTS.

I ALMOST EXPERIENCE MORE LUST AND ROMANTIC LONGING HERE THAN I EXPERIENCED IN CIVILIAN LIFE. IN CIVILIAN LIFE I WAS BORED BY THE MEN I KNEW, BUT HERE I LIVE WITH MEN WHO SHARE MY BELIEFS AND VALUES.

FORGIVE ME FOR SAYING THIS, MASTER, BUT THE MAN WHO IS MOST OFTEN ON MY MIND...

THE MAN I LUST AFTER THE MOST...

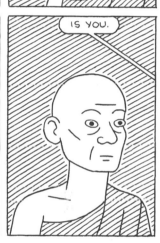

IS YOU.

I KNOW IT'S COMPLETELY ABSURD TO LUST AFTER MY MASTER, WHO'S MILES BEYOND ANIMALISTIC PASSION, BUT I CAN'T HELP IT.

I FEEL VERY ASHAMED TELLING YOU THIS, BUT I HAD TO GET IT OFF MY CHEST. I—I DON'T KNOW WHAT TO DO.

WELL, ANASTASIA, THERE DOES EXIST A SPECIAL TECHNIQUE THAT IS SURE TO COOL YOUR DESIRE. HOWEVER, IT MAY NOT BE THE TYPE OF TECHNIQUE YOU'RE EXPECTING.

WHAT IS IT?

IT IS AN INCREDIBLY EFFECTIVE TECHNIQUE, AND ALSO A VERY ANCIENT ONE. SO ANCIENT, IN FACT, THAT IT EVEN PREDATES THE TEACHINGS OF THE BUDDAH HIMSELF.

REALLY?

YES.

MASTER, I — I BELIEVE I'VE GUESSED THE TECHNIQUE YOU'RE SUGGESTING.

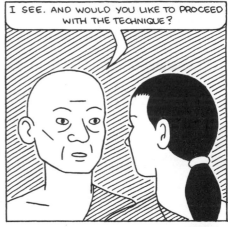

I SEE. AND WOULD YOU LIKE TO PROCEED WITH THE TECHNIQUE?

YES, VERY MUCH.

?

136

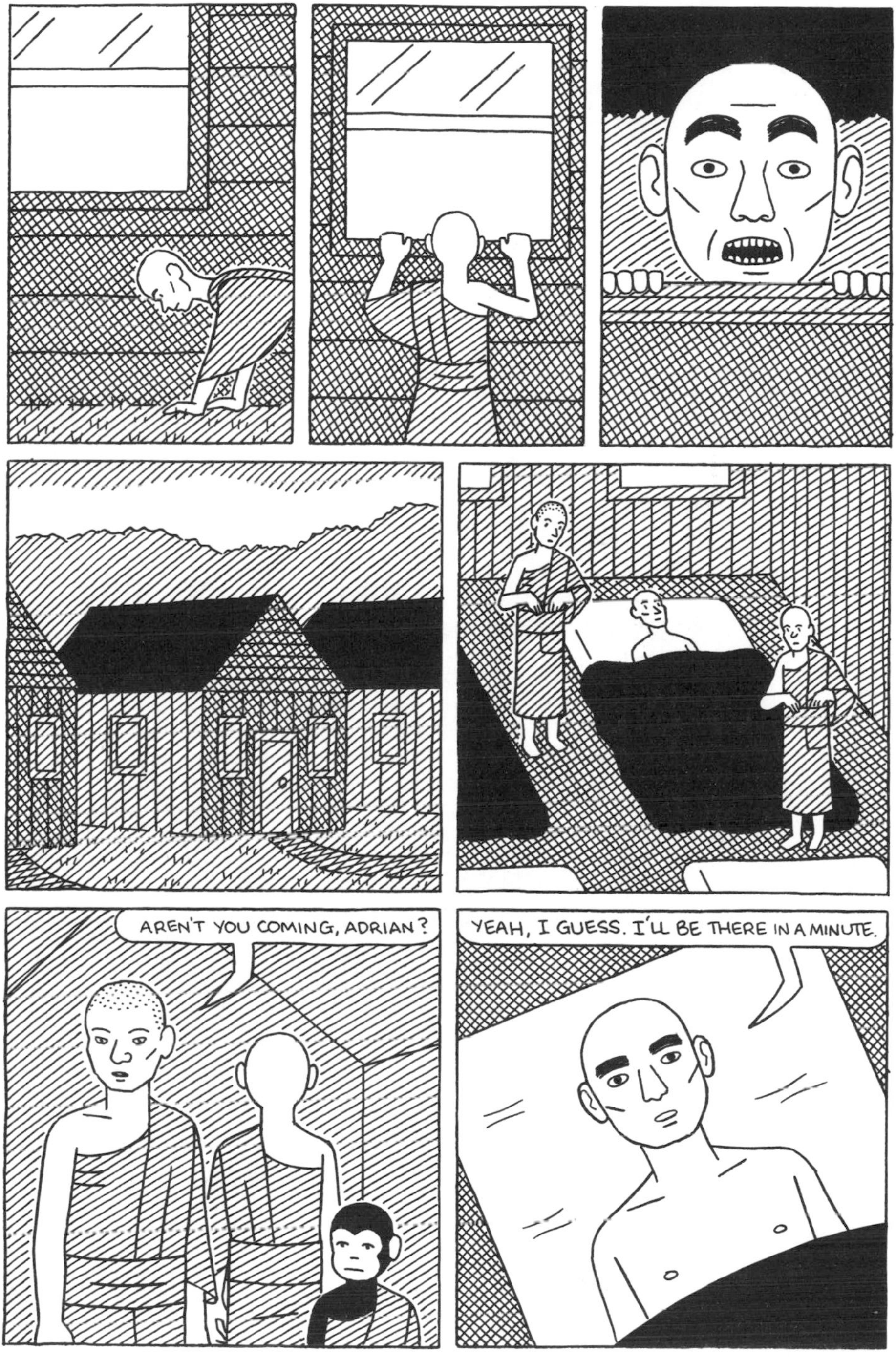
AREN'T YOU COMING, ADRIAN?
YEAH, I GUESS. I'LL BE THERE IN A MINUTE.

GOOD MORNING, EVERYONE. LET US BEGIN OUR MORNING MEDITATION.

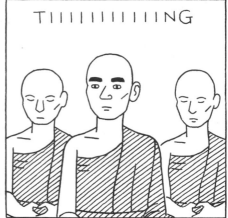

TIIIIIIIIIING

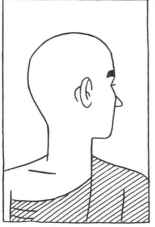

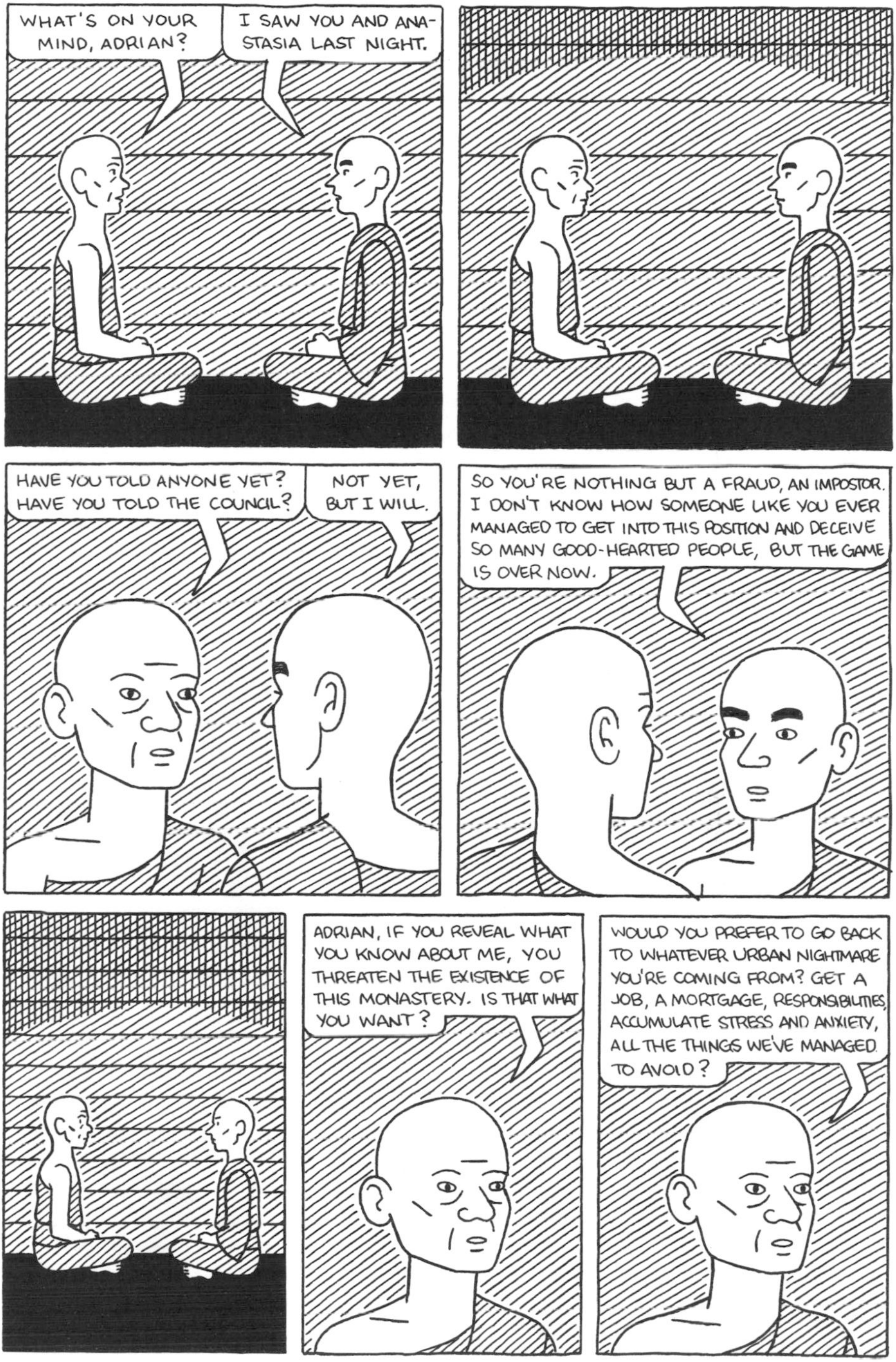
WHAT'S ON YOUR MIND, ADRIAN?
I SAW YOU AND ANASTASIA LAST NIGHT.
HAVE YOU TOLD ANYONE YET? HAVE YOU TOLD THE COUNCIL?
NOT YET, BUT I WILL.
SO YOU'RE NOTHING BUT A FRAUD, AN IMPOSTOR. I DON'T KNOW HOW SOMEONE LIKE YOU EVER MANAGED TO GET INTO THIS POSITION AND DECEIVE SO MANY GOOD-HEARTED PEOPLE, BUT THE GAME IS OVER NOW.
ADRIAN, IF YOU REVEAL WHAT YOU KNOW ABOUT ME, YOU THREATEN THE EXISTENCE OF THIS MONASTERY. IS THAT WHAT YOU WANT?
WOULD YOU PREFER TO GO BACK TO WHATEVER URBAN NIGHTMARE YOU'RE COMING FROM? GET A JOB, A MORTGAGE, RESPONSIBILITIES, ACCUMULATE STRESS AND ANXIETY, ALL THE THINGS WE'VE MANAGED TO AVOID?

YOU HAVE THE OPTION OF KEEP-
ING WHAT WE HAVE HERE ALIVE.
IF THAT'S WHAT YOU CHOOSE,
PERHAPS YOU'D BE INTERESTED
IN ADOPTING MY LIFESTYLE. YOU
CAN BE LIKE ME AND PRACTICE
THE ART OF HAVING IT BOTH WAYS.

IT WOULDN'T BE HARD FOR YOU
TO FIND SOMEONE HERE WHO'S
WILLING AND ABLE. THEY'RE ALL
READY TO SNAP.

JUST AS LONG AS YOU'RE
DISCREET ABOUT IT, OF COURSE.

AND I WOULD BE HERE TO
TEACH AND GUIDE YOU.
FOR INSTANCE, I BET YOU'RE
STILL A VIRGIN. I CAN HELP
PREPARE YOU FOR SEX. I CAN
TEACH YOU ALL THE THINGS YOU
NEED TO KNOW TO PLEASE A WOMAN.

THIS COULD BE A GREAT OPPORTUNITY FOR YOU.
WHAT DO YOU SAY?

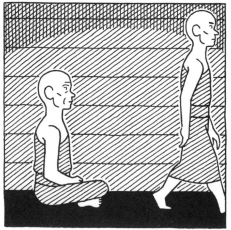

THINK
ABOUT IT.

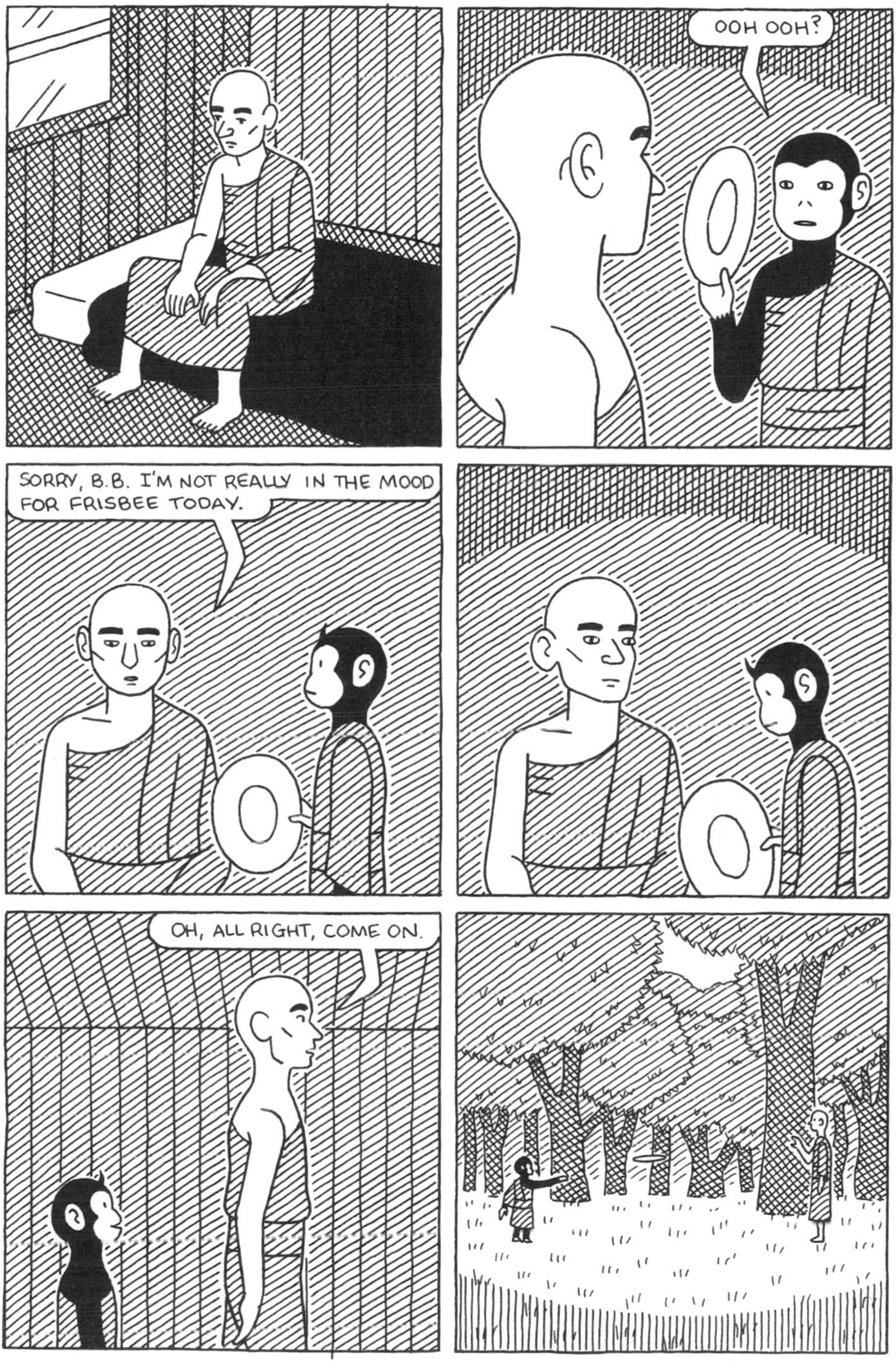
OOH OOH?
SORRY, B.B. I'M NOT REALLY IN THE MOOD FOR FRISBEE TODAY.
OH, ALL RIGHT, COME ON.

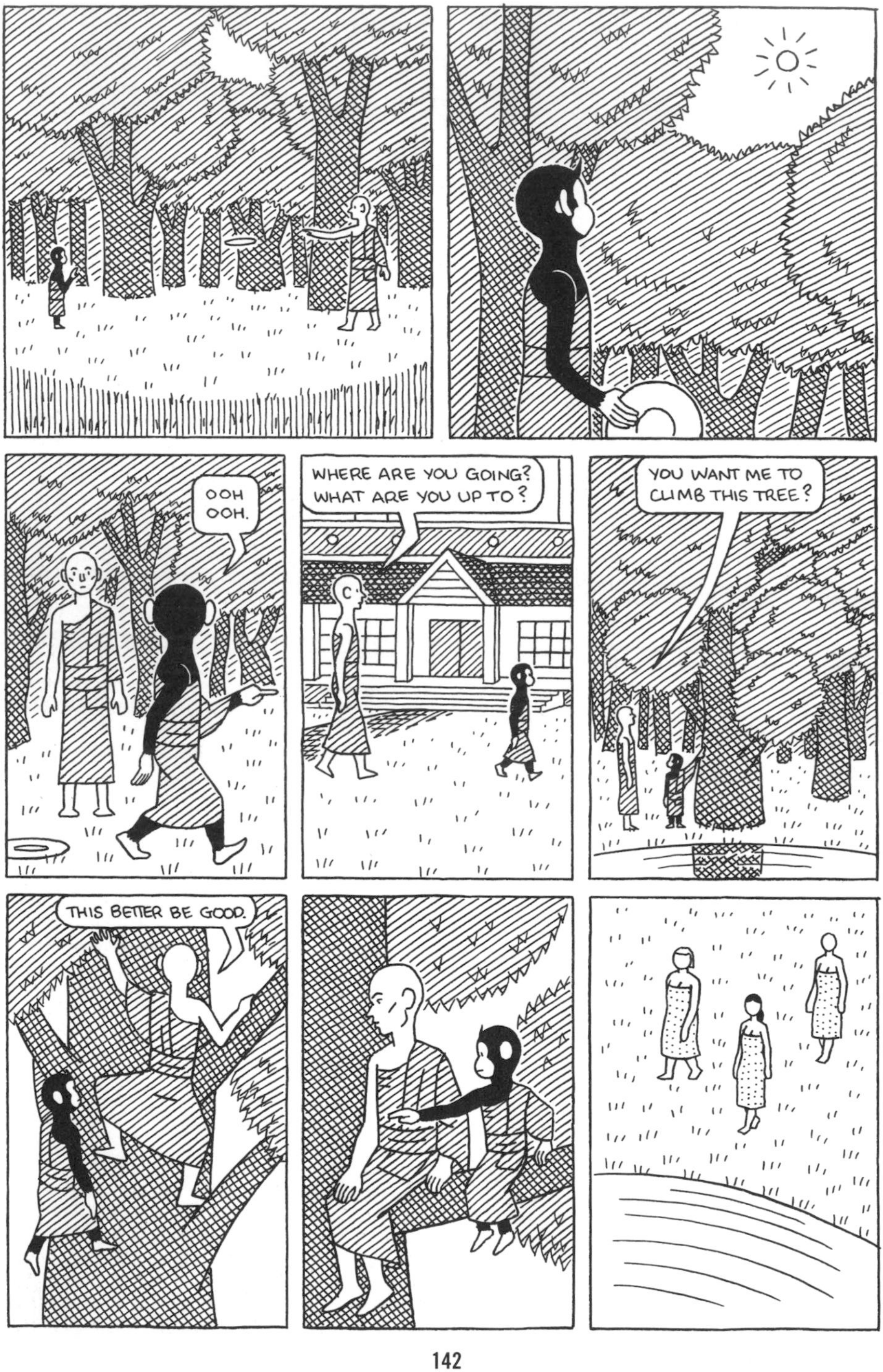
OOH OOH.
WHERE ARE YOU GOING? WHAT ARE YOU UP TO?
YOU WANT ME TO CLIMB THIS TREE?
THIS BETTER BE GOOD.

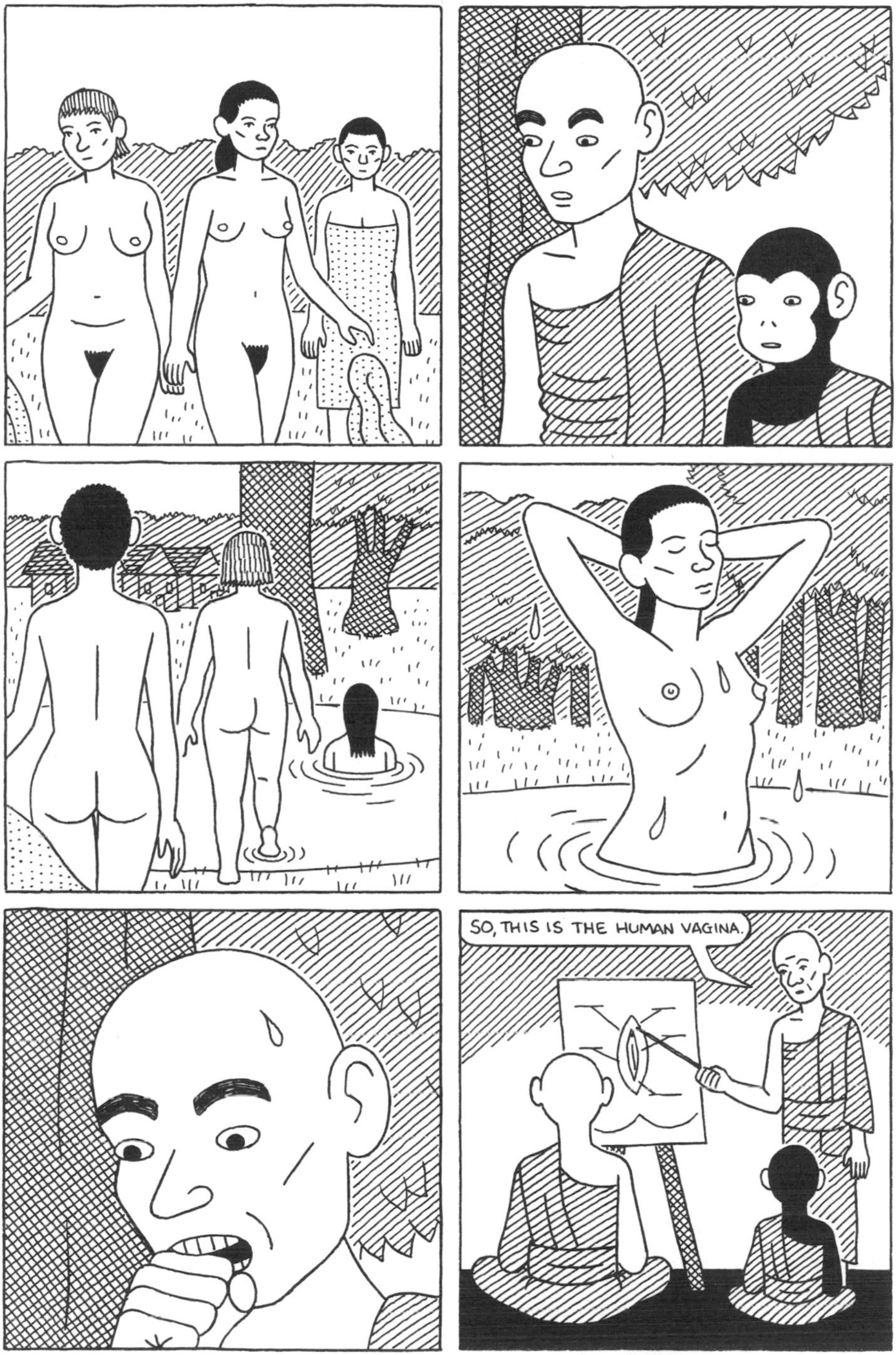
SO, THIS IS THE HUMAN VAGINA.

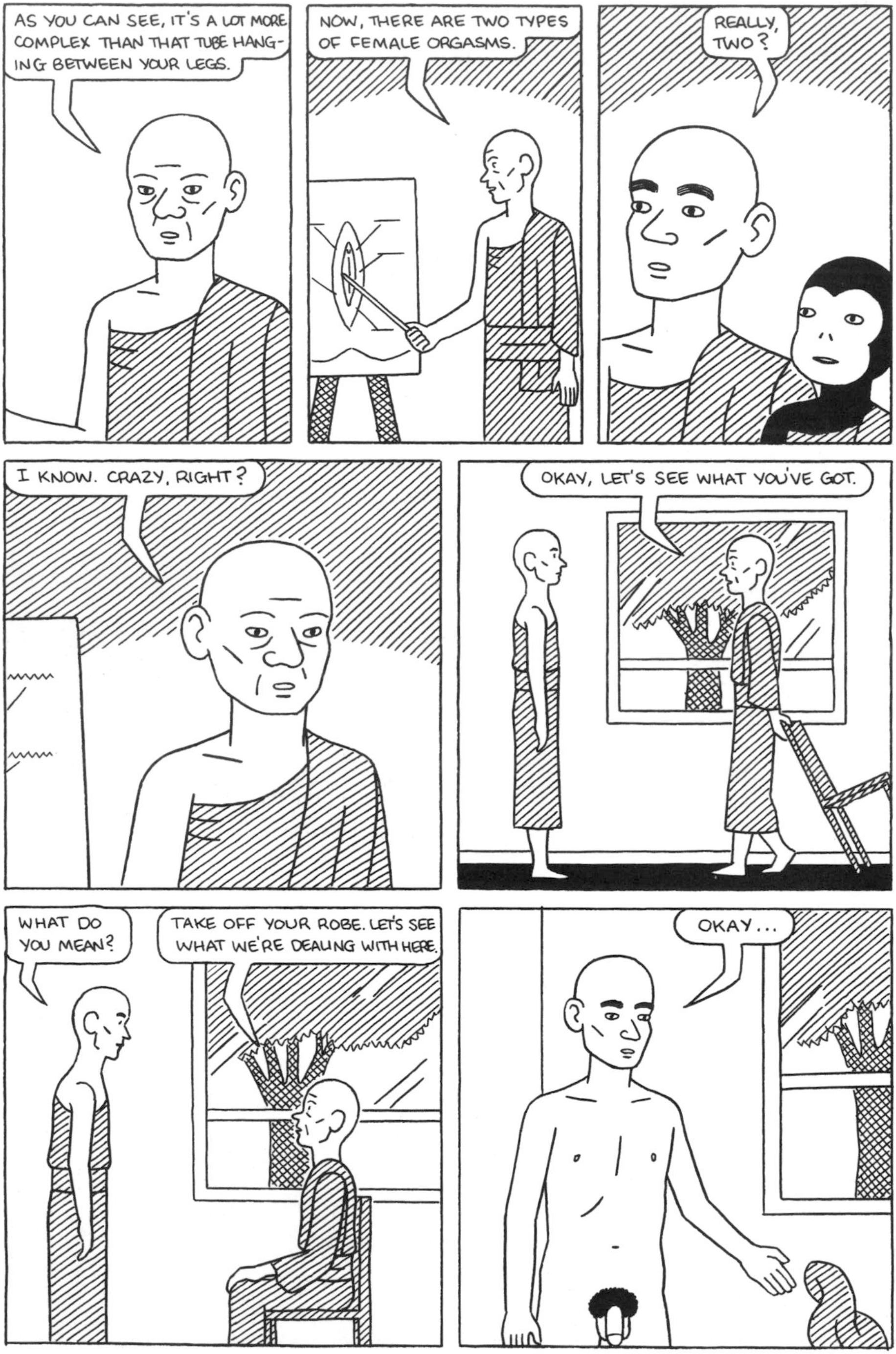
AS YOU CAN SEE, IT'S A LOT MORE COMPLEX THAN THAT TUBE HANGING BETWEEN YOUR LEGS.
NOW, THERE ARE TWO TYPES OF FEMALE ORGASMS.
REALLY, TWO?
I KNOW. CRAZY, RIGHT?
OKAY, LET'S SEE WHAT YOU'VE GOT.
WHAT DO YOU MEAN?
TAKE OFF YOUR ROBE. LET'S SEE WHAT WE'RE DEALING WITH HERE.
OKAY...

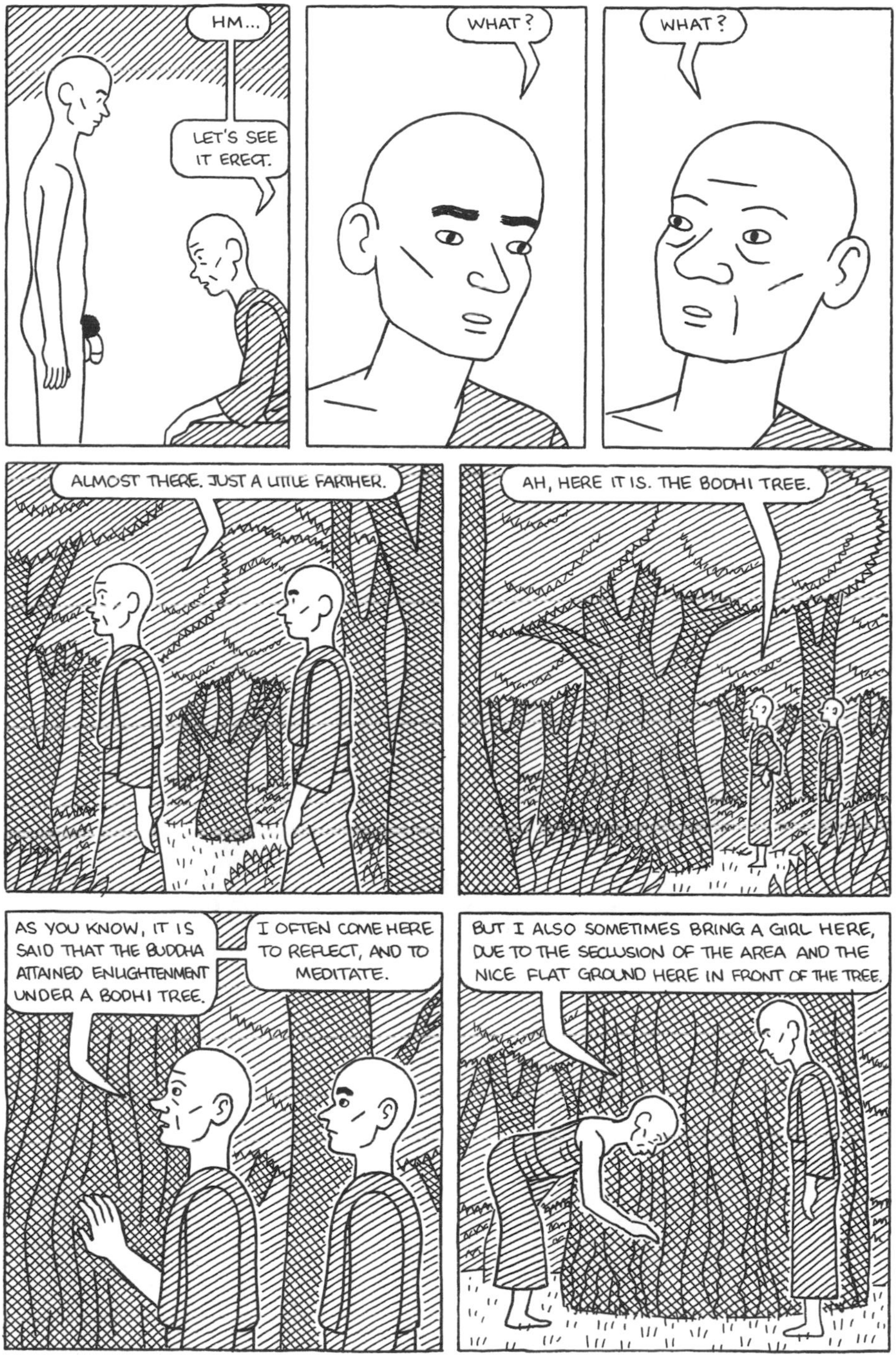
HM...
LET'S SEE IT ERECT.
WHAT?
WHAT?
ALMOST THERE. JUST A LITTLE FARTHER.
AH, HERE IT IS. THE BODHI TREE.
AS YOU KNOW, IT IS SAID THAT THE BUDDHA ATTAINED ENLIGHTENMENT UNDER A BODHI TREE.
I OFTEN COME HERE TO REFLECT, AND TO MEDITATE.
BUT I ALSO SOMETIMES BRING A GIRL HERE, DUE TO THE SECLUSION OF THE AREA AND THE NICE FLAT GROUND HERE IN FRONT OF THE TREE.

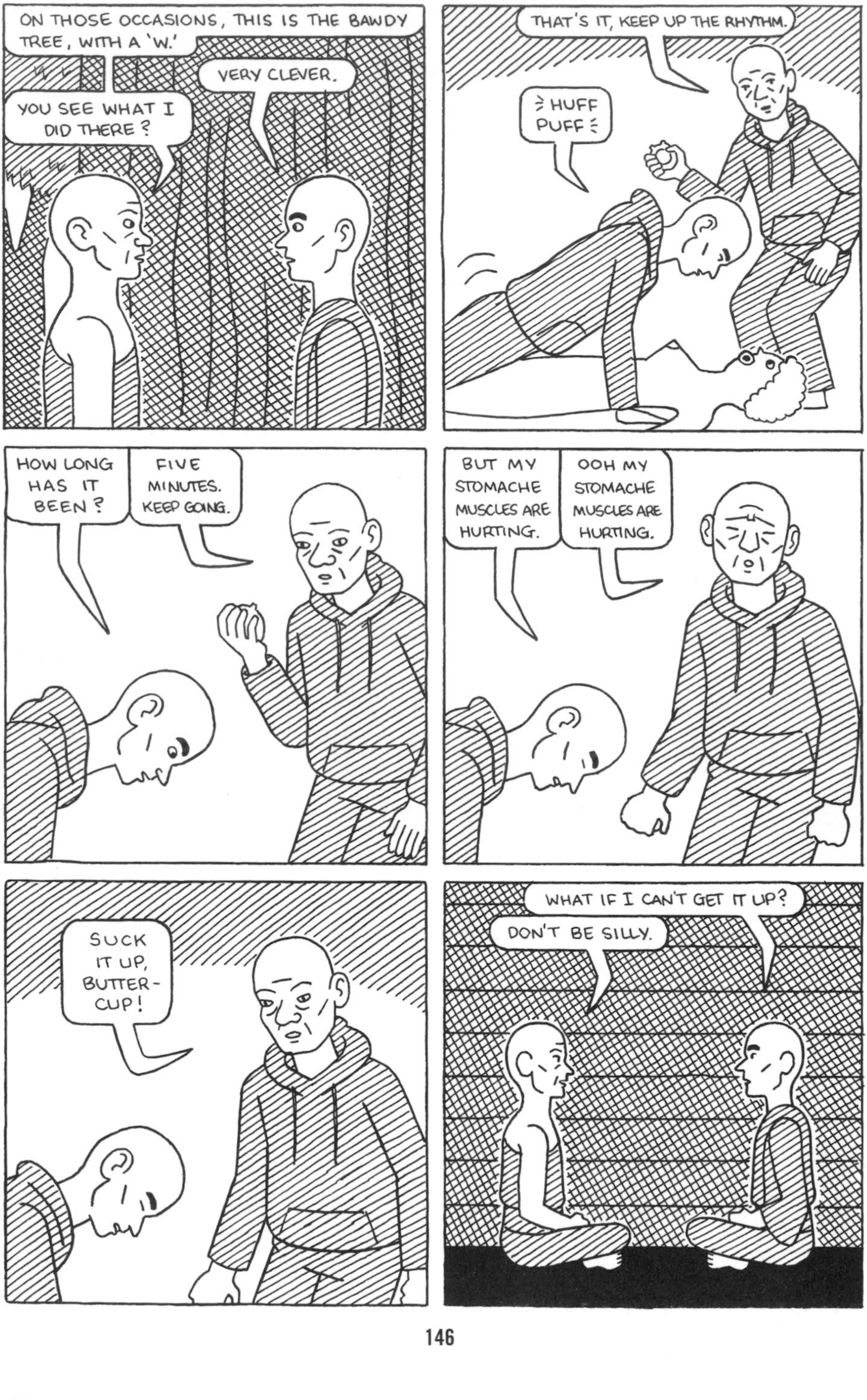
ON THOSE OCCASIONS, THIS IS THE BAWDY TREE, WITH A 'W.'
YOU SEE WHAT I DID THERE?
VERY CLEVER.
THAT'S IT, KEEP UP THE RHYTHM.
HUFF PUFF
HOW LONG HAS IT BEEN?
FIVE MINUTES. KEEP GOING.
BUT MY STOMACHE MUSCLES ARE HURTING.
OOH MY STOMACHE MUSCLES ARE HURTING.
SUCK IT UP, BUTTER-CUP!
WHAT IF I CAN'T GET IT UP?
DON'T BE SILLY.

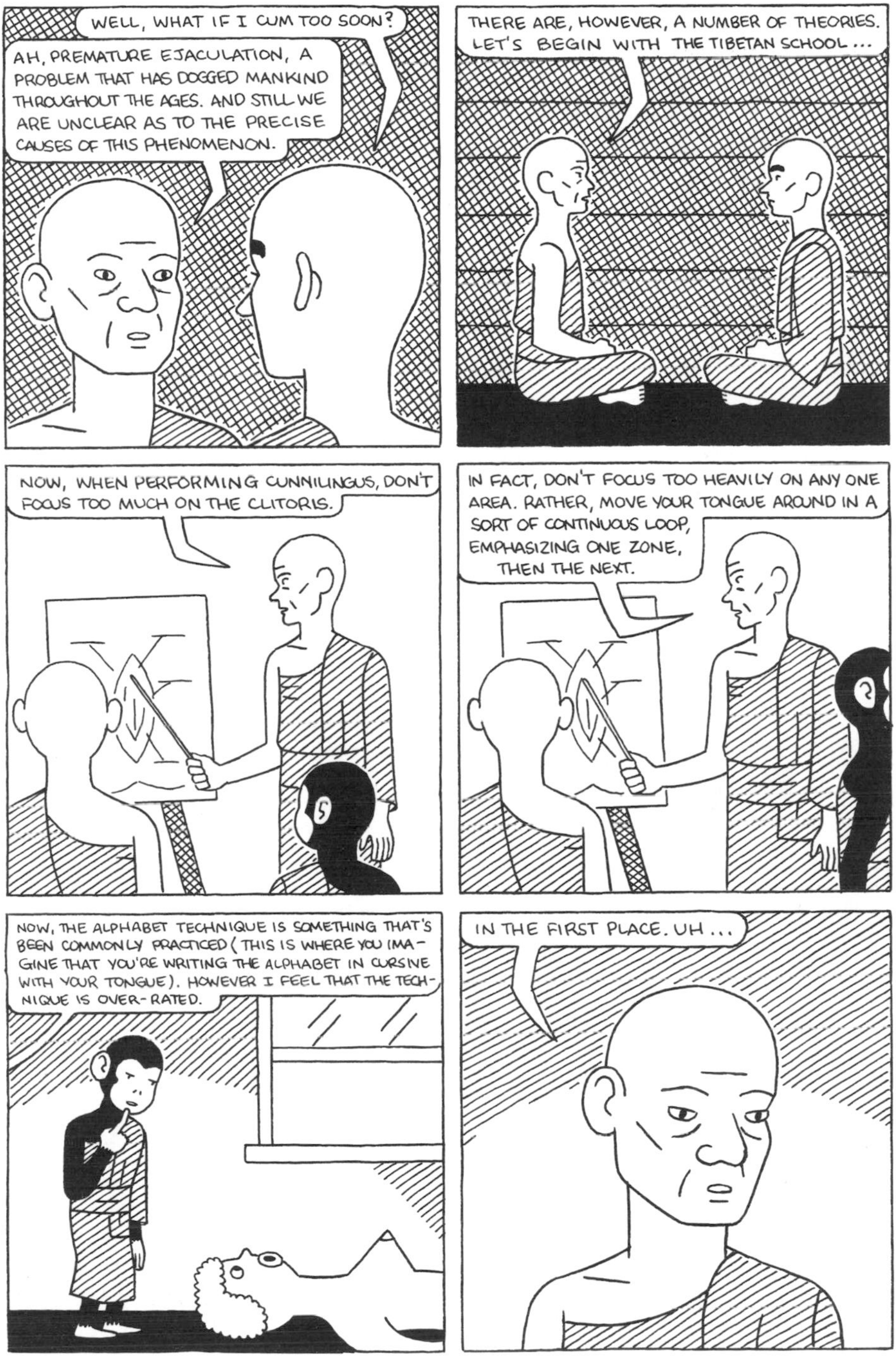
WELL, WHAT IF I CUM TOO SOON?
AH, PREMATURE EJACULATION, A PROBLEM THAT HAS DOGGED MANKIND THROUGHOUT THE AGES. AND STILL WE ARE UNCLEAR AS TO THE PRECISE CAUSES OF THIS PHENOMENON.
THERE ARE, HOWEVER, A NUMBER OF THEORIES. LET'S BEGIN WITH THE TIBETAN SCHOOL...
NOW, WHEN PERFORMING CUNNILINGUS, DON'T FOCUS TOO MUCH ON THE CLITORIS.
IN FACT, DON'T FOCUS TOO HEAVILY ON ANY ONE AREA. RATHER, MOVE YOUR TONGUE AROUND IN A SORT OF CONTINUOUS LOOP, EMPHASIZING ONE ZONE, THEN THE NEXT.
NOW, THE ALPHABET TECHNIQUE IS SOMETHING THAT'S BEEN COMMONLY PRACTICED (THIS IS WHERE YOU IMA-GINE THAT YOU'RE WRITING THE ALPHABET IN CURSIVE WITH YOUR TONGUE). HOWEVER I FEEL THAT THE TECH-NIQUE IS OVER-RATED.
IN THE FIRST PLACE. UH...

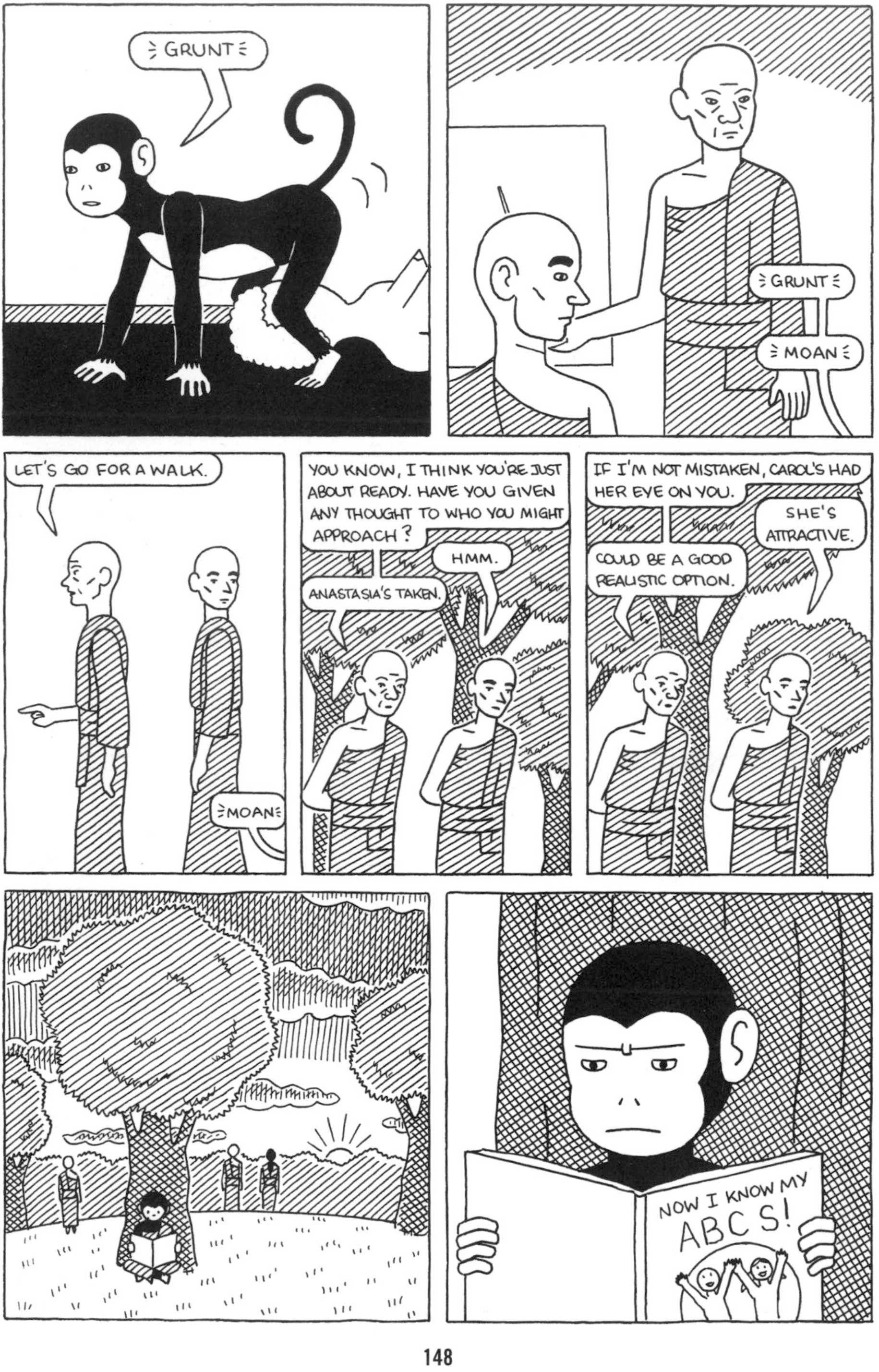
GRUNT
GRUNT
MOAN
LET'S GO FOR A WALK.
MOAN
YOU KNOW, I THINK YOU'RE JUST ABOUT READY. HAVE YOU GIVEN ANY THOUGHT TO WHO YOU MIGHT APPROACH?
HMM.
ANASTASIA'S TAKEN.
IF I'M NOT MISTAKEN, CAROL'S HAD HER EYE ON YOU.
SHE'S ATTRACTIVE.
COULD BE A GOOD REALISTIC OPTION.
NOW I KNOW MY ABCS!

IT'S A BEAUTIFUL SUNSET TODAY.

YES.

DO YOU EVER FIND IT DIFFICULT LIVING HERE?

IN WHAT WAY?

WELL, TO BE FRANK, THE SEXUAL FRUSTRATION IS A LOT WORSE THAN I THOUGHT IT WOULD BE.

WHAT IF I WERE TO TELL YOU I KNOW OF A SPECIAL TECHNIQUE THAT'S SURE TO COOL YOUR DESIRE?

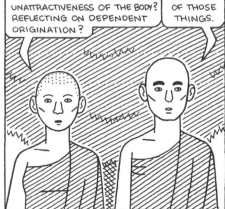

WHAT IS IT, REFLECTING ON THE UNATTRACTIVENESS OF THE BODY? REFLECTING ON DEPENDENT ORIGINATION?

NEITHER OF THOSE THINGS.

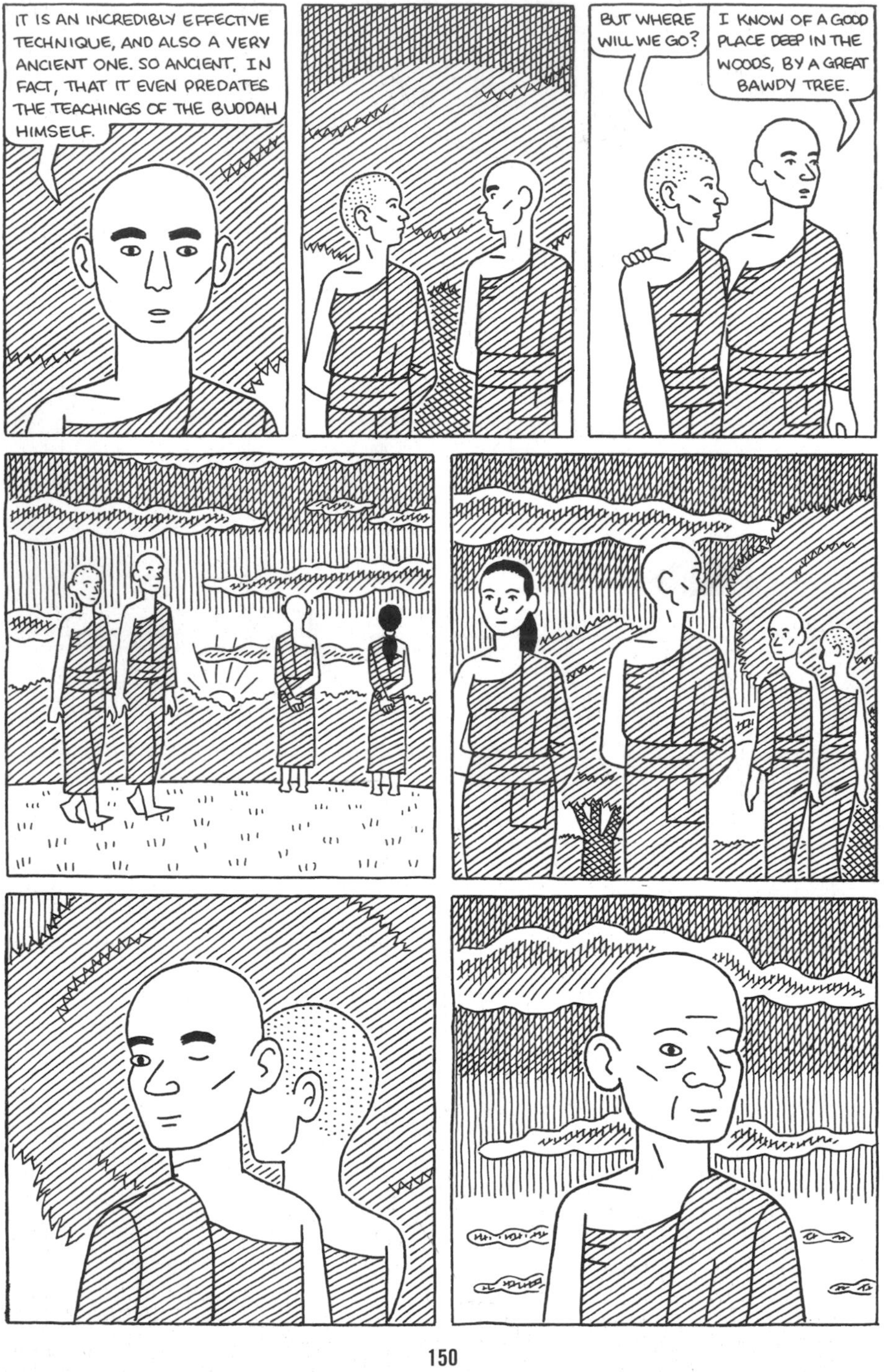
IT IS AN INCREDIBLY EFFECTIVE TECHNIQUE, AND ALSO A VERY ANCIENT ONE. SO ANCIENT, IN FACT, THAT IT EVEN PREDATES THE TEACHINGS OF THE BUDDAH HIMSELF.
BUT WHERE WILL WE GO?
I KNOW OF A GOOD PLACE DEEP IN THE WOODS, BY A GREAT BAWDY TREE.